Chasing Frank and Jesse James

ALSO BY WAYNE FANEBUST

*Brigadier General Robert L. McCook
and Colonel Daniel McCook, Jr.: A Union
Army Dual Biography* (McFarland, 2017)

*Major General Alexander M. McCook, USA:
A Civil War Biography* (McFarland, 2013)

Chasing Frank and Jesse James

The Bungled Northfield Bank Robbery and the Long Manhunt

WAYNE FANEBUST

McFarland & Company, Inc., Publishers
Jefferson, North Carolina

LIBRARY OF CONGRESS CATALOGUING-IN-PUBLICATION DATA

Names: Fanebust, Wayne, author.
Title: Chasing Frank and Jesse James : the bungled Northfield Bank robbery and the long manhunt / Wayne Fanebust.
Description: Jefferson, North Carolina : McFarland & Company, Inc., Publishers, 2018 | Includes bibliographical references and index.
Identifiers: LCCN 2018003900 | ISBN 9781476670676 (softcover : acid free paper) ∞
Subjects: LCSH: James, Jesse, 1847–1882. | James, Frank, 1844–1915. | Outlaws—West (U.S.)—Biography. | Bank robberies—Minnesota—Northfield.
Classification: LCC F594.J24 F36 2018 | DDC 364.15/520922 [B] —dc23
LC record available at https://lccn.loc.gov/2018003900

BRITISH LIBRARY CATALOGUING DATA ARE AVAILABLE

ISBN (print) 978-1-4766-7067-6
ISBN (ebook) 978-1-4766-3189-9

© 2018 Wayne Fanebust. All rights reserved

No part of this book may be reproduced or transmitted in any form or by any means, electronic or mechanical, including photocopying or recording, or by any information storage and retrieval system, without permission in writing from the publisher.

Front cover images of Frank James (Clay County, Missouri, Photograph Collection [P1112]. 023962. State Historical Society of Missouri, Photograph Collection) and Jesse James, ca. May 22, 1882 (Library of Congress)

Printed in the United States of America

McFarland & Company, Inc., Publishers
  Box 611, Jefferson, North Carolina 28640
  www.mcfarlandpub.com

Table of Contents

Preface and Acknowledgments — 1

1. Pen Pictures of the James Brothers — 5
2. A Long Way from Home — 20
3. Deadly Debacle at Northfield — 33
4. Six Men on Five Horses — 45
5. The Two That Escaped — 60
6. A Ride for Life — 73
7. Dakota and Devil's Gulch — 83
8. A Wild State of Excitement — 98
9. Northfield Avenged: The Capture of the Youngers and the Killing of Charlie Pitts — 111
10. Missouri Outlaws Face Minnesota Justice — 126
11. The James Brothers Go In and Out of Iowa — 136
12. The Dark River — 151
13. A Desperado Dies — 165
14. A Gathering of Death Deniers and Myth Makers — 182
15. Outlaw Stardom — 194

Chapter Notes — 215
Bibliography — 229
Index — 233

Preface and Acknowledgments

From 1865, the year the Civil War ended, to the 1880s when the last of the James–Younger gang had been killed, imprisoned, or had simply disappeared, there was a tension among the people of Missouri between the need for law and order and the desire to protect certain outlaws, their comrades, the last Rebels. The James brothers and their cohorts were the products of the Confederacy and the war it fought against the Union in defense of secession and slavery. The defeat of the Southern army created lasting bitterness in the South and a burning desire to "right the wrong," so to speak.

At the same time the James gang was robbing banks, stagecoaches and trains, others were busy re-writing history, creating the myth of "the Lost Cause," a false picture of the Confederacy and the Civil War. The never-say-die outlaws played into that narrative by refusing to lay down their guns and put their shoulders to the plow. Instead they attacked "Yankee" banks and committed other acts of violence to remind the less daring Southerners that the war was not really over.

The bandits were sticking it to the authorities in a manner that some men admired but could not bring themselves to act out. So they watched the violence from the sidelines, secretly or openly supporting the criminal acts of the James gang, including the Younger brothers—all heroes in the minds of the grim and melancholy Southern patriots, the believers in wholesale redemption. The lack of effort from law enforcement was a re-enforcement of the public apathy or sympathy for the outlaw. It was plain to the casual observer that little or nothing was being done to capture or kill the outlaws. And when they were not out freebooting, robbing, and killing, the outlaws moved freely and openly from place to place almost as if flaunting their lawlessness, seemingly daring someone to make a move against them.

When the Civil War ended, the James brothers and Cole Younger, all former guerrillas under the vicious William Clark Quantrill and William

"Bloody Bill" Anderson, were denied amnesty, but it is not certain that they would have accepted it had it been offered. Instead they turned to a life of crime, using the refusal of amnesty as an excuse. From 1866 to 1876, they were successful in robbing, killing and spreading terror and escaping punishment. From the Missouri governor on down, there was very little enthusiasm for rounding up the criminals and putting an end to the robbery and murder. The state government at Jefferson City was seemingly out to lunch, with a blind eye toward the crime and carnage, and the cost in lives and money.

But while Missouri, sneeringly dubbed the "Robber State" or the "Bandit State," was at best ambivalent in its attitude toward putting a stop to the crime epidemic, the northern states were firm in their denunciation of outlawism, and they offered no sympathy, nor did they look upon the banditti as bold, daring heroes. To people outside of the South, the James brothers and their associates were bad people, criminals who committed terrible crimes, men who deserved hanging. They were recognized as being very good at their line of work, but not invincible.

So it was a huge mistake for the James–Younger gang to venture forth into Minnesota, looking for fat bank to rob. It was extremely arrogant of the Missouri outlaws to think that the hard-working farm and business people of the northern prairie would simply run away once the shooting started. And when the shooting started at Northfield, Minnesota, the townspeople offered stiff and brave resistance, exchanging gunfire with gunfire. When the shooting stopped, two outlaws lay dead in the street, and the rest were shot up and sent riding for their lives. Two citizens of Northfield were killed in shocking crime that set in motion, one of the greatest and most exciting manhunts in American history.

This book is about that manhunt, that great escape by Frank and Jesse James through southwestern Minnesota, southeastern Dakota Territory, and thence into Iowa and finally back home in Missouri. The bank robbery itself and capture of the Younger brothers will also be explained in some detail, but the meat of the book will be an account of the mile by mile, day by day escape by the James brothers, both of whom were wounded and in need of medical care. That they were able to keep out the grasp of the numerous bands of man hunters, find food at homesteads, get directions from kind but unknowing settlers, cross rivers and creeks and steal horses when needed, until at long last, they reached Clay County, Missouri, their home base, has to rate as one of the most unlikely and sensational accomplishments in the history of the American West.

But it is a subject the James brothers never talked about, or if they did, the discussion never found its way into print. And yet the Northfield raid and the great escape combined to form the vehicle that sent the James brothers speeding into history, riding an express train of unparalleled popularity and notoriety. Books, stage presentations, Wild West shows, re-enactments, and finally movies and television, all tell their story with varying degrees of accuracy and truth. But it matters not, for Frank and Jesse James are America's most famous outlaws. They earned the award the hard way, and in the American mind, they have a strong and lasting grip on the trophy.

One day while talking to some friends about my writing projects, I mentioned that I was working on a book about Frank and Jesse James. Not surprisingly, I was questioned about the subject: What could I possibly write about them that was not already in print? Good question, of course, but I replied that the great escape from Northfield was the one part of their lives that others have ignored or glossed over, and yet, to my thinking, it was the greatest and most singular achievement of their outlaw careers. So I forged ahead with the project and I now lay it before the reading public, armed with the thought that there is room on the bookshelves of America for one more book about the James brothers.

The research and writing of this book was a mission of pleasure, made relatively easy by the newspaper archives in the Library of Congress. The digitizing of millions of newspaper pages, and the ease with which one can access the site called Chronicling America, has brought to light a vast number of newspapers that had seemingly disappeared from memory long ago. Having the resource available allowed me to find useful and relevant information that has never before appeared in print.

Even though the modern researcher works mainly from his or her computer, libraries have not lost their value. For me the people at the Siouxland Library in Sioux Falls, South Dakota, were exceptionally helpful and always friendly and respectful, handling my requests for inter-library loans, and I thank each and every member of the reference staff. Other research was conducted at the library of Augustana University in Sioux Falls, and at the public libraries at Pierre, Canton, Yankton, Mitchell and Vermillion, South Dakota, and Luverne, Minnesota. I extend my sincere thanks to the staffs of those facilities. I also appreciate the kind assistance from the librarians at the public library in St. Joseph, Missouri, where I spent an afternoon going through a file on the James brothers.

I wish to thank my friends and colleagues who have encouraged me and supported my writing, among them David Swan, Richard Nordstrom, Steve Bointe, Bill Waggoner, Harry Thompson, Ron Robinson, Steve Cosulos, Tom Maldari, Dave Davis, Matthew Dorweiller, Beverly Boehrns, Paula Habbena,

Dorinda Daniels and each and every member of the Minnehaha County Historical Society, Sioux Falls, South Dakota. I also want to salute and thank the South Dakota State Historical Society, the Center for Western Studies at Augustana University, the Minnehaha Century Fund, and the Westerners Sioux Falls Corral, along with the membership of the San Diego Independent Scholars, with special thanks to Sam Gusman and Gerry Horwitz.

A writer invariably meets new people during course of writing a book. It was my pleasure and luck to meet Joseph K. Houts, Jr., of St. Joseph, Missouri, who, like me, is a lawyer and author. Joe very kindly took time from his busy work schedule to give me and my sister Connie Lilla a tour of the museums and other historic sites in St. Joseph, and a look inside the house were Jesse James as shot and killed in 1882. Thanks very much, Joe.

My family always gets the last word in the preface and acknowledgments of a new book. My brother Dave, sisters Connie, Elleen and Twyla, have been faithful and steadfast in their support of my writing and I thank them very much. The same goes for my brothers-in-law, all of whom are loyal and honorable members of my family. I know I speak for them all when I say that we shall always love, honor and remember the loved ones who have passed on.

To my daughter Danae, her husband Steven, granddaughter Angelina and grandson Hunter, I love you all very much and at this and every future moment of my life, I will hold and keep you in my heart.

1

Pen Pictures of the James Brothers

"There is a certain halo of romance around the name of the outlaws, on the general principle that distance lends enchantment to the view."
—J. A. Derome in the *Daily Argus-Leader* (Sioux Falls, SD), April 5, 1924

Americans have long and openly expressed mixed feelings about crime and criminals. It seems as if we are never able to simply reject all bad behavior in favor of good conduct. Instead, we freely grant some bad people a free pass on their way to the throne of judgment by history. We carry on as if we feel sorry for certain lofty, colorful criminals, many of whom—like splashy, rebellious characters in a novel—we have learned to like and admire. Although we have always been a people sharply divided by race, religion and politics, we all seem to agree that when it comes to crime, there are, invariably, shades of gray. Indeed, legends, songs and stories are created out of the mysterious ambiguity.

Investigations, arrests, trials and punishment have combined to provide an intense and over-arching drama that is often more appealing than the creative efforts of the best writers of fiction. While most of these colorful episodes have faded away with the passing of time, the stories about Frank and Jesse James, from Missouri, have retained their luster and staying power. Other outlaw gangs robbed banks, stagecoaches and trains, but none ever matched the cunning, daring, finesse and success of the James brothers, along with their companions the Younger brothers and other gang members. If there was a gold standard for outlaws, the James–Younger gang owned it.

The daring lives of outlaws such as the James brothers contributed to the proliferation of "dime novels." Seemingly cranked out by a myth-making machine, these inexpensive, short works of fiction were very popular in the late 19th and early 20th century. The cheap books that sold for ten or 15 cents often featured stories about western characters, both outlaws and honest men, engaged in violence and vice or thrilling acts of heroism. If they were written about a real person, there was little, if any, truth in the narrative. They were marketed to young, impressionable boys, and although they contributed to literacy, they were often blamed for leading youth into crime. The James brothers were "dime novel" heroes that long ago endeared themselves to the public despite their actual record of robbery and murder, and other forms of violent, self-indulgent behavior. They were not good role models, but the endearment has stood the test of time.

The penultimate takers from the money-makers, these villains openly, and without shame or regret, simply did what many other men of their time secretly wanted to do: recover their fair share of the wealth that the ruling class kept in banks. Rich people rode on trains and stagecoaches too, so these carriers were fair game.

For their leading role in a bizarre form of class warfare, the James brothers have laid claim to our lasting fascination. Not for the good they have done, for they have done no good, but for their wild, independent, bold, point of a gun lifestyle, all of which has, ever so strangely, placed the Missouri-born brothers, and other outlaws of the Old West, on a pedestal next to Americans worthy of respect and fame. For proof we need only look at the number of books written and movies made celebrating the lives and exploits of outlaws. Without a doubt, there will be more for there is much good in being bad.

Of course the American Civil War had a hand in the bad business. For in addition to causing suffering and death, the war—like all wars in general—tended to inspire the development of new and more advanced weaponry. And thanks to men like Winchester, Remington and especially Colt, America found itself much better armed after the war than before the shooting started. The romance of the gun was in full swing in the 1870s, a decade marred by gun violence.

So it is true that the Civil War, and the frontier experience that followed in its wake, gave guns to America, and guns have, in turn, helped to create a false history of the American West. Seemingly transfixed by a distorted view of the history of the frontier, many people find it impossible to separate themselves from guns, those iconic symbols of the past. The thought of the James brothers in a shoot-out with a posse stirs the blood. Owning handguns and rifles—things that provide a sense of fulfillment, security and power—connect well because of our fascination with the frontier past.

People do so without a clear historic understanding about frontiersmen, including outlaws, and their guns. The men and women of the frontier, both good and bad, were not engaged in acting out, and there was no glamour or ego in wearing a gun. Unless you were an outlaw and needed a gun to commit crimes, firearms were a necessary tool, a utilitarian object like an ax or a plow. But over the years, novels, television and movies have infiltrated the American psyche, presenting a fictionalized if not altogether false evaluation of guns and their role on the frontier. We believe, or want to believe, what we see in the movies and on television is a truthful version of the Old West, when, in fact, much of it is a fable, something akin to folklore.

No one understands exactly why it happened, and the debate is ongoing, but the gunfighter long ago emerged as an American folk hero. The shootist became the ultimate individualist in the age of rugged individualism, symbolic of all that was wild, dangerous and brave.

Jesse James and other bad men of the 19th century unwittingly created—from the hoof prints of a dusty trail—an indelible image that has inspired a nostalgic longing for guns by so many moderns. Like the readers of "dime novels" of the 1870s, many people secretly, or openly, want to be like the bold men of the old days, and to step into those worn out boots, they include guns in their wardrobe. We can't travel back in time, so we can't escape the shackles of the present, but with gun in hand we can at least get a feeling for the frontier past.

Guns served society by bringing law and order to a lawless land. But when the smoke cleared, it was not always the lawman that emerged as the hero; it was the gun—the transcendent gun—that looms above all else, even the outlaw. The gun makes daring and bravery relevant in the minds of those who accept, as truth, the mythic view of the Old West. For the myth-makers and their followers, the use of a gun in a shoot-out is more important than the outcome, because it is the gun that made it all possible. Throwing stones at 20 paces, for example, would not provide the necessary thrill.

The characters in this book could not have succeeded in pulling off crime after crime without access to guns and ammunition. As to the ability of the James and Youngers to shoot fast and straight, the record is mixed. It was, however, their willingness to shoot and kill people that set them apart from others, and contributed to a criminal success story that is unparalleled in American history. In most respects they were just ordinary and average men who had survived the Civil War. But they were also Yankee-hating Southerners who were motivated by feelings of outrage toward the victors. The war taught them how to kill without remorse, and that lack of empathy allowed them to turn away from the mundane lives that one might expect from ordinary men.

Their suffering during the war does not, of course, excuse nor mitigate their lawlessness. That they refused to accept defeat and go on with their lives simply means that they snubbed reality and were not willing to make peace with the winners, nor would they accept that they were losers. Motivated by emotion rather than reason, Frank, Jesse, Cole Younger and his brothers chose a life of crime, and therefore did not represent the many thousands of bitter, war damaged, ex-Rebels who returned to their homes and rebuilt their lives under the American flag and within the confines of the law.

The purpose of this book is not to further applaud the lives of the law breakers. In fact this writer believes it is okay to call one who commits a crime a criminal. So rather than passing out further accolades to the infamous brothers in crime, the author of this book will attempt to provide readers with a dispassionate, fact-based narrative and leave the glorification to others. The main thrust of this book is to explain the remarkable escape from Northfield, Minnesota, over a span of 400-plus miles, by the James brothers, with special emphasis on their brief Dakota sojourn.

It was the miraculous, unbelievable "Great Escape" that catapulted the James brothers into permanent and lasting fame that climaxed in a barrage of Wild West shows, books, theatrical performances and movies that have celebrated their lives. These extravaganzas, following the death of Jesse James, were attended by huge cheering crowds, the kind of attention usually reserved for good people who perform outstanding, unselfish and truly heroic deeds. But the American people had bestowed that kind of honor on a pair of legendary killers and robbers, and nothing has been able break the public gaze; there has been no force powerful enough to disturb the strange fixation. Both Frank and Jesse James, each larger than life, speak loud and clear to the secret outlaw in every man. Sometimes false gods are destined to be heard and believed.

Alexander Franklin James was born on June 10, 1843, on land that was very close to where the James farm was later located. His brother Jesse Woodson James was born on September 27, 1847. The boys had a rural childhood that was typical for children of the Missouri countryside. Their parents were Robert and Zerelda James. Their father was a college-educated Baptist minister, including a master's degree in art from Georgetown University. Their tall, broad-shouldered mother was a strong, independent and aggressive woman, devoted to her family and afraid of no one. Zerelda Cole was also said to have been a refined woman, having been educated "at a convent in Lexington, Kentucky," and she could say, with pride, that her grandfather had served as a soldier in the American Revolutionary War.[1]

Better off than most, the James lived on a 275-acre farm near Kearney, Missouri, 17 miles northeast of Kansas City. Robert Sallee James was the pas-

1. Pen Pictures of the James Brothers

This is one of the earliest photographs of Jesse James, taken in 1864, during the third year of the Civil War. Young Jesse was a member of William C. Quantrill's guerrilla fighters. A strident Confederate and a believer in slavery and a state's right to secede, Jesse joined the guerrilla unit in 1864, at age 16 or 17. He acquired a reputation as a fearless fighter and a vicious killer, whose hatred of Yankees knew no bounds. While trying to steal a saddle, Jesse was shot in the right breast, the bullet passing through his body. Although the wound was serious, Jesse survived, thanks to the care he received from his cousin, Zerelda Mimms, the girl he would eventually marry (Library of Congress).

tor of the New Hope Church, preaching to a sizable congregation. He was a co-founder of William Jewell College, established in 1849 in Liberty, Missouri.[2] His only daughter, Susan Lavenia James, was born on November 25, 1849. Everything about the James family seemed calm, quiet and prosperous. But Robert S. James was apparently not fully satisfied with a peaceful family life. The man was bright and full of promise, but there was no pill for the restlessness he felt. Reverend James was seemingly mesmerized by sweet song of a distant siren. In 1850 he went to California, in search of gold, and possibly to visit his brother Drury James, who was prospering in the far West. What, if any, gold he found will never be known, for not long after his arrival on the West coast, he died of fever.[3]

Two young boys and a little girl, who would have no knowledge of her father, except what she was told by others, were left fatherless. It was reported by an Indiana newspaper that the "distinguished Baptist clergyman," Robert S. James, father of three, "was driven from his house by the mother," the forceful and demanding Zerelda James, causing him to die alone, "in exile."[4] It was also claimed that he became a 49er to make money to pay for the education of his children.[5]

Whatever the truth, the death of their father was a severe loss for the James children, but fortunately for the boys and their sister, their mother did not falter; she eagerly took up the task of providing for her family. In fact, it appears that the rambunctious boys got their derring-do from their mother. Unlike her studious and religious husband, Zerelda came from a family that owned a tavern, reputed to be a place where wild, bizarre and immoral behavior ruled the day. In her younger days, Zerelda was said to be "a daring horsewoman, a good dancer, and not afraid of the devil himself."[6] Her influence on her sons was exceedingly strong. Her neighbors stated that she "transmitted to her boys 'all the deviltry,' that distinguished their career."[7] William Pinkerton of Chicago's famous Pinkerton Detective Agency thought she was a criminal by nature, calling her "a regular Tartar."[8]

The bold and brassy Zerelda married Benjamin Simms in 1852, but that marriage failed because he could not get along with his stepchildren. It ended with his death in a horse accident. Never one to quit trying, the widow Simms married Dr. Reuben Samuel from Kentucky, and found the relationship to be a good fit. He was described as "small, meek and quiet," and she was large and loud and "wore the pants."[9] It was also a good deal for in a pre-nuptial agreement Zerelda retained ownership of 200 acres of land and six slaves.[10] It was not a plantation and the Samuels were not a part of the Southern aristocracy, but they had the advantage of land and expectation that they were in an upwardly mobile position.

Susan Lavenia James Parmer, the younger sister of Frank and Jesse James, was born November 25, 1849. Little is known of her life except that she grew up in troubled times when her native state of Missouri was embroiled in the savage politics of slavery and states rights, a political struggle that culminated in the Civil War. For four long years, Susan was forced to bear witness to violence and destruction on a scale no one could have predicted. At age 14, Susan and her mother were arrested and temporarily imprisoned for failing to cooperate with the federal authorities. A true Southern woman, she married Allen H. Parmer in Clay County, Missouri, in 1870. Her husband had served with Quantrill's raiders during the Civil War. The couple lived in Texas. Susan died March 3, 1889 (The State Historical Society of Missouri).

Then disaster struck and a great unraveling began that would in the end destroy the old South and along with it dramatically change the lives of countless thousands of people. The 1860 election of Abraham Lincoln to the presidency followed by the secession of several Southern states sent shock waves through America. Missouri felt it too. It was a border state with considerable slaves in the southern counties, but it had a cosmopolitan aspect with strong ties to the Union in cities such as St. Louis. The Civil War began when men stopped talking and started shooting. Confederate artillery fired on Fort Sumter in the Charleston Harbor on April 12, 1861, and it wasn't long after that Missourians were up in arms.

Although Missouri stayed in the Union it was not spared the ravages of war. It was a sharply divided state, setting off neighbor against neighbor violence resulting in bloodshed on a scale that no one could have anticipated. Clay County, where the Samuel family lived, was in the thick of the backstabbing, guerrilla-style struggle that threatened to tear the state apart; indeed, Missouri was caught up in its own civil war and was destined to reap a whirlwind of suffering and sorrow.

The staunchly, pro–Confederacy Samuel family was not spared, and they too suffered. One day a group of Union soldiers arrived at the Samuel place

Zerelda Samuel had three husbands during her long and tumultuous life, and two of them were the fathers of her seven children, five of whom lived to be adults. Her first husband, Robert S. James, was a prominent Baptist minster who gave up a comfortable life in order to search for gold in faraway California. He died there, leaving Zerelda to handle the responsibility of child raising and managing the family farm near Kearney, Missouri. Her second marriage to Benjamin Mimms lasted just a short time. Her third husband was Dr. Reuben Samuel, a mild mannered physician who seemed to be satisfied that his domineering and fiercely independent spouse "wore the pants" of family. It was believed the fiery, tall and broad-shouldered Zerelda passed on to Frank and Jesse her fearless and aggressive nature. Zerelda died in 1911 (The State Historical Society of Missouri).

while the doctor and his step-son Jesse were working in their cornfield. The visitors demanded of Samuel that he tell them where they could find the Rebel guerrilla leader William Quantrill. The doctor told them he did not know and the men found that answer unsatisfactory. They took Dr. Samuel to a tree and with a rope around neck he was raised off the ground, left to strangle for a short time and then lowered. This was repeated three times, and the suffering doctor was left "senseless and bleeding." All this was done with Jesse helplessly watching in horror.

But Union men were not finished. They turned on young Jesse and "with a whip he was scourged up and down corn rows, prodded with bayonets." Not satisfied yet, they roughly demanded that Zerelda tell them the whereabouts of the terrorist guerrilla Quantrill. She rose up and with a strong voice answered: "what I know I will die knowing." They did not kill her, though, no doubt, she convinced them that she would have chosen death.[11]

This incident had a telling and lasting effect of Jesse and Frank. In their anger, the young men saw it as their duty to oppose the Union. "A teenaged Frank James joined a company of the Missouri State Guard in time to participate in the battle of Wilson's Creek, near Springfield on August 10, 1861." It was an especially savage and brutal battle with high casualties on both sides and resulted in victory for the Confederates. In the winter of 1861–62, Frank got the measles and was captured. He was later paroled and permitted to return to Clay County, where he eventually took the Oath of Allegiance to the United States and posted a $1,000 bond to back it up.[12]

But Mr. James was probably not all that sincere about taking an oath to uphold the U. S. Constitution, for his next move during the war was to join a band of marauding, bushwhacking guerrillas. When he learned that William Clarke Quantrill was recruiting men to join his gang of pro–Rebel fighters, Frank signed on in May of 1863, and he met and became good friends with Cole Younger. With two young and fiercely dedicated Rebels among the throng, the band went on a long raiding and killing spree in Missouri, Kansas and as far south as Texas, attacking and killing Union soldiers and other groups and individuals who opposed "the cause." There can be no accounting of the number of people Frank James killed during his stint as Missouri guerrilla, under the leadership of the merciless butcher Quantrill, known to be a "demon in battle."

Frank's younger brother, Jesse, aggressive by nature, was anxious to be a part of the action, but he was at first rejected by the gang because of his age. Forced to stay at home and mind the farm and younger siblings, it would be just a matter of time until he saddled up and rode away. He was just too motivated and energetic, and had seen too much of the strong-armed tactics of the Union soldiers to simply stay at home and wait out the war. He hated Yankees and wanted to kill his share and then some. He fit in nicely with the "take no prisoners" attitude of Quantrill.

Most likely it was in the spring of 1864 that Jesse James joined Quantrill's gang of wanton killers. In the late summer or early fall, Jesse was shot in the right breast, while trying to steal a saddle, the bullet passing through his body. After suffering a wound that could prove fatal, Jesse managed to ride, with Frank's assistance, four miles to the house of his uncle by marriage, John Mimms, and was cared for by his cousin Zee Mimms (short for Zerelda). Though his wound was severe, he survived, for he was both young and strong. He rejoined his brother on September 20, 1864.[13]

The painful experience reinforced his determination to strike the enemy. As a guerrilla fighter, Jesse acted out his hatred of the Union and its soldiers. He was described by a companion as essentially fearless and "that he was brutal none will deny." He shot and killed a "St. Louis drummer" who was simply walking down a street, out of "pure wantonness." It was also reported that Jesse—a man of deep

This photograph shows a young Frank (sitting) and Jesse James (right) and a comrade named Charles Fletcher Taylor. Taken in 1864, this is proof that the brothers took time off from raiding and killing, so they could be memorialized in a Civil War photograph. Frank James joined the Southern army in 1861, not long after the war commenced. He fought in the battle of Wilson's Creek near Springfield, Missouri on August 10, 1861, that resulted in a Confederate victory. The following winter, Frank took ill and was captured by Union soldiers. He took an oath of allegiance to the United States, but soon broke it and joined forces with William C. Quantrill, serving as a raider and killer until the end of the war (The State Historical Society of Missouri).

religious faith—angrily shot and killed a man who "doubted the existence of a hell." He was a poorly educated young man who nonetheless became "thoroughly posted on the affairs of the day." The man, who learned to use the news media to his advantage, was "licentious and cruel," and yet able to develop strong, caring relationships with "good women." With other women, "who were not pure," he freely indulged in "liaisons with hundreds" of them. An exaggeration no doubt, but it was claimed that as a result of his promiscuity, he fathered a girl who in 1882 was living in Howard County, Missouri.[14]

The dangerous life on the trail, coupled with their dedication to the Confederacy, caused the two wayward brothers to become close and protective of each other. It was said that Jesse's love for Frank "was always like that a woman has for her child."[15] It was also said that the bookish, introspective Frank "always lacked initiative."[16] But that Frank could count on Jesse no matter what the circumstances was seemingly written in letters of blood at an early age.

The brothers served under Quantrill's associate, William "Bloody Bill" Anderson, a psychopathic killer who loved his work. It wasn't enough for him to simply kill or see men die; he sought to terrorize his victims, he found pleasure in bringing about death of others in a cruel, sadistic manner. Unfortunately for the civilian population of Missouri, Anderson assumed control over most of the guerrillas. He proved to be far more reckless and bloodthirsty than Quantrill who had become marginalized as a leader. The members of his gang either gravitated toward Anderson, or, like Cole Younger, joined the regular Confederate army.[17]

Anderson's conduct was looked upon as so horrible as to be unacceptable by ordinary Rebel officers and men. But they did nothing to stop him for the Confederate high command understood the value of terror and torture. Confederate president Jefferson Davis, his cabinet and generals were interested in winning the war and were willing to look the other way to avoid facing the atrocities of Bloody Bill Anderson, who massacred people with joyful exuberance. Anderson and his comrades were "land pirates and [they] carried a black flag." Their brand of warfare was one of savagery, a series of sneak attacks.

Among the many blood-lettings under Anderson's banner was the "massacre at Centralia," a railroad village in Boone County, Missouri. Bloody Bill and about 80 bushwhackers took over the town in the morning of September 27. They ransacked two stores, found a barrel of whiskey and got rip-roaring drunk, but they were just getting started. Before lunch they robbed a train, stealing from both pro–Union and pro–Confederate people alike, after which they captured and severely beat about 25 Union soldiers returning from a furlough. Not yet finished with their fiendish business, they set the train on fire and then sent it "racing down the tracks to the west." Then they burned the depot and another train. Later that afternoon, the drunken killers ambushed a detachment of the 39th Missouri Infantry, killing the commanding officer, Major A. V. E. Johnson, and 148 other men, all shot in the head. Seventeen were scalped and one man had his privates cut off and stuffed in his mouth. Jesse James was credited for killing Major Johnson, according to his brother Frank.[18]

Around the time of the Centralia massacre, young Jesse earned the nickname "Dingus," and it would stay with him for the rest of his life. While he was cleaning his gun, he accidently cut off the tip of his middle finger, left hand. He reacted by blaming the gun, calling it a "dodd-dingus pistol."[19] Of course the missing fingertip would be something that could be used to identify him as the years went by. And throughout the years, he regularly wore gloves in public to conceal the tip-less finger.[20]

The carnage and savagery at Centralia was certain to be met with retribution, and the Union forces were determined to hunt down and kill Bloody Bill Anderson. A contingent of Union troops led by Major Samuel P. Cox, from Gallatin, Missouri, was detailed to do the job. An informant told Cox that Anderson was camped near Orrick, in Ray County. On a balmy afternoon in October of 1863, Cox decoyed Anderson's men into a trap and with Yankees on both sides of the road they opened fire. One of the casualties was Bloody Bill Anderson. His body was taken to Richmond, the county seat, and photographed. Later his head was severed and placed on a telegraph pole, after which his headless body was rudely dragged through the streets.[21]

With the loss of Anderson, the guerrillas were in disarray but not defeated. In late December 1864, Quantrill decided to reunite the remnants of his band. Frank James rejoined Quantrill on a long raiding odyssey into Kentucky, but Jesse and others went south into Texas, looking for the scattered pieces of Anderson's gang. The South was clearly losing the war, but no one, it seems, had had enough of killing.

Quantrill's men worked their way across Kentucky, at times dressed in federal uniforms, stealing horses and other supplies, and killing men who opposed them. Frank James shot and killed a Union lieutenant, upon orders from his boss, Quantrill.[22] Their seemingly aimless trek through Kentucky came to an abrupt end on January 29, 1865, when the "scouts" of Captain James H. Bridgewater caught up with the guerrillas near Harrodsburg. In a shoot-out with Union troops, some of the raiders were killed and many were captured, including Jim Younger. Frank James managed to escape and went back searching for Quantrill.

Quantrill's men scattered in the woods, horseless and barefoot in the February cold and snow. Their ranks seriously thinned out, they retreated to the west, stealing horses when the opportunity presented itself. Finally, on May 10, in gun battle on a farm between Taylorsville and Bloomfield, Quantrill was mortally wounded. Frank James was about 15 miles away, and when he learned of Quantrill's condition, he rode to the farm house where the Rebel leader lay paralyzed from his wounds. There was the realization among those gathered around Quantrill's bed that there nothing left to do but surrender.[23]

In March or April of 1865, Jesse James had rejoined what was left of Anderson's brigands in Texas. A new company of 144 men was created under the leadership of Archie "Little Archie" Clements. They lit out for Missouri. On May 7, well after General Robert E. Lee had surrendered to General U.S. Grant at Appomattox, the raiders struck the town of Kingsville, Missouri, where mostly Unionists lived. They sacked the town and burned five houses, killing eight men. Jesse is credited with killing the postmaster, Leroy Duncan, putting a bullet in his forehead.[24] The war was grinding to a halt but the crazed killers would have none of it.

But all came to a head on May 15, 1865, when a strong Union force hit the guerrillas near Lexington, Missouri. Jesse James later explained that he and other raiders were going to Lexington to surrender when they encountered some "drunken soldiers." James recalled that his horse was shot and so was he.[25] For all practical purposes, when Jesse fell, the Civil War was over. War can prove to be tiresome and ultimately it will grind to a halt, but in the waning days and hours, there is one singular desire in the mind of every combatant: no soldier wants to be the last casualty of war. This was especially true for a man who would remain for the rest of his life an unrepentant Rebel.

Strangely enough, a northern soldier, John J. Jones, serving with the 3rd Wisconsin Cavalry, may have been the man who shot and wounded Jesse James. In 1904, after Jesse James had been immortalized in death, Jones came forth and made two audacious claims: On May 17, 1865, while chasing the enemy, he fired the last shot in the Civil War, and when he pulled the trigger, he was aiming at the guerrilla Jesse James. In his own words, Jones explained that his unit was on patrol on the Warrensburg Road near Lexington, Missouri, when they came upon a party of Rebel "bushwhackers," one of whom was Jesse James. A fire fight broke out and Jones shot and wounded Jesse James. Jones did not explain how it was he knew his target was a teenager turned guerrilla fighter, a lad who would one day become America's most famous bandit. But 40 years is a long time, plenty of time for Jones to work out the details of his claim to fame.[26]

But the painful truth, however, is that someone, Jones or another man, had shot Jesse James, but not fatally. With admirable toughness, he ran from the soldiers through the woods with blood spurting out of his wound. Fortunately he was found by friends and was taken in a wagon to Lexington where he was put up in a hotel. At this point, there was nothing left to do but surrender. The name "J. M. James" was on a list of those who surrendered on May 21, 1865, and took the oath of allegiance. About a month later, Jesse James was taken to the home of John and Mary Mimms where he was once again nursed back to health by his relatives.[27]

Next, it was Frank's turn to give up the fight. On July 26, 1865, the name "Alex James" was one of 14 survivors of Quantrill's gang who turned themselves in. Under the terms of their surrender, they were allowed to keep their horses and side arms and were all paroled based on their written agreement not to take up arms against the federal government.[28] All in all, exiting the war went well for the James brothers, both of whom were cold-blooded killers who deserved hanging. Although Jesse had to suffer through another long and painful recovery, recover he did, thanks in part to a long and restful stay at San Luis Obispo, California.[29] As an adult he was described as clean-cut and handsome, with "clear steel-blue eyes and the physique of an athlete."[30]

Both men ignored their so-called allegiance to the United States that seemingly meant very little because as ex-guerrillas they were pursued and harassed by the authorities. So instead of starting their lives over as law-abiding citizens, they began planning for a career outside of the law. The deadly, serpent-like entity known as the James–Younger gang had emerged from the poisonous, polluted dirt of the Civil War. It was their connection to Quantrill and "Bloody Bill" Anderson that would prove to be a liability that neither brother could overcome.

Still, there was some semblance of decency in their lives. Frank was married on June 6, 1874, to Annie Ralston, of Jackson County, Missouri. Her father, Samuel Ralston, a Unionist and high-ranking personage in Independence, Missouri, strenuously disapproved of the marriage so the couple eloped. An outlaw-friendly newspaper, *The Kansas City Times*, crowed: anyone who knew "anything of the career of the James brothers would [not] expect them to woo, win and marry like other people," certainly not the "dashing and daring" Frank James, "the bold train-robber."[31]

Annie was said to be a beautiful and intelligent girl, but quite sentimental; she was also well educated, which probably suited Frank's love of Shakespeare and classical literature.[32] They met by chance and she was smitten; a clandestine wedding was arranged and the vows were exchanged in Omaha. It was said she was carried away by her "romantic temperament," enhanced by the dangerous exploits of her beau and his gang.[33] She left a note that simply said: "Dear Mother: I am married and going West."[34] Unfortunately, there was negative fallout after the wedding; she was disowned by her heartbroken parents,[35] and she was snubbed and deserted by some of her friends who disapproved of her choice for a husband.[36]

Jesse beat his brother to the altar. On April 24, 1874, in Kearney, Missouri, at the residence of Zee's sister, Jesse married the girl who had nursed him back to health during his guerrilla days: his cousin, the quiet, introspective Zerelda "Zee" Mimms, "born in Kentucky of old revolutionary stock."[37] Their uncle, Reverend Billy James, performed the ceremony. But he did so only after the groom convinced the good pastor that he was not the notorious outlaw that many believed him to be. The bride's mother also disapproved of her daughter's choice for a husband.

The wedding was duly performed despite the sudden appearance of two detectives, both of whom Jesse spooked out of their boots with a clever ruse. When he learned the detectives were entering Kearney, he wrapped Zee in a feather bed, and then mounted his horse and waited at the back of the house. As the detectives were entering the front door, Jesse raced around to that entrance and caused a disturbance that distracted the lawmen, both of whom returned to the front door, went out and got on their horses. As the frustrated members of the legal fraternity were chasing after the phantom rider, Jesse re-entered by the back door and retrieved his gentle bride-to-be from the tender folds of the feather bed.[38]

Jesse was kind, gentle and loving to his wife and she returned that love and loyalty to him, and in the virtuous entwinement lay the path to a successful and lasting marriage. Trust and loyalty from his wife would prove to be essential to Jesse's success in his chosen field. Likewise the trust and loyalty of friends and comrades was the character trait that Jesse valued the most, and pity the person who betrayed his trust. It was said that he once claimed that he would kill a woman who betrayed him as quick and easy as he would kill a man for the same offense.[39]

Zee—who would always be faithful—was a public-school teacher at the time she married Jesse. To Zee, Jesse was a man of good habits; he never used foul language in her presence. He didn't drink alcohol, nor did he smoke or chew tobacco.[40] She once described him as "a reticent man, and he never told me where he intended going, but I always had an idea what he was doing." In the same interview she said rather coldly, "there's one thing certain, what I do know of Jesse will never be made public. I'll go to my grave without telling anything."[41]

Like Frank's spouse, Zee was devoted to her husband, and maintained that devotion until the day she died. Both women shared their husbands' "fear of detection and arrest."[42] Both women would be forced to ride the roller-coaster of emotion as each day brought excitement, apprehension, relief or threats of retribution from the gun or the rope. Although their spouses had many friends and sympathizers in Missouri, as time went on, a large measure of men wanted the James brothers locked up and hung or simply shot dead. After having lived through four years of savagery during the Civil War, some men were disappointed that post-war Missouri was still awash in violence and crime. They wanted an end to the outlaw activity; they just wanted ordinary peace and quiet. But that worthy goal was not something looming on the horizon, and Missouri, along with the rest of the country, was forced bear witness to a crime wave of long duration.

2

A Long Way from Home

"The gang that rode into Minnesota did not plan any particular robbery. It was a sort of bandit's outing party."
—*The Fulton County News*
(McConnellsburg, PA), June 27, 1901

September 7, 1876, was a calm and peaceful day in the town of Northfield, Minnesota, as people went about their daily affairs, meeting and greeting each other with friendly words and gestures. The southeastern Minnesota town, along with much of the northwest, had suffered through the great grasshopper calamity of 1876, the clouds of insects in the millions having destroyed countless acres of crops. Many a farmer had been "grasshoppered," some worse than others, but despite the insect infestation, Northfield had the look and feel of peaceful prosperity, amid the "stagnation, depression and suffering" elsewhere in America.[1]

Pioneers were an optimistic and resilient bunch; they took a punch, and if they went down, they got back up. Besides, the rich soil of the Minnesota prairie had been good to them. They were believers and they lived with the prospect of future harvests of grain and other crops to put food on the table, and fatten the bank accounts of merchants and other business.

Although the life of the pioneer was dominated by hard work, the mundane rhythm of life never succeeded in destroying the romance of life. Autumn was the time of year of the "Harvest Moon," and of the atmospheric magic of "Indian Summer," a strange, unseasonably warm weather event, peculiar to the northern plains. Appearing like something that comes out of a magician's hat, it creeps across the landscape without warning, but always with an indescribable feeling of pure enchantment, that once experienced is never forgotten.

Northfield—just 40 miles south of St. Paul—wore the appearance of a conservative, orderly town, a place no one would expect to see violence on a large scale. It was a peaceful city of approximately 2,000 people, all of whom seemed satisfied with their lives, their prosperity and future prospects. A Minneapolis newspaper described them as "notably of the undemonstrative character."[2]

The city got its start in 1855, when John W. North chose the site for a new town.[3] The city center was a short distance away from the bridge over the Cannon River that ran in a north to south direction, dividing the town. It was home to two colleges, Carleton College and St. Olaf College, the places of learning that gave the town a certain sophistication, something that might impress the Yankee east. It had a good baseball team, the Silver Stars. The main street, Division Street, stretched out in a north and south direction, featuring the Dampier Hotel, a drug store, a couple hardware stores and dry goods shops. It was peopled primarily by Scandinavians, some of whom did not speak English. For clever and daring outlaws, Northfield was like tempting, sun-ripened fruit, ready to be plucked and bagged. Something was approaching and it wasn't "Indian Summer."

Adelbert Ames, a decorated Civil War veteran, and the former Reconstruction governor and U.S. senator from Mississippi, was in Northfield assisting his father Jesse and brother John at the family flour mills, a business they established in 1869. John was the mayor of Northfield. In the afternoon of September 7, Adelbert and his brother crossed the bridge over the Cannon River, going in the opposite direction of three well-armed strangers on horseback, all of whom bore the look of grim determination. One of them recognized Adelbert as the former governor of Mississippi. He apparently thought nothing of it, but soon the Ames brothers' attention was drawn to the sound of gunfire coming from the central part of the city.

The Massachusetts native and combat veteran, who had been severely wounded at the battle of Bull Run, did not hesitate. He ran toward the gunfire and discovered that some citizens and a band of outlaws were engaged in a shoot-out, following an attempt by the outlaws to rob the First National Bank of Northfield. Located in the rear of the two-story Scriver Building, it was the only bank in town. Serious, bloody crime was playing itself out in the heartland. Ames watched as the brave townspeople drove off the desperadoes, killing two of the outlaws and wounding others. In a letter to his wife, Ames jocularly compared the experience to the fiery nature of post-war Mississippi politics.[4]

No one knew it at the time, of course, but the bank robbers were not ordinary outlaws. They were members of the notorious James–Younger gang from Missouri, all seasoned professional brigands, some of whom had honed their deadly skills while fighting for the South in the Civil War. The principals were the brothers Jesse and Frank James, Thomas Coleman "Cole" Younger and his two younger brothers, James and Robert. Lesser known, but no less dangerous, Bill Chadwell, Clelland "Clell" Miller and Charlie Pitts were also part of the gang. An article in a Kansas City newspaper suggested that the plans for the elaborate and risky Northfield caper were discussed and agreed upon at the St. Joseph, Missouri, home of "Doc" H. S. Miller, a brother to gang member Clell Miller and the "boon companion of Jesse James."[5]

For the past several years, the James brothers and their gangs had made a living robbing banks, stagecoaches and trains. But for Jesse James, the unrepentant Rebel, the Northfield raid had political underpinnings, for he wanted to strike a blow at the federal policy of Reconstruction. The hated, post-war policy threatened to elevate the freed black people to the status of full citizenship, and thereby dim the prospects for the restoration of the Old South. The antebellum days were dead, stone-cold dead, but restoring life to the dead past was an obsession to Jesse James. It was never too late, the ghosts were never too stale, and the dream of full redemption was not beyond restoration.

Some months before the Northfield raid, on August 31, 1875, a son, Jesse Edwards James, was born to Jesse and Zee James. But father was not content to stay with his family and enjoy the tender company of his infant son. Instead, the restless father chose to venture far from family, home and hearth, at the risk of never seeing his son again, or fathering another child.

Cole Younger was—like Jesse—an outlaw through and through, but

This is probably the best known photograph of the handsome, steely-eyed Jesse James. He sat for this photograph in 1875, in Nebraska, where the James-Samuel family had lived for a time during the Civil War. When the James-Younger gang left Missouri for Minnesota in search of adventure and a bank to rob, Jesse looked like the image reflected by this picture. It was said that Jesse and Frank James were always well dressed when they held up banks, trains and stagecoaches. They preferred to look like businessmen rather than travel about in dirty or ragged clothes, like ordinary saddle tramps. They took special pride in their dangerous work and felt the same about their appearance in public. Image was important to the legendary James brothers (Library of Congress).

while the latter was thought as inflexible and merciless, the former was considered rather kind-hearted and pragmatic. Still stories were circulated that painted a much different picture of the man with a balding head, commanding presence and powerful physique. One such story has Cole Younger—a member of Quantrill's band—in possession of an Enfield rifle that he used to shoot 15 captured Kansas jayhawkers. It was claimed that he wanted to learn more about the killing capacity of the Enfield, so he lined up all 15, took aim and fired. The first shot killed three men and a disappointed Younger supposedly, finished off the rest of them with six more shots.[6] Younger, of course, denied ever having done anything remotely that vicious and heartless, and the story is probably just that.

The Younger family was headed by Henry Washington Younger, a lawyer, legislator, judge and all around good citizen, but like countless others, his life was rudely disrupted by secession and Civil War. Henry came from Kentucky, and settled near Lees Summit, Missouri, on a farm of 600 acres. He was a slave holder but a staunch Union supporter, nevertheless. "The war ruined the Younger family," and worse yet Henry was ambushed and killed and robbed by "Kansas Jayhawkers and Red Legs" near Independence.[7]

The death of Henry W. Younger occurred after his son, Cole, had joined the Quantrill band of terrorists, and after Kansas federals had attacked and looted Henry's stable at Harrisonville, Missouri, stealing horses, wagons and carriages worth thousands of dollars.[8] The raid at Harrisonville had been conducted by troops under Charles R. Jennison, a man just as ruthless and vicious as his counterpart, William C. Quantrill. In connection with the raid, Cole Younger was captured and sentenced to death. A hanging was scheduled, but Cole took "the rope provided for his death," and escaped from a window, rejoining the guerrillas.[9]

While death of his father and subsequent events lit a fire of vengeance in Cole, turning him firmly against the Union, it nevertheless appears that he emerged from the horrors of the Civil War with a somewhat pragmatic attitude, realizing that most men in both armies were, at heart, honorable men. He had killed his share of the enemy but he reconciled himself with the defeat of the South and attempted to put it behind him. It could stay there, too. For as long as he could find his place in the new scheme of things, Cole was satisfied. Jesse James could harbor no such thoughts.

The loquacious Cole Younger liked to blame others for crimes committed by him and his colleagues. It was in 1868 that he made the switch from an industrious farmer to a dangerous desperado. It was at a bank in Russellville, Kentucky, that Cole Younger cut his criminal teeth, not only admitting he participated in the crime, but declaring when questioned: "To tell you the truth, I was there, and we got $19,000.00 in cash."[10]

Although he had participated in some of the riskiest armed robberies, Cole insisted years later that he was opposed to the Northfield adventure. In an 1889 interview, Cole said, "the Northfield affair was a very foolish piece of business."[11] He only went with the majority after he was overruled.[12] Besides, he had to go with the gang to look out for his younger brothers.

One of those who voted against him was his brother James Hardin "Jim" Younger, also a Civil War veteran on the side of the South. The introspective member of the Younger clan had once been a policeman, having joined the Dallas police department in the winter of 1872–73.[13] Usually called Jim, he quit the police department and opted for California, where he apparently prospered in the sheep business, for it was reported in a newspaper that he financed the entire Northfield operation, after he was convinced to leave the West and join the gang.[14]

Most likely, however, the expedition was funded by the $15,000 that the gang took during a train robbery near Otterville, Missouri, that took place on the night of July 7, 1876.[15] One of the eight gang members, a newcomer named Hobbs Kerry, was arrested not long after the heist. When pressed by the authorities, Kerry—who had no prior criminal record—confessed in great detail, in writing, and named all the other gang members including the James brothers and Cole and Bob Younger.[16] Ratting on your fellow robbers is not what the experienced outlaws had in mind when Kerry was added to the gang, and the naming of names may have motivated the gang to head for Minnesota.

That the lawmen were frantically searching for the James and Youngers is well established in the newspaper record. In early August, the home of Samuel Ralston, father-in-law to Frank James, five miles east of Kansas City, was visited one night by an unruly trainload of detectives from St. Louis and Cincinnati. Breaking and entering in the middle of the night, they pounced upon and arrested an "innocent and astounded farmer," the "supposed Jesse James." No doubt they were looking for Frank or Jesse, but had they known how much Ralston hated his son-in-law, the detectives may not have conducted the raid.[17]

It is generally believed that the outlaws traveled north on horseback leaving the Clay County home of the mother of the James boys on August 15, 1876, traveling in small groups with Jesse and Frank riding together, which they typically did while on a raid. It has also been written that they rode on horseback from Clay County to Council Bluffs, Iowa, where they boarded a train.[18] But this version was disputed by Cole Younger in one of his many self-serving interviews with the news media. In 1889, Cole said that "seven of us had left Missouri by train." At Council Bluffs, they "accidently" met Jim. He had been in California with the Younger's uncle. Jim was convinced to join the group, "the trip being merely for a few weeks of pleasure among the lake resorts of the northwest." Cole claimed that each man had several hundred dollars cash to spend. "Robbery was furthest from our minds."[19]

In March of 1903, Cole Younger told a different story. He said that they all traveled in the same train, from Joplin, Missouri, to Mankato, and then on to Minneapolis and St. Paul, where they spent about two weeks. They all bought horses and their outlaw paraphernalia in Minnesota,[20] including four horses that were purchased in Red Wing.[21] The chief of police for St. Louis believed and was quoted as saying the gang met at a "ranche [sic] near Sherman, Texas," on August 23, "and went by rail to Minnesota."[22]

Then there is a story about the gang crossing the Missouri River near Yankton, Dakota Territory, on their long trek to Minnesota. According to H. N. Cooper of Canton, Dakota, B. M. Bottalfson, helped "ferry the James brothers and their gang, across the Missouri River at Yankton." Bottalfson recalled that it was a cold, windy and stormy day, and the ferry crew expressed their displeasure at having to make a perilous crossing over the often dangerous Missouri River. But they were persuaded take the risk when "the bandits demanded action." The ferry, the crew and their outlaw passengers all made it across safely, and the riders continued on their way.[23]

It seems highly unlikely that the James–Younger gang would have diverted so far to the west when the map they were looking at made it clear that going directly north through Iowa, would get them to the destination much quicker than a long meander toward Yankton. Quite likely, the ferry man did transport some outlaws across the Missouri River, for there were so many hard men of questionable backgrounds on their way to Dakota in 1876, due to the Black Hills gold rush. But it is likely that Bottalfson claimed that he gave the James–Younger gang a river ride in order to burnish his Wild West credentials and lay claim to a tale to repeat over and over again to enraptured listeners. It would be one of many tales, however minor, inspired by the exploits of the James–Younger gang, America's best-known outlaws.

There was something about life on the wild frontier that went to a man's head, and if he told his story a certain way, over and over again, people believed it almost as if a nugget of truth had emerged from the fool's gold. For example, it was believed that in the mid–1860s, the James brothers came to Dakota Territory to hide some stolen gold in the high Missouri River bluffs of southern Charles Mix County. The story had legs that carried it to the 20th century, and in the summer of 1908, a man named J. C. McGarvan emerged as "the lucky discoverer" of the "several thousand dollars of the filthy tainted lucre." The story of the lucky find found its way into a newspaper and a reporter coyly predicted that there will be an end to the "dream which has hung on to the skirts of time."²⁴ Perhaps, but tales of the James brothers bold and mysterious exploits would continue to rise up like forbidden fruit to tempt and feed the hungry minds of incredulous people.

Assuming the boys did have bank robbery on their agenda, why the gang chose Northfield when there were so many banks in Iowa, Kansas and Missouri to hit is a question that comes up from time to time. Aside from the political considerations already mentioned, there are other reasons laid out in books and articles. One is that Jesse James, along with Bob Younger, discussed robbing a Minnesota bank. The 22-year-old Bob had grown fond of Jesse and the daring, outlaw attitude he projected, but Bob had found love and wanted to settle down. But first he needed money. Jesse proposed that they gather the gang together, make the long trek to Minnesota and rob a bank, so Bob could buy a farm, marry his girl and settle into the life of a farmer.²⁵

Another version is that the Jameses and Youngers were drawn to Minnesota because they were bent on killing a lawyer named Samuel Hardwicke. Hardwicke had represented a member of the Pinkerton detective agency that threw a "hand grenade" through the window of the James' home in Kearney, Missouri, killing their 14-year-old half-brother, Archie Samuel, and tearing off the right arm of their mother Zerelda. It was not a hand grenade but rather a shell containing combustible material in it, and when Dr. Samuel, using a shovel, tossed it into the fireplace, it exploded.

It mattered not just what it was that caused the damage and suffering, Hardwicke was a marked man. At first Hardwicke stayed in Missouri, moving from place to place, always well armed and fearful that "he could be shot down at any moment." After receiving "dozens of letters" that "threatened his life," he went to St. Paul to live. With vengeance on their minds, the James–Younger gang set out to kill Hardwicke and then rob a bank to, as the old saying went, "replenish their exchequer."²⁶

Other sources suggest the influence of Bill Chadwell, whose real name was said to be Bill Stiles, was a deciding factor. He talked to the others about his knowledge of Northfield, and its bank "in which a large amount of cash was always kept."²⁷ Chadwell, said to be a Minnesota-born horse thief, who had spent time in the "Indian Nation," was most likely the idea man behind the "failed journey" to Northfield, a plan he sold to the rest of the gang. According to a Texas newspaper, Chadwell and one of the Youngers traveled in advance, to "recononiter" several days before the others departed Clay

County, Missouri, in August 1876, to join their comrades and rob the bank.[28] But none of this was true; Bill Chadwell never used the name Stiles and he was just visiting Minnesota, hoping to leave richer than when he arrived.

Bob Younger simply stated in a jailhouse interview that although they considered other banks, they chose Northfield because they believed it was "a wealthy bank, the only one in the village."[29] But like much that came out of the mouths of the Youngers while in jail, it was subject to change, and in another interview, he said they chose Northfield because Adelbert Ames, the former military governor of Mississippi, had "money there."[30]

A Northfield newspaper, the *Rice County Journal*, reported, with a generous dose of sarcasm, that after the gang had "examined Red Wing, Faribault, Mankato and other places," they resolved to rob the bank in Northfield, "owing to our quiet dove-like reputation."[31] Of course the world was about to learn that the people of Northfield were anything but "dove-like" when confronted by hardened criminals.

The least likely reason for the Northfield raid comes from a Sioux City, Iowa, newspaper. The writer of the article claimed to have interviewed "Judge Younger, of St. Clair County, Missouri, uncle of the notorious Younger brothers." The "Judge" offered that it was the James brothers who insisted on the robbery. "They were going to the British Dominion" with a view of settling down "in peace." But problems popped up along the way because "the James boys got to gambling and lost all of their money," and worse yet, they lost all the money of the other men who rode with them. "The James boys swore they wouldn't travel without money, and resolved on the bank robbery."[32]

Cole Younger contributed another explanation while in the sunset of his life and in doing so he confirmed the explanation given by his brother Bob, back in 1876. In his memoir, Younger declared that the gang chose Northfield because Adelbert Ames and Benjamin Butler, both Union generals in the Civil War and both well hated in the South, had money in the Northfield bank. Since the James and Youngers, all former Rebel soldiers or sympathizers, never accepted the surrender of the Confederacy, the war did not end and they were simply attacking Yankees. Younger complained that the gang had been falsely blamed for every robbery, far and wide, and the outlaws grew tired of the accusations, so it was the plan to hit Northfield, take the loot and retire in Cuba or Australia.[33]

If the gang was looking to retire in some faraway paradise, striking out at and harming Adelbert Ames would have given Jesse James special satisfaction; he could then sit back and sip his tropical drink with a smile. Ames was a public figure, often in the news, while he worked hard to convert Mississippi into a state that accepted freedom and full participation in public life for the black man. For that he had made enemies in the South, in great abundance, and he left Mississippi under cloud created by trumped charges against him.

Ames was an easterner, an urbane man of learning, culture and sophistication who believed in equal rights for all including black people. These radical qualities riled Jesse beyond measure for he was opposed to everything that Ames stood for; they stood poles apart on the great social issues of the day, symbolic of the divided nature of America. Oh yes, Jesse James most definitely sought to bring down the "villainous Yankee," the hated Adelbert Ames.[34]

Many years after the Northfield incident, a man interviewed in a Pennsylvania newspaper claimed that he was acquainted with the James and Youngers, and therefore spoke authoritatively and with a dash hero worship. He said that the Younger brothers "were the brains of the party" and "men of good presence." Cole Younger, the eldest, was described as a quiet man, deeply religious, and sure to be welcomed into any congregation. Bob was handsome and athletic, and "the best shot of the three,"[35] while Jim was the "politician of the trio," a man who could talk to others and "get their confidence."

A convincing and disarming gift of gab was a skill that would be very useful when the gang members gathered at Minnesota "resorts" on their way to Northfield. They were way off the beaten path in the heart of the North, and they leisurely "touched elbows with people," taking time to learn about the towns in the area.[36] They posed as surveyors, and in a sense, they were, for they studied "the topography of the country for miles about Northfield, particularly to the south and southwest."[37] They also claimed to be cattle drovers and at yet another place, they were explorers from Kentucky bound for the Black Hills.[38]

While all this was going on, *The Kansas City Times* was busy with alibi-like reporting, making a case to show that the James brothers did not travel to Minnesota. That newspaper asserted that the "majority of the people in this section of the country, do not believe that Jesse and Frank James or the Younger boys are guilty of all the great robberies charged against them." In fact, Jesse "is now residing in Kansas, a peaceable citizen, under a false name," and that he "reads daily papers" and occasionally visits relatives in Kansas City.

The *Times* wanted its readers to believe that all the wild talk about Jesse James, the outlaw, was pure bosh. As proof, it published a letter purported from Jesse W. James dated August 14, 1876. In it Jesse called Hobbs Kerry a "liar, thief and a robber," and went on to state that he knew nothing about

Charlie Pitts and Bill Chadwell until after Kerry was arrested. He further claimed that he had the statements from eight "good and well-known men of Jackson County" to prove that he was not a part of the gang that pulled off the Otterville robbery.[39]

But Jesse wasn't finished. In another letter dated August 18, from "Safe Retreat," he called Kerry's confession "a pack of lies." Detectives, he said, "have been trying for years to get positive proof against me for some criminal offence." Later in his angry letter he indicated that Congress might "grant us a full pardon." Then, realizing he just incriminated himself, he shifted gears quickly, writing, "I will not say pardon, for we have done nothing to be pardoned for."[40]

But it was all false. The gang of eight went north to Minnesota in conformance with its line of work. But before they got down to bank robbing, they took time to let loose and have fun. Six of them made an ugly scene at the Nicollet Hotel in Minneapolis on August 23, 1876, where they worked out final details of the Northfield bank robbery. The James brothers and one other man, who pretended to be sick, checked in to the hotel, using aliases. Claiming to be grangers, they signed the guest register with smooth, fine hands belied their alleged status as hard-working farmers.

The next day, they were joined by three others who also registered using false names.[41] Appearing on the balcony, decked out in linen dusters and white hats, the flamboyant Missourians amused themselves by tossing down coins to the "crowd below."[42] The boisterous outlaws made a scene in the dining room, acting in a loud, crude and boorish manner that upset management and other guests. They were carefully watched by the hotel watchman and it was said that everyone present "saw through them with ease."[43]

They tried their luck at gambling in a prominent St. Paul gambling saloon. The weather being warm, they took off their coats, unstrapped their gun belts and laid their pistols and knives aside. This display of "their warlike character" created a "profound sensation in the gambling room." But lady luck was not on their side, for "our St. Paul sharper's relieved them of about two hundred dollars of their surplus Missouri cash."[44]

Cole's 1889 interview is in accord with the foregoing account. He said that after "making a circuit of the resorts we landed in St. Paul." There the men indulged in "gambling and drinking," and having lost all their money in high stakes poker, the topic of bank robbery came up. It had worked before so why not try it again?[45]

One night they hired a hack and patronized a Minneapolis brothel run by Mollie Ellsworth. She was dressing herself for the evening when a man, armed with "three or four large revolvers," casually walked into her room.

After staring at her for a moment, he asked if she once "kept a house in St. Louis" using the name Kitty Traverse. She replied in the affirmative and in that instant, knew that she was looking at Jesse James, a man she had met in St. Louis. Mollie questioned Jesse about his presence in Minneapolis, and the outlaw simply said that he and his friends were checking out the area, and when they were finished with their tour, he would come back and take her to the Centennial Exposition in Philadelphia.

"I know it was Jesse James," Mollie insisted when she was interviewed by a St. Paul newspaperman. In telling her story to the reporter, Mollie called Jesse "good looking," and added, "they will never catch him. I have known him for twelve years and he always has been a thief. The men are not smart enough to catch him."[46]

The Kansas City Times reported the story too, and with other details. Mollie stated in an interview that in late August "three of the robbers visited my house." One, of course, was Jesse James, heavily armed and carrying a lot of money. She cautioned him to not find trouble, to which Jesse said: "I shall die like a dog or eat the hatchet." Mollie was being civil to Jesse, but in her interview, she let on that she disliked the Missouri legend, a man that "would just as soon shoot a person as to shoot a dead dog." Mollie let it be known that if Jesse ever again showed up at her house, she would "drop him into a hat," meaning she would turn him in to the authorities. In closing her remarks, she said that Jesse was wearing mismatched boots, and that he had a very small foot, "and could wear my shoe."[47] Yes, Mollie—claims to the contrary notwithstanding—Jesse James was in Minnesota in the summer of 1876.

Another person, W. H. Stevens, a reporter for the *St. Paul Weekly Dispatch,* was certain that he saw Jesse James in St. Paul, in the company of four other "suspicious looking men riding up Fifth street" a few days before Northfield was hit. He claimed he was able to get a good look at all of them, and later said, "I have good reason to believe that Frank was not there." Much later in 1886, when Stevens was doing newspaper work in Missouri, he saw Frank James in person, but he did not bear any resemblance to "any of the robbers," that he had by chance, seen in St. Paul in 1876. On the other hand, he said "I recognized Jesse James at sight, at the time of his assassination, as being one of the party I had seen in St. Paul."[48] But his suggestion that Frank James was not in Minnesota, is flawed because he had only seen five of the eight outlaws, meaning quite simply, that Frank could have elsewhere, alone, or with the other two. It is well established that the only time all eight were together was when they were robbing the bank in Northfield.

As the James and Younger gang was zeroing in on their target, a St. Paul newspaper was taking aim at them and their reputation for violating the law and escaping punishment. The article appeared in print on September 1, 1876, just six days before the epic robbery in Northfield. The piece revealed a number of crimes that the Jesse James gang had been accused of committing. Despite reliable evidence against him and his fellow gang members, a number of "good citizens" would invariably step up and by word of mouth give Jesse and his men an airtight alibi. In other words, the crime of perjury covered up the crime of robbery and murder, and no one seemed to be concerned. It was just the way it was in rural Missouri in the 1870s.[49]

According to Cole Younger's account of the daring, September enterprise, the gang didn't confine their activities to Minneapolis or St. Paul, but they prepared for their crime by ranging far and wide taking in Madelia and eastern Cottonwood County, getting to know roads and terrain. They gathered together in Mankato and bought horses, then divided into two groups and set out for Northfield.[50]

Younger doesn't mention any other activity in Mankato, but a latter-day newspaper report states that they were prepared to rob the bank, but were dissuaded from doing so by the presence of large group of men on the sidewalk. Some of them suspiciously "pointed to horsemen." Thinking that "they had been discovered," they "left Mankato in a hurry." The reporter decided that an old saying was worth repeating: "the wicked flee when no man pursueth."[51] Cole Younger vehemently denied there was any plan or attempt to rob the bank in Mankato.[52] But then Cole spun many a yarn when it was convenient to do so.

At some point in time, the gang decided to rob the bank in Northfield. On Monday, September 4, the "wicked" gang was in Le Sueur Center where they spent the night on the floor of a hotel, because court was in session and the beds were all taken by lawyers and court personnel, all of whom "had a high old time that night." Tuesday night they were at the small town of Cordova and on Wednesday night, the eve of their date with destiny in Northfield, they slept at Millersburg, 11 miles west of Northfield. In the morning, they split up again and reunited outside of Northfield west of the Cannon River. Late morning they entered the town, checked out the bank and had lunch "in various places," attracting attention because of their dress and fine horses adorned by silver studded bridles and saddles.[53]

They also attracted attention at J. G. Jeft's restaurant "on the west side of the Cannon River," where they openly and casually discussed politics. When one of the group, "to all appearances the leader of the gang," paid his bill, he boldly "offered to bet the ... proprietor one hundred dollars that this state [Minnesota] would go Democratic."[54] The challenge was not accepted.

After lunch and their final peruse of the town, they returned to their camp outside of town to review the details of their plan.[55]

When they emerged from the woods southwest of town, someone claimed that there were nine riders, thus giving life to the rumor of the "ninth man." The "ninth man" supposedly was given the role of guarding their camp, from which they planned to make their getaway after the robbery business had concluded.[56] But no such "ninth man" is mentioned in Cole Younger's memoir so it is a story that over the years has not gained sufficient credence in the minds of most historians. The *Minneapolis Tribune* declared that "there were only eight men engaged in the affray."[57]

Eight outlaws, all with experience at killing and robbing, all done according to a routine that had been successful in the past, were about to test their skill and luck in Northfield, Minnesota, and in so doing, they were making their grand entrance into annals of historic crime.

3

Deadly Debacle at Northfield

> "The daring attempt to rob a bank at Northfield, Minnesota, ... by eight desperadoes ... is one of the marvels of crime."
> —*Daily Press and Dakotaian* (Yankton, DT), September 21, 1876

By mid-afternoon on September 7, the eight outlaws were ready. They were all mounted on fancy horses, adorned with McClellan saddles, heavily armed with navy revolvers and well-stocked cartridge belts, concealed by long, linen dusters, a popular garment for riders on the prairie and plains. They approached their target in groups in accordance with a well-laid plan. With the collective look of grim determination, they were ready to rob—but there is some confusion in the record as to the identity of the men who entered the bank. A Minnesota newspaper contends that the men were Bob Younger, Charlie Pitts, and a "red-whiskered" man, who was not named in the article.[1]

Another source states that the group of three consisted one of the James brothers, most likely Jesse (whom Cole called Howard), Bob Younger and Samuel Wells who went by an alias, Charlie Pitts.[2] They pulled up in front of Lee and Hitchcock's store on Division Street and dismounted. They lounged around "with an indifferent air." There was a certain swagger about their behavior that drew suspicious glances. Nevertheless, some Northfield men believed they were simply cattle buyers, legitimate business men.

A third source, writer Marley Brant, who had access to descendants of the James and Younger families, states that it was Frank and Jesse James, and Bob Younger who went into the bank.[3] But among them, only Bob Younger would admit that he was "one of the number who went into the bank."[4]

It has been argued by another writer that it was Jesse who led the trio that had entered the bank, at the rear of Lee and Hitchcock's store, and did so for "practical reasons." The rumor was that Jesse did not like shootouts and furthermore he was a bad shot. It was said that on one occasion, he fired six shots at a man and "missed every time." Since he was the acknowledged leader of the gang, he could have exercised his right to work inside the bank, rather than in the street, according to his preference.[5] To add further confusion to an already muddled narrative, a reporter for the *New York Sun* claimed to have interviewed a man who was acquainted with Jesse James. This man said that Frank James was sick on the day of the robbery, and did not participate. He did guard duty that day only, and then rode away "and joined them," when their bloody work was finished.[6]

At some point in every narrative, where there are conflicting statements in the telling of the story, a writer has to make a stand. This writer concludes, based on an evaluation of the books and many newspaper articles, that Jesse James, Frank James and Bob Younger were the three outlaws that entered the First National Bank at Northfield, all three with unlawful intentions and wicked thoughts, expecting a big payday. What they probably didn't know is that less than a month before the historic robbery, bank officials proudly announced that improvements in the form of "double doors" to the vaults, along with "a new steel burglar proof safe with a chronometer lock," had been made to better safeguard their customers' money.[7]

The improvements were about to be tested, for when two other riders, Cole Younger and Clell Miller, rode up, on cue, the three outlaws selected to take on the hardest challenge, entered the bank.[8] Meanwhile, the last three, Jim Younger, Bill Chadwell and Charlie Pitts,

Joseph Lee Heywood was the assistant cashier for the First National Bank of Northfield. He and two others, Frank J. Wilcox and Alonzo E. Bunker, were on duty on September 7, 1876, when three men burst into the bank with guns drawn. A demand was made to open the safe but Heywood refused. The safe was, in fact, unlocked, but the outlaws believed otherwise, and as they exited the bank, one of the three shot and killed Heywood. The identity of the killer has been the subject of debate among writers and other outlaw enthusiasts. The prevailing belief is that the man who murdered Heywood was one of the James brothers, most likely Frank (*St. Paul Pioneer Press and Tribune*, September 28, 1876).

crossed the river and waited by the bridge, on their horses, a short distance away, watching for a signal to join the rest of the gang.

There were three bank personnel on duty that day, namely, the bookkeeper Frank J. Wilcox, teller Alonzo E. Bunker and Joseph L. Heywood, the acting cashier and the man in charge. Heywood was also the Northfield city treasurer and the treasurer for Carleton College, and, overall, one of town's most beloved and respected citizens. All three were brave men and as such the outlaws met with considerable resistance and without the expected cooperation.

When the three outlaws—who Cole alleged had all been drinking—entered the bank, they drew their guns and jumped over the counter, ordering all three men to get down on their knees. They didn't have to say it, but one of the outlaws informed the startled bankers that the bank was being robbed, and that if they failed to cooperate, their brains would be blown out to decorate the drab interior of the small financial institution. To the terrified hostages, the proceedings in the bank were far from what was normally all in a day's work.

Wilcox was interviewed the day after the robbery. He told a reporter that the robbers abruptly stated that "they intended to rob the bank." Wilcox went on to say, "I believe this was stated by the small man of light complexion who seemed to be in command and who was first in getting behind the desk."[9] Another report describes "the leader of the band" as "slim, muscular ... clean cut features, no beard" and about five feet, six inches tall. He was "quick in his movements, well dressed," wearing a linen duster and white gloves.[10] The second man was described as "a large, heavy built fellow with a black heavy mustache cut rather stubby short." The third outlaw "also a large man and wore a beard."[11]

The robbers' objective was a safe inside the vault. The gunmen demanded to know which man was the cashier, for he would be the man who would know how to unlock it. Heywood calmly replied that the cashier was not in. It was a correct response because the cashier, George M. Phillips, was far away, enjoying himself at the Centennial Exposition in Philadelphia. In fact, Heywood and his wife were planning on a Centennial visit as soon as Phillips returned to Northfield.

Heywood's tepid response did not sit well with the impatient intruders. They turned to the other men, still on their knees, and asked each if he was the cashier, and each man denied it. The scene inside the small bank lobby was growing extremely intense as the outlaws shouted questions and demands at the frightened men in rapid fire fashion. The three men knew that their lives were in danger, but they also understood that the bank held money

The First National Bank of Northfield had offices in a small section in the rear of the two-story building on Division Street, shown in this photograph. The bank was equipped with a walk-in vault that contained a safe that held the money of many hardworking people. On September 7, 1876, three members of the James–Younger gang entered the bank with guns drawn. The great Northfield bank robbery was underway, setting off a gunfight, the likes of which was totally out of character for the peaceful town. When it was over, two outlaws, Bill Chadwell and Clell Miller, lie dead in the street. Inside the bank lay the body of Joseph L. Heywood, the assistant cashier, shot to death by one of the robbers. Another bank employee, Alonzo E. Bunker, was shot and wounded but survived. A Swedish immigrant, who understood little or no English, was mortally wounded in the street fight. It was a violent and tragic day that the town of Northfield, Minnesota, would long remember (Northfield Historical Society, Northfield, Minnesota).

belonging to a number of people and businesses; there was no government guarantee to cover losses, and money taken by force could never be replaced.

The low-key Heywood had some experience dealing with the stress of deadly force, for he was a Civil War veteran and had seen action at Vicksburg and Arkansas Post as a member of the 127th Illinois Infantry Regiment. When ordered by the outlaws to "open the God-damned safe," Heywood said it was impossible because the safe was on a time lock. Just then one of the robbers saw that the vault door was not closed tight, so he opened it and dashed inside, whereupon Heywood bravely slammed the vault door shut, momentarily trapping the robber inside. Another robber grabbed Heywood by his shirt collar, drug him away from the safe, then released the trapped outlaw.

The man who appeared to be in charge, Jesse or Frank James, pulled out a bowie knife, and held it to Heywood's throat, inflicting a cut "across his esophagus, drawing blood." Then, with special emphasis, Jesse or Frank demanded that Heywood "open that door or we'll cut your throat from ear to ear." Somehow, Heywood managed to break free and yell, "Murder!" This infuriated his attacker beyond all restraint and he beat Heywood with his pistol, causing the poor man to collapse into a state of semi-consciousness.

Meanwhile the other outlaws were hounding Wilcox and Bunker with demands and threats, should they not lend their complete cooperation. But the two bank employees were right about one thing: they couldn't unlock the safe because it was, in fact, unlocked. In desperation, Bunker tried to sneak over to where he had a small Smith & Wesson pistol, but seeing this one of the outlaws, most likely Bob Younger, took possession of the weapon. Bunker got off his knees hoping that someone might see him and sound the alarm. When Younger saw this, he angrily forced Bunker's head to the floor, pointing a revolver at him, while threatening to shoot the terrified man.

But Bunker was determined to break away and while Jesse or Frank was working on Heywood, he, in a moment of desperation, jumped up and made a dash for the back door.[12] Darting into the alley with escape on his mind, Bunker was pursued and shot in the shoulder by Bob Younger. It was only a flesh wound, and he was able to run away to safety, yelling that the bank was being robbed.[13]

Bunker survived his wound and lived to be an old man, but the horrors of September 7, 1876, had a profound and lasting effect on him. In 1922, Bunker was a resident of Los Angeles, where the old man kept a scrapbook of all the articles he had collected over the years about the great raid and robbery.[14] He had escaped the deadly clutches of the outlaws, but he could never escape his role in one of the most daring bank robberies in the history of American crime.

When Cole Younger and Clell Miller rode up to the bank, they were dismayed to see so many townspeople gathered near it. Were they tipped off? Maybe, but there was no sign of a sheriff or other law enforcement, and if someone was certain that there was about to be a robbery, surely he or she would have alerted the law officers.

It is possible that the presence of so many people in town was caused by the scheduled appearance of "Professor Lingard, an Australian illusionist." The magic show that would be highlighted by the release of two hot-air balloons labeled (Samuel) Tilden and (Rutherford B.) Hayes, the Democratic and Republican candidates for president.[15] Since these traveling shows were infrequent entertainments, people typically came in from miles around to attend.

The balloon ascension was scheduled for 6:45 p.m., at which time the outlaws planned to be miles away. But first they had to complete their dangerous work that, from the outset, promised that it would be done in a manner that was something other than neat and tidy. Sensing that a fight was in order, Clell Miller lit his pipe with grim determination and with the intent to smoke it throughout the ordeal.

Trouble erupted in the street when J. S. Allen, a hardware store proprietor, and two other men started talking about the possibility that a raid on the order of the famous St. Alban's bank robbery, by Confederate operatives, near the Canadian border in northern Vermont in 1864, was about to occur. Allen walked toward the bank after the three robbers had entered. Seeing this Miller intercepted Allen and seized him by the coat lapel. Then the outlaw drew his gun and fired several shots in the air while shouting: "Get out of there you sons of bitches." Allen jerked away and ran toward a store yelling, "Murder! Robbers!" An outlaw fired two shots at Allen, missing him both times.[16]

After Allen sounded the alarm, the townsmen got their guns, an odd collection of weapons at that. It was prairie chicken hunting season and men were out and about with their fowling pieces, but all of a sudden, the guns were aimed at human targets. C. E. Bates had been checking out the trusses in a store near the bank when he heard shots fired. Thinking the bank was in danger, he grabbed a shotgun, ran to the back door, aimed at a well-dressed bandit and pulled the trigger, but "the gun would not go off." He dropped the shotgun and picked up a seven-shooter revolver only to discover that it was not loaded. Undismayed, he pretended it was loaded, and as the outlaws rode by, he took aim at one of them and called out, "Now, I've got you." Hearing this, the riders "turned their horses and fired at Bates, the balls crushing through the plate glass." He bravely kept up the ruse and luckily he was not shot.[17]

For seven to ten minutes, chaos, fear and gunfire reigned supreme in Northfield. The poorly armed citizens made a noble effort, doing the best with whatever they had. For example, the town marshal, Elias Hobbs, had no firearms but he nevertheless "went into the street and hurled stones at the robbers with coolness and bravery."[18]

Despite the erratic gunfire, there were some folks in town who were completely out of sync with action in the street. A lady thought that the shooting was from men "advertising" for an "Indian show" that was scheduled for the evening. Theodore Miller (no relation to Clell Miller), whose undertaking business was right next to the bank, "thought there was going to be a circus in town, and I stood and watched them." Miller, who was nearly deaf, failed to hear the outlaws yelling at him, and simply stood still while shots were fired in his direction. Suddenly his wife came dashing down the stairs and convinced her husband that he was in danger, at which time the horrible truth sank in and he ran to safety.[19]

The gunshots attracted the attention of the editor of Northfield's newspaper, the *Rice County Journal*. At 2 o'clock in the afternoon, that fateful September 7, he was sitting at his desk when he was "aroused by firing in the street." Knowing that there was a city ordinance that prohibited the firing of weapons in the city, the editor assumed that something unlawful was happening.[20]

He was right and the gunfire was about to get louder. The three outlaws waiting near the bridge rode up toward the bank, shooting in the air and yelling at people to get inside. Their job was to clear the street without killing anyone, if possible. But the impossible was happening: the so-called docile townspeople did not meekly retreat; they rose up and fought back. A Minneapolis newspaper rather blithely described the street fight as "an exciting interchange of leaden courtesies."[21] The continuous fire from both sides of the battle, along with the outlaws' display of "excellent horsemanship,"[22] was long remembered by the people of Northfield.

It was all that and more. With a full-bloom shootout between the five mounted outlaws and the indignant citizens of Northfield, the three men in the bank concluded their work, having failed to get into the safe. It was unlocked so all they had to do was turn the handle, open it and load the cash into a bag. But it was the successful ruse and bravery of Heywood and his co-workers that prevented the outlaws from getting access to it. There would be no big robbers' payday in Northfield, even though the bank was well stocked with cash.

As the three robbers exited the bank, without a bagged bonanza, one of them, Jesse or Frank James, shot and killed Joseph L. Heywood in the presence of Wilcox. It was a cold-blooded murder that attracted national attention; outraged Americans, including those in the press, rose up in anger and defiance. Wilcox—who probably wondered why he wasn't killed too—claimed that the "small man" of "light complexion," who appeared to be the leader, and the last one to leave the bank, placed his "revolver to Haywood's [sic] head, fired, shooting him dead."[23]

Jesse was a little shorter than Frank, and a lot shorter than Bob Younger, so Wilcox seems to point to the younger of the James brothers as the infamous killer of the temporary cashier. Bunker, who was outside of the bank when Heywood was shot and killed, averred that "one of the James brothers" murdered the temporary cashier.[24]

In a front-page article, the *Minneapolis Tribune* stated, "Heywood was shot by Frank James." Then, in another column in the same piece, the *Tribune* declared that Jesse James shot Heywood, because "Jesse James is always ready for murder."[25] That accusation was echoed in an article in the *Rice County Journal*. A Cincinnati detective, Larry M. Hazen, came to Northfield, and after listening to the descriptions of the three that went into the bank, he concluded that Jesse James was the killer of the assistant cashier. Hazen and other detectives had been tracking the James–Younger gang since Otterville robbery, exactly two months earlier than the Northfield criminal episode. Hazen was certain that both crimes were committed by the same gang.[26] Another Minnesota newspaper, *The Faribault Democrat*, declared that the killer was the "red-whiskered man."[27] A Kansas newspaper stated point blank: "Jesse James killed Cashier Haywood [sic] in cold blood for refusing to open the vault."[28]

The question of which outlaw killed the gallant Heywood has concerned researchers and writers for generations. In 1897, in an article about Frank James, the journalist stated that "Frank James is credited with murder of Hayward [sic]."[29] Of course, the reporter didn't get that from Frank.

The general consensus is that it was Frank, or Jesse, with emphasis on the former. Cole Younger once said in an interview: "I shall never tell who shot Cashier Heywood,"[30] but in his memoir, published in 1903, he declared that the killer was a liquored-up Pitts who "shot him through the head."[31] This would be consistent with Younger's attempts to convince the public that the James brothers were not in Northfield and therefore did not participate in the crime. Besides, Pitts was long dead and in no position to refute Cole's allegation.

Another source was decidedly undecided, saying that if Frank was the James brother inside the bank, he could have fired the fatal shot. But Frank was "known as being bitterly opposed" to killing anyone during a robbery, while Jesse was, by reputation, far more ruthless.[32] Another recently published book places blame squarely on Frank James who, with "the expression of a very devil in his face," put his pistol to the cashier's head and pulled the trigger.[33]

Writer Marley Brant gets the last word on the subject. Frank was the killer of the assistant cashier. On his deathbed, Cole Younger told the son of Jesse James and another relative, Harry Hoffman, that the rider of the "dun horse," Frank James, the last man to exit the bank, killed Heywood. It is the general consensus of the descendants of the James family that Frank fired the fatal shot, thus launching Heywood into the role of hero and martyr: a state of grace that he has occupied for many generations.[34]

When the men inside the bank hurried out of the door, they were shocked to see three bodies in the street and one dead horse. Among the mortally wounded was Nicolas Gustavson, a stranger in town. This unfortunate victim, who stepped out of a saloon at a very bad time, was a Swedish immigrant knew no or very little English, and thus failed to respond to the outlaws' demand that he go back inside. It was said that Cole Younger put a bullet in his head,[35] but it is possible he was hit in the crossfire. He would die as a result.

The dead bad men were Clell Miller, veteran outlaw and longtime member of the gang, and Bill Chadwell. Miller had been hit with a blast of bird shot from a shotgun borrowed by Elias Stacy from J. S. Allen. In pain, bleeding and stunned but not totally disabled, Miller got back on his horse. A few minutes later he was shot and finished off by Henry M. Wheeler, a medical student who was in town on vacation. Wheeler had been relaxing in the Dampier Hotel, while admiring a Civil War carbine on the wall "behind the counter." The gun was loaded, and after hearing the shooting outside, Wheeler took it off the wall, rushed to the balcony, and shot the desperado, Clell Miller, dead, in front of the bank.[36] Wheeler and the other men that fought back that day in Northfield would receive death threats by mail for their role in breaking up the James–Younger gang.

Bill Chadwell fell dead after a concealed Anselm R. Manning, a hardware store proprietor, with a Remington repeating rifle, took careful aim and fired. An unidentified robber dismounted where Chadwell lay dying. After conceding his comrade was dead, the man "took his [Chadwell's] cartridge belt and two pistols, and, remounting his horse, rode off."[37]

Writing about the street fight in 1930, the son of a Minnesota pioneer compared it to a "regular western movie."[38] While there were comparatively few gun battles in the streets of frontier towns, it seems as if the movie business had, by 1930, intercepted the truth and twisted it into a shape, a thing, or a formula, that captured the imagination of the public. In the "western movie," the novelists, the playwrights and the cinema, using certain foundational facts, had created the mirror opposite of the true West. The emergence of what has become known as the "Myth of the West" has been thoroughly woven into the historical narrative of the real West, and we are stuck with it. It refuses to die; it will not die, for it has been given a life of its own.

And so it went that September afternoon. Although the entire nation had knowledge of the James–Younger gang, none of the Northfield people knew they were shooting at a band of well-known, seasoned criminals. They were simply shooting at men who started the fight. What is important to understand is that the men of Northfield refused to be cowed by a band of slick and arrogant outlaws; instead they had fought fiercely to protect their bank and town and, although they suffered severely, they had won the day. If there was a lesson in it for the outlaws, it was to never underestimate the determination and fighting spirit of ordinary pioneers. Never challenge an opponent whose cause is greater.

On the whole, it was a badly bungled bank robbery by men who might have been expected to do better. As Bunker explained, they missed the obvious and failed to capitalize on opportunities that experienced robbers would have seized. He said that there was more than $15,000 in the safe and that it and the vault could have both been opened simply "by turning the handles." There was also a drawer, "immediately beneath the one in which they found the nickels and a small amount of scrip," that contained about $2,000 in cash. All they had to do was open it up and grab the cash. In an interview while still convalescing, Bunker said the "villains seemed to have blundered all through this transaction."[39]

Fortune did not favor the bold. For example, the death of Chadwell presented a serious problem, for many historians have believed he was a Minnesotan and had been tasked to guide the gang in its retreat out of Minnesota. His death also played into a minor mystery in connection with the "ninth man" theory. It started in 1876, not long after the robbery. The *Minneapolis Tribune* contained an article that stated, "It is also a theory advanced by some that there were nine … robbers connected with the Northfield job." The ninth man was "supposed to have been the one who set up the job," but he did not ride into town with the other eight.[40]

The story of the "ninth man" was revived in 1913, when an old man made his way to Los Angeles for the purpose of robbing a train. After arriving in the City of Angels, he ducked into the Union Rescue Mission to avoid curious glances from lawmen. Inside the mission he experienced a sudden and dramatic conversion; he had seen the light and the truth and would thereafter live a just life. Suddenly, it all came clear to him; he would, at some point in time, reveal his true identity to the public. He claimed to be the mysterious outlaw, William "Bill" Stiles, who had survived the robbery at Northfield. He was the "ninth man" assigned to guard the escape route, and furthermore, the man killed in the street fight was really Bill Chadwick, alias Chadwell, said to be a member of a prominent Minnesota family, a good boy gone wrong.[41] The old, repentant man, the "real" Bill Stiles, had escaped the disaster at Northfield, and if people wanted to believe he had been using the name Chadwell, and had died in the street fight, he could live with that—that is, until he found religion.

Stiles got a job at the mission as a night watchman and gained a reputation for respect and loyalty. In short, he was popular and well liked. Finally, in an interview on July 8, 1931, the old man "made a full confession as to his true background." He explained that he had ridden with the James–Younger gang and participated in the Northfield bank robbery, but only the extent that he was the "ninth man." Stiles claimed that on the day of the robbery, while stationed in the rear, he heard shots and rushed into town, where he assisted his companions, but took "no part in the actual fighting." He escaped with the rest of the gang on a "black stallion."[42]

The reformed outlaw spoke in great detail about the raid, which, of course, he could have learned from many printed sources. He claimed that his own father came down to Northfield, from Grand Forks, Dakota, examined the body of Chadwell, and left convinced that the deceased man was not his son, Bill Stiles.[43] On the whole, the sad old man convinced some of his listeners and his story was repeated in letters, articles and newspaper reports. One of those who ran with the story was William A. Corey, a newspaperman from Pennsylvania, who promoted it with great vigor, even though he was persuaded that Stiles would "carry to his grave" certain secrets.[44]

All outlaws have their secrets, of course. But the unintentional secrets, the good and beneficial life they may have led before choosing a life of crime, are matters that are usually forgotten. In the case of the actual Bill Stiles, it was revealed that he had a Dakota connection. Both he and his father had worked as carpenters in 1874, on the construction of the Headquarters Hotel in Fargo, Dakota. After that Bill strayed from the path of honesty and "did a thriving business ... selling whiskey to Indians." He was arrested but escaped and went to Texas, where he continued his downward spiral. It was revealed by knowledgeable men that the death of his mother was the cause of great sorrow that sent him "going from bad to worse."[45]

The old man who claimed to be Bill Stiles died in 1939, leaving the James–Younger theorists in an oceanic tizzy: to believe or not to believe, that was the agonizing question. The waters have calmed over the years and the outlaw scholars and history buffs have moved on, leaving the "ninth man" theory swirling in the dying light of fiction. Bill Chadwell, just 23 years old, died an outlaw's death in the streets of Northfield, having been shot through the heart. That much is settled. Chadwell was not an alias for Stiles and the latter was not one of the Northfield robbers. According to many 19th century newspapers, there were eight men, all of whom were accounted for in the record, and it was only two—not three—that escaped.

The quaint old man who insisted that he was the outlaw Bill Stiles inserted himself in the James–Younger narrative. In doing so he slipped into the skin and reputation, so to speak, of the "ninth man" who lingers, ghostlike, on the edges of the grand narrative. The old man simply and effectively took a shadowy young outlaw into old age, thus creating a more meaningful life and better end for both men.

4

Six Men on Five Horses

> "There are all sorts of rumors as to the robbers, some believing them to be some of a gang heretofore operating in Missouri or Kansas"
>
> —*The Daily Journal* (Sioux City, IA), September 8, 1876

"For God's sake don't leave me boys, I'm shot," cried Bob Younger as he watched his companions mount up.[1] Hearing this, his older brother Cole took hold of Bob and got him safely mounted on the back of a horse that would have to carry two riders. In the next instant, six stunned, wounded and dispirited men, astride five horses, rode away in haste. After a costly and deadly operation of about seven minutes, they left town with a total of $26.70,[2] a pittance compared to the $63,000 that was reported to have been inside the safe.[3] According to an eminent Minnesota historian the robbers "did not get a dollar."[4]

What they got was a lot of inspired attention. The loss of two gang members and three horses, and the shock of being outgunned by ordinary men, caused the shot-up survivors to mount their remaining horses and retreat, knowing that they would soon be pursued by an angry posse, determined to capture or kill them.

But who were they? What kind of men would plan and perpetuate such a brazen and shocking crime? One immediate suspicion was that the robbers were members of the James gang from Missouri. A Minneapolis police officer, Patrick Kenny, claimed that he had seen and talked to "one of the gang in this city" about two months previous and recognized him as a man who had been arrested some years ago in Iowa. The man had served time in prison and told Kenny that he was "doing better now" and that he had plans to go to the Black Hills. Kenny was certain that the man, whom he did not name, "had previously been connected with the notorious James boys."[5] *The Faribault Democrat*, a Rice County, Minnesota, newspaper, boldly suggested in a headline, that the robbers were the "Celebrated James Brothers."[6]

That same newspaper reported that a man named Charles Robinson, from Maryland, had recently been in Mankato, where he claimed he saw Jesse James, "whom he knows ..., a few days previous to the attempted robbery." Robinson claimed he spoke to Jesse and asked him what he was doing in Minnesota, but "he received no answer." But having seen Jesse James, Robinson warned the Mankato bank to be wary. The talk among men throughout southern Minnesota towns was about seeing well-dressed strangers, off and on, for a period of two weeks prior to the Northfield incident.[7]

Wild rumors hovered over Northfield like birds of evil omen as anxious men speculated about the identity of the robbers, while lamenting the loss of two worthy citizens and a beautiful horse. Although reeling in shock and sorrow, the townspeople could take heart in that they had driven the invaders off, whoever they were, and that the outlaws departed without having taken the cash stashed in the bank safe. The Rebel yell and the demand that people get off the street may have worked in Missouri, but it utterly failed in Minnesota. Still there was much sadness to contend with, a terrible crime had been committed in their peaceful town, and some of their best blood had been shed in defense of the bank and the town. The bravery of the citizens of Northfield, however, would not go unnoticed or unappreciated. Just then all of Minnesota was singing the praises of the residents of Northfield, for they had shown the outlaws that "the people of Minnesota are made of different stuff."[8]

Among those with the right stuff, Adelbert Ames, the Civil War veteran, was a witness to all the shooting, but managed to keep away from the intersecting bullets. Later, Ames felt compelled to write a letter to his wife, Blanche, with a brief description of all the deadly excitement, comparing the shootout to a typical, post-war Mississippi election. He recalled that the bodies of the two dead outlaws were loaded in a wagon and put on display for those with inquisitive minds.[9]

After news of the robbery reached surrounding towns, the evening trains into Northfield were filled with the curious, all of whom wanted to know the terrible details of the crime and take a look at the two dead criminals and view the broken windows and bullet-scarred buildings. The following day the crowds were so huge that the unidentified bodies were brought out into the "open square, which was soon packed with people."[10] More than 50,000 photographs of the dead outlaws would eventually be sold.[11]

Because they lacked any papers to identify them, the authorities were caused to think the dead men were "professional brigands, probably from Missouri or Kansas."[12] Curiously, the larger of the two dead men was wearing "mismatched boots."[13] The clothes of the dead men were searched, and on the body of the "shortest man," searchers found an expensive gold watch, a small amount of money and a "pocket map of Minnesota" that had been purchased in Minneapolis.[14] Two "heavy eight-inch Smith and Wesson seven shooters" were taken from each of the deceased outlaws.[15] The dead men, cleaned, embalmed and photographed, were again put on display for the throngs of the curious.

At some point a man in the crowd was heard to exclaim: "I know that man!" The man he was looking at would later be identified as Bill Chadwell, but the excited witness said the deceased was William "Bill" Stiles (also Styles) and that he had been born near Monticello, Minnesota. To further bolster his credibility, the stranger said that "deceased boarded with him at Cannon Falls, two years ago, for a month." The witness, who was not identified by the *Tribune*, said the father of the dead outlaw was living in Grand Forks, Dakota Territory, and that "about two months ago the deceased [Stiles] wrote deponent from Middletown, Texas, stating that he had made a good haul." He also mentioned that he was planning to travel to Minnesota, where "they could make another good haul."

A Northfield man came forth and identified the dead body as that of his ex-brother-in-law who once lived in Cannon Falls. The man claimed that the deceased robber "married and deserted his sister four years ago."[16] This added substance to the claim of the stranger in the street, and many historians throughout the years have believed that Bill Stiles had been a member of the James–Younger gang under the alias Bill Chadwell.

A few days later, a letter from Grand Forks arrived in Northfield. It was from Elias Stiles, father of the Bill Stiles, the wayward son that Northfield citizens believed had carried on a life of crime under the cognomen Bill Chadwell. "I thought he was in Texas. I suppose he got in with a lot of them damned pirates." The elder Stiles sadly confessed that his son "had always been a wild boy" but he was not "vicious." Vicious or not, the 23-year-old man, who once sold illegal whiskey to Indians in Dakota, died an outlaw's death in Minnesota, or so many believed.[17]

Though both were young outlaws, Bill Stiles and Bill Chadwell were two entirely different men. Thanks to sterling research by writer Mark Lee Gardner, it can be established that Bill Chadwell was not born in Minnesota, but rather in Illinois and had lived in Kansas before joining the James–Younger gang. For one thing, the man shot in the street identified as Bill Chadwell was a strapping six feet, four inches tall while Stiles was said to be only to five feet, eight inches in height. Additionally, Elias Stiles angrily denied that his son was an outlaw traveling under the name Bill Chadwell, for having seen the picture of the dead outlaw he declared that he was not looking at the body of his son.[18]

Further proof that Chadwell was not a Minnesota lad acting under an alias came from a woman in Cato, Kansas, who, after viewing the published photograph, insisted that she knew the young man and his family, that his mother was a fine Baptist woman and that the family was poor but respectable. The letter writer recalled that young Chadwell, at age 18, had worked for her husband. He was not "particularly brilliant," but was "harmless" until he was led astray by a vile and corrupt man. Lamenting the death of young Chadwell, she confessed that she would "drop a tear of regret over his terrible fate."[19]

A whimsical Minnesota editor tossed out a different sentiment over Chadwell's death as an outlaw. "Altogether there is still considerable doubt whether the villain was Bill Stiles or Bill Chadwell ... [but] it is quite certain that ... he was a bad Bill, and is now beyond redemption."[20]

But that wasn't the last word about Bill Chadwell, for about a year after the Northfield excitement subsided, a Godfrey, Kansas, woman, claiming to be the widow of the slain outlaw, wrote to Rice County Sheriff Ara Barton, "asking that if the dead robber left any property it might be forwarded to her." In her letter, signed "M. E. Chadwell," the claimant revealed that she last saw Bill Chadwell on August 3, 1876, but knew not where he went. Then she "saw his name connected with the Northfield tragedy as being killed." She wrote to someone in Northfield but got no answer. The alleged widow described her man as "six feet two inches in his boots," weighing 200 pounds, with curly dark auburn hair "and small gray eyes." She urged the sheriff to reply "whether the man answers to this description or not."

According to *The Faribault Republican*, the sheriff wrote to Cole Younger in an effort to corroborate the information in the letter from M. E. Chadwell. Although Younger was very tight-lipped about naming names, he had no problem discussing Bill Chadwell with the sheriff since it was apparent that "Chadwell's family did not care to have his name kept secret" and further that the "woman's representations were correct, and that she was entitled to the property." But the paper trail seemed to end, for there were no follow-up articles in the *Republican*, leaving the matter in a state of mystery.[21]

Ultimately, it was agreed upon that the dead outlaws were Bill Chadwell and Clell Miller, both of whom were reportedly dumped in a hole in a corner of the Northfield cemetery. Sometime later, the bodies "found their way to a certain medical college" for anatomical study.[22] That medical college was the University of Michigan. The *Ann Arbor Register* claimed that "the two Northfield, Minnesota robbers who didn't escape" had been turned over to the "interests of science" and will be "closely guarded by the University authorities."[23]

But wait, for the mystery deepens. It was written that Miller's embalmed body was shipped from place to place and put on display at various events in Minnesota. Eventually, his family claimed and buried his body. A recent book says that the remains of Clell Miller eventually found rest in the Muddy Fork Cemetery in Clay County, Missouri. Chadwell's remains "somehow ended up in the possession of Henry M. Wheeler."[24] In a 1930 South Dakota newspaper article, a reporter rather cheekily remarked that Dr. Wheeler, from Grand Forks, North Dakota, had "a skeleton in his closet," and further claimed that the bones were those of the man he killed during the Northfield shootout, meaning Clell Miller.[25]

Another source supports the North Dakota boast, claiming it was Miller's body that found no rest. A. E. Bunker, the wounded assistant cashier, stated with eyewitness conviction, in a letter dated January 15, 1924, that "Dr. Wheeler had the flesh taken from the bones of Clell Miller." Rather strangely, he said, "I saw the skeleton in the doctor's office at Grand Forks, N. D." That was an odd statement, for he failed to explain how he could identify someone by looking at his bare bones. Nevertheless, Bunker further stated that "if the body of one of the bandits was sent to relatives, it was probably that of Stiles—or Chadwell."[26] Be that as it may, there is a gravestone in the Muddy Fork Cemetery, Clay County, Missouri, bearing the name "Clelland D. Miller," and date of death is September 7, 1876.[27]

In another strange twist to an already bizarre story, it was Henry M. Wheeler, the future doctor, who had assumed the ghoulish role of grave robber. He went to the cemetery during the night and surreptitiously performed a "resurrection."[28] Miller's body was reportedly shipped from Northfield to St. Paul in a barrel labeled "rot gut whiskey."[29]

The macabre act of grave robbery—not all that uncommon in the 1870s—cast another long, dark shadow over Northfield. The participants in the tragic drama were unable to shake off the horror, and the terrible memories would long linger. It was said that the terror and excitement felt in Northfield as a result of the robbery and shootout was unequaled in the memory of Minnesotans, with the exception of the "Indian outbreak" of 1862, when hundreds of people were massacred.[30] It was stories like this and others pertaining to the Northfield raid that caused Minnesota newspaper sales to soar.[31]

It would take time, but the great excitement in Northfield would subside and folks would continue with their lives. But the bold and brazen robbery had set in motion the greatest manhunt in the history of America, a pursuit that would command the attention an entire nation, whose collective focus was on vengeance. "Minnesota blood is up!" declared the *Minneapolis Trib-*

une. The anger among the people was as red-hot as was the Minneapolis newspaper, thus the "fleeing murderers" could expect that a fiercely determined attempt would be made to catch them.[32] Another angry editor said that Minnesotans "ought to teach the border ruffians that this so-called cold Minnesota climate is entirely too hot for men of their ilk."[33]

The robbers failed to cut the telegraph lines, and this omission facilitated the response of law enforcement and ordinary citizens. News of the robbery was telegraphed as far south as Faribault, arousing the citizenry, calling all brave men who believe in justice to take action, while in the East "the news of the Northfield raid and murder emphasized the many legends about 'the wild and wooly west.'"[34]

Among the first to enter the chase were Mayor John Adelbert, his father and about a dozen others from Northfield.[35] Henry Wheeler was a member of the makeshift posse, and he jumped on his horse, not even taking time to put on his boots.[36] Outlaws and killers had been pursued before, but in the history of the great Northwest, never had so many men mounted up to run down six criminals. Like the hounds of perdition, dozens of excited and determined men were sent scouring the state. More than a thousand armed men would eventually be in pursuit of the James–Younger gang.[37] The leader of one band of outlaw hunters boldly declared that "we start this morning, and will camp on their trail and follow them to Missouri if necessary."[38]

The fleeing criminals had many concerns, among them were the wounds inflicted during the street fight and while exiting Northfield. While Jesse and Pitts may have avoided Northfield bullets and buckshot, Frank took a bullet in his right leg. The Younger brothers had all sustained injuries; Cole had three bullet wounds and Jim had been hit in the shoulder, but Bob was in the worst shape, having been shot in the right elbow. Yelling to his companions that he was shot, Bob grabbed the outstretched hand of his brother, and, although in great pain, he managed get on the back of Cole's horse.[39]

They rode out of Northfield, southwest, toward the town of Dundas, a decision that undoubtedly was made in advance. About halfway to Dundas, they helped themselves to a horse belonging to a farmer. It was a work horse but the big animal was better than nothing. It belonged to Phillip Empey who was absent at the time, enjoying himself at the Centennial celebration in Philadelphia. While Empey's hired hand was being relieved of the horse, two scouts from among the pursuers approached, oddly enough, on horses that once belonged to the robbers. But as they were outnumbered, the scouts retreated.[40]

When asked about the incident in 1924, Empey's sister Nellie E. Odell—then a resident of Sioux Falls, South Dakota—remembered seeing riders going through Dundas a "break neck speed." Next she saw their hired hand walking into town, complaining that "some gentlemen knocked me on the head and took my horse." The stolen horse was eventually found about 30 or 40 miles from Dundas.[41] That's all it took. Odell was hooked and she kept a scrapbook that included newspaper articles about the robbery. Most important, perhaps, she had her very own Jesse James story to tell.

Word of the escaping bandits was telegraphed to Dundas, but to no avail, for the operator was "not at his post."[42] Passing through Dundas, they stopped at the store of George Sexton. He and C. W. Brown were standing in front of the store, and Sexton, thinking they were a "crew of drunken rowdies," called out to them in an insulting manner: "are you a cavalry regiment?" The outlaws' response was to pull their pistols on the two men, causing Brown to challenge one of the men to a fight. The outlaws simply rode away without a word. Later, when Brown learned that the strangers had robbed the bank at Northfield, he was pleased that he did not undertake to give "them a lesson in good breeding."[43]

The great get-away did indeed create many memories. For example, after the incident at Sexton's store, they stopped at Robert Donaldson's place, "about a half a mile from Dundas." There they got a pail of water and one of the men poured it on Bob Younger's wounded arm. Donaldson asked how it was the poor man came to be shot and was told that a "blackleg from Northfield" did the deed and paid for it with his life. Donaldson then asked for the name of the blackleg killed and the terse response was "Stiles."[44]

After passing through Dundas, they took a saddle from another farmer, explaining they were lawmen in pursuit of outlaws.[45] They rode to Millersville at full speed and after passing through that town the fugitives continued on toward Shieldsville. Before reaching that hamlet, they stopped a man named McMurtrie with a view of taking his horses, "but his team did not seem to suit them so they passed on."[46]

Their next stop was in the hamlet of Shieldsville, 20 miles southwest of Northfield, where they availed themselves to water from the town pump. They washed their wounds, while inside the Haggerty saloon four men whose intent was to capture or kill the robbers took in what was commonly called "liquid courage." Foolishly, the outlaw hunters had left their guns outside with their horses.

Bob Younger passed out in front of the saloon, due to the loss of blood, attracting the attention of an old man. The rest of the fugitives simply said that Bob was a horse thief they had just captured. The old man inquired about what they had planned for the horse thief. "The leader" rudely stated that they were going to "hang that d—d cuss," while pointing to poor, suffering Bob, all covered with blood.[47]

But the old man acted like he was not convinced, although he was most certainly concerned. He entered the saloon about the same time as the liquored-up posse came out to find that they were looking at drawn guns. Having mastered the situation, the James–Younger gang took their wrath out on the town pump, and after shooting it up, they rode out of town, without taking the guns or horses from the would-be pursuers. The show of force was enough to frighten the poorly armed townspeople. It was also reported that, as they were leaving, "one of the highwaymen turned and fired a shot which grazed a little girl who was standing by the door."[48]

The thrill of the chase, and undoubtedly the wounding of the girl, trumped the stern warning from the fugitives, and soon about a dozen men were mounted up and on the trail. At a ravine about four miles west of Shieldsville, the opposing groups exchanged gunfire that ended when the robbers disappeared into a wooded area. Only one bullet hit a target; Cole Younger was struck in his "crazy bone" while he was leading Bob's horse, but aside from a little excitement, it had no effect on him.[49] In the excitement, Bob, who was riding the Empey horse, was thrown off, and after the "saddle girth broke, the horse was abandoned."[50] So they were back to five men on six horses, and it would only get worse for the Missourians, for by sundown as many as 200 eager men had joined the chase, armed with whatever they had including handguns, shotguns and muskets.[51]

Keeping track of the fleeing outlaws was impossible until and unless they waylaid some unsuspecting person. On their first night on the trail, they stopped and "called on a farmer named Sager, and borrowed a horse," after telling their host that they were part of the larger group pursuing the outlaws. When Levi Sager asked them what authority they were acting under, he was told to "go to hell." The horse proved balky and uncooperative, so once again they went back to six men on five horses. Sager, however, was not off the hook, and he was forced to guide the gang to the road leading to Cordova. He left them at a spot about five miles north of Waterville. It was speculated that they would press on to the Minnesota River, but the smart money was on the belief that they entered an area called the "Big Woods," a good place to hide.[52]

It was also thought that they had spent the night in a house in the woods near Waterville. The next morning two of the robbers went to the house of man named George James (no relation to the notorious brothers), inquired about roads, and politely asked Mrs. James if she had seen "two small black mules that had been stolen." They left the James house and attempted to cross the Cannon River but were unable to do so. Next they crossed the Cordova road four miles northwest of Waterville, where they encountered a crew working on the road, informing the workers that they were looking for the robbers. Apparently the road workers were not convinced and soon a group of armed men appeared and one of them took a shot at the robbers. One of the gang members yelled out: "we must take to the woods."

The outlaws then rode along the Cannon River to a narrow point where they made a crossing and once again the pursuers lost track of their quarry. They headed west and when they reached Elysian Township, they stole a work horse from two boys named Rosenhall, who were out plowing. One of the boys was recruited to act as a guide "through the timber until they reached the Elysian Road."[53] Their next stop was the home of Asa Swain, where they helped themselves to more horses. They reportedly stopped at a farmhouse, and being ravenously hungry, they "took possession of all the cooked provisions."[54] It was getting interesting and frustrating at the same time.

The chase was just getting started and the early reports about the massive effort were indeed as mixed up as were the so-called leaders of the angry and nervous pack. The local people were in a panic as if there was a "robber behind every bush."[55] The St. Paul boys were "often mistaken for bandits and the people run from them like mad." The complaint is they looked fierce and dangerous and people could not readily tell the difference between the good guys and the bad guys. At times the amateur outlaw hunters themselves panicked and ran. It was said that some men "were scared at the sight of a stump." One terrified man lost "his false teeth. Another threw away his gun."

But wait, good help was on the way in the person of the experienced St. Paul detective John B. Bresette. He was in the process of organizing "a picked company" of experienced, stalwart fellows, and would soon commence scouring the woods.[56] Other key players included Sam Dunham, chief of police at Faribault, who was reputed to be an "experienced tracker of horse thieves," and Colonel Streeter of Northfield, who had been "shot at six times" during the street fight in Northfield and was itching for revenge.[57]

At Faribault, a large crowd of eager, would-be outlaw hunters gathered on the morning of September 10. The town was "full of rumors," hit by a wave of speculation so overwhelming that it was impossible to discern a particle of truth or good sense. A St. Paul reporter following the pursuit suddenly realized he was standing amid hundreds of milling men, not unlike a recruiting center for new soldiers preparing for war, and Rice County Sheriff Ara Barton was acting as a "generalissimo." Among the mass of volunteers was a "lad with a decrepit wooden leg … mounted on a bad looking nag." He was armed with "a double-barreled fowling piece full of buckshot," along with a "horse pistol" stuck in his pocket. "He was accepted promptly as his pluck was unquestionable."[58]

And who was it, exactly, that the chaotic masses of men were looking for? Within two days of the bank robbery, an Iowa newspaper attempted to answer the question: "the general impression seems to be that the robbers are members of the famous Younger and James Gangs."[59] By September 11, the *Minneapolis Tribune* was blaming the James and Younger gang for the crime, calling Cole Younger the "captain of the gang."[60] Several men from the South were just then in Minnesota and when the outlaws were described to them, the Southerners said, "beyond a doubt the robbers are the James–Younger brothers gang, and we have big game to bag."[61]

A luckless man was bagged on September 10 and brought into the town of Janesville that evening. He was captured "in the woods near where the Northfield robbers were uncovered this morning." The suspect claimed to be a detective named Sprague from "Pittsburg [sic]" and insisted that he was "acquainted with the James and Youngers," having met them at "horse races in Missouri." The man was simply part of the massive effort, on foot and on horse, "in the woods," looking for the real brigands.[62]

Excitement was heaped upon excitement, and danger seemed to be lurking in every dark shadow, as the state of Minnesota rallied around its wounded and suffering constituents at Northfield. Railroads were advised to be watchful, and on September 12, 1876, Minnesota governor John S. Pillsbury, announced a reward of $1,500 for the entire gang but quickly increased it to $1,000 for each robber.[63] The governor didn't say anything about taking the robbers dead or alive, but most men would have preferred to see bodies draped over a saddle or dangling from the branch of a tree. Either way, the amount offered would only go higher. The scent of money in the air only added to individual alacrity and quickened the pulse and pace of enlistment in the great Minnesota manhunt. Trainloads of armed men were on the move.

Minnesota men were pouring into the Northfield area in droves. The influx of law officers and other volunteers caused the *Minneapolis Tribune* to declare that "it may look ridiculous for a thousand men to hunt down six outlaws." But the gravity of the crime and the heavily wooded terrain necessitated the need for a large force of men. Besides, "the people of the section where the robbers have been discovered are ignorant, superstitious Bohemians, who could readily be made the obedient tool of the men who scruple at nothing." The *Tribune* wanted "every foot of the ground" covered and warned that those doing the covering should expect to do some shooting.[64] A wiseacre among the large crew of reporters declared that one thing was certain: "it will not be safe for any man with a linen duster … in this part of the country for some time to come."[65]

While there was some attempt to coordinate the mammoth undertaking, it was, from the start, a disorganized and inept mob that became the butt of jokes. A chaotic mass of excited men all of whom dreamed of personal glory and a share in the reward had turned itself loose in the woods and prairies of Minnesota, but not a cent was available to "pay for provisions or forage."[66] When there was so little organization and so much dependence upon luck, the only hope for success was that someone would get lucky.

A mound of dirt that looked like a grave was thought of as a lucky find. It was discovered by a "scouting party" at Waseca. It was believed that it had been "dug by the robbers ... for the purpose of burying the wounded man." The "grave" was examined but it contained no body.[67] "About one mile north of Marysburg," in the afternoon of September 11, searchers came upon a spot where "the robbers had camped this morning, the ashes of their camp-fire still being warm."[68]

There were signs and sightings enough to maintain an interest in the chase. Horses and saddles, believed to be those of the outlaws, were found in the "timber near Cleveland on the Waterville road." This was cause for the outlaw hunters to believe that the fugitives made their way through the dragnet. Disappointed, many of the pursuers went home. Spirits rose when the sheriff of Faribault County reported seeing five men matching the description of the robbers near Indian Lake, three miles from Mankato. Soon thereafter, a force of men was in pursuit.[69]

Although the human herd was guided by a strong sense of optimism, some intervention was needed—human, divine or natural—to slow down the outlaws, who, lacking a guide, needed sunshine, blue skies, food and binoculars. But as the riders entered an area commonly called the Big Woods, the weather turned against them. A hard, cold September rain soaked men and horses alike, day after day, thus adding to their misery. Bob Younger's suffering was especially horrible. The constant pain was exacerbated by the fact that, so long as they were running, he would get no medical treatment for his shattered elbow. He could do nothing but endure the pain with the stoic attitude of a man who accepted that as an outlaw he might someday be shot.

While the befuddled and suffering outlaws were desperately trying to get out of Minnesota, a man claiming to be Jesse James stomped into the office of the *Leavenworth Times*, in Leavenworth, Kansas. The man was a fine mess. A tobacco stained vest, dirty, uncombed hair, slurred speech and breath reeking with the smell of liquor combined to make him a very unwelcome visitor. The unkempt lout demanded to see the editor, complaining that he, Jesse James, had been wrongly accused of train robbery, and to right the wrong, he asked for the loan of a quarter. The request was denied, and after exchanging a few more words, the drunken, deluded man left the office, telling the assistant editor: "Don't forget to say in your paper that I've been here."[70]

The real Jesse James was known to be a voracious reader of newspapers. He was also noted for his ability to use and manipulate newspapermen, but on September 11, 1876, when the bumbling, phony Jesse attempted to impress the Leavenworth newsmen, the noted Missouri outlaw and his friends were mired in a crisis far more serious than disputing an article that falsely blamed them for a train robbery.

Public interest in the outlaws' current dilemma was heightened when, on Tuesday, September 12, news filtered back to Minneapolis about two horses that were found on a road near the town of Elysian. Detectives riding with the posse claimed they were familiar with the horses and that they were "brought from Missouri." One horse was "Jesse James' famous brown mare," and the other was "Clell Miller's bay jumping horse."[71] No further explanation was offered by the detectives, who were in error. The gang bought their horses in Minnesota, having traveled up by rail.

A total of five horses were found, said to be "fine looking animals," but all of them were sore, gaunt and in bad shape, having been abandoned by the outlaws. An equal amount of saddles was found at a campsite, near German Lake. Some of them were the McClellan brand. One saddle bore evidence of having been hit by two bullets. The searchers surmised that the "robbers carried away all the bridles and good blankets."[72]

But there was more troubling news for eager readers to ponder. Minneapolis detective Mike Hoy was known to be a bully who liked to "kick, beat and otherwise maltreat unarmed, defenceless [sic] men."[73] One day on the trail of the outlaws, he slipped into the role of a vigilante, when along with his companions he "visited the house of a fellow named Conway, a leader of a gang of horse thieves." Conway was not there but the outlaw hunters found a "boy named Dolan," who was said to be an ex-convict. Believing that Conway might have been the "eighth man of the gang," Hoy questioned Dolan, and not getting any answers, his interrogation suddenly changed and he prepared to hang the boy. A rope was placed around his neck and the other end tied to a tree limb, and although Dolan was thoroughly frightened, he said nothing, most likely because he knew nothing. Hoy and friends abruptly cancelled the hanging and moved on.[74]

While the obnoxious Hoy was threatening to choke information from the young man, another group of outlaw hunters were staking out a "notorious bagnio" at the town of Janesville. It was known that when the gang was on its way up to Northfield, they "several times" stopped at the brothel, so it was thought that "they were making again directly for that point." But an evening stakeout was unavailing, for the outlaws failed to appear.[75]

Early in the morning on the 13th, the six outlaws showed up at the farm of Henry Shaubert, three miles north of Mankato, at a place called Union Junction.[76] There they "made a prisoner" of Shaubert's hired man, demanding that he provide breakfast for them and further that he "pilot them around the city to a point south." The hired man had just entered the woods to look for cows when he came upon the six most wanted men in America.

The captured a man was Thomas Jefferson Dunning, who was, classically, in the wrong place at the wrong time. An article in the *Minneapolis Tribune* claimed that the outlaws told Dunning they were members of a posse on official business, that is to say, "in search of the robbers." One of them asked Dunning if he knew "where they came from." He nervously answered that he guessed they were from Missouri, to which an outlaw said, "it was a d—d sight further than that!" At all times during the discussion, Dunning's life seemingly hung from a thread.[77]

Although thoroughly scared, Dunning had the presence of mind to take a careful look around and make some mental notes about the outlaws. He said they were all large in size, and "all wore black rubber coats, and each had woolen blankets about them." They carried their bridles with spurs tied to them. They wore heavy boots. He noticed that there were "two revolvers on each ... navy pistols twelve inches long, all black except the one carried by the leader that had a white handle."

He was in their custody for about an hour. They spoke among themselves in hushed tones, but when they turned to talk to him, he had no trouble hearing them. He was asked if he knew of any "skiff on the river below Mankato and St. Peter," and about the nature of the country side in general, and finally, "had he ever been a soldier?" They told him point blank that they were the "men that tried to rob the Northfield bank, and that if Haywood [sic] had opened the vault they would not have shot him." The outlaws talked about shooting their hostage too, should he lead them to a place where they would be in danger.[78]

What the outlaws wanted from Dunning, they got. He took the Missourians to a road "which they wished to find." Instead of thanking him, they tied him to a tree and debated whether they should let him go or "kill him on the spot." According to one story, they took a vote and it was the "no" vote of Charlie Pitts that saved Dunning.[79]

According to another story, it was Bob Younger who saved Dunning's hide. One of the James brothers warned Bob that if Dunning—the accidental victim and celebrity of the moment—was allowed go free, "he will have the whole country after us within twelve hours and with your broken arm we cannot possibly get away." But Bob would not give an inch and Dunning was released.[80]

Another report hints that Dunning's quick thinking may have saved him. While the outlaws were deliberating his fate, Dunning said that he "was subject to heart disease and if he was away [too] long his folks would" send out a search party, and more people searching was something the fugitives did not need. When Dunning left, one of the group said that if they "got home all right, they would send him a nice present."[81]

The Dunning incident was covered by several newspapers. An Iowa report states that an outlaw described as "the red-whiskered man" wanted to kill Dunning—who had been, early that morning, out searching for missing cattle—but due to strong protests from the Youngers, the man was spared after he swore he would not reveal the location of the fugitives. It was a promise he did not keep, however, and Dunning has been credited for providing the information that led to the apprehension of the Youngers.[82]

There is the follow-up story in an Iowa newspaper that Dunning, a German immigrant, was so unnerved by the experience and his "memorable interview" with the James and Youngers that he pulled up stakes and left Minnesota. The frontier having proven to be very dangerous owing to the presence of desperate men, Dunning set sail for the old country. He feared that the "revolvers of the bandits or other avenging weapons would fail to reach him" if he was safely across the Atlantic Ocean, beyond the reach of his "freebooting captors."[83]

This report was lambasted by the *Weekly Pioneer Press* in St. Paul. Thomas Jefferson Dunning was no German, no Dutchman, not even an immigrant. He was an honest-to-goodness American originally from Indiana. He had moved to Blue Earth County, Minnesota, and had never been to Europe. The *Press* defended Dunning after the capture of the Youngers, and castigated several newspapers that had published false stories making fun of the unfortunate man, who just happened to fall into the hands of outlaws, and lived to talk about it.[84]

The news about Dunning's outlaw encounter set Mankato afire, and by 5 o'clock on the 13th, "hundreds of men are on the streets, awaiting the arrival of couriers." Whenever a man, a stranger, arrived in town, he was "besieged by questions" from over-eager questioners. One interesting piece of news was that two "suspicious characters" were arrested at St. Peter, thought to be "confederates of the robbers." They said they were John Schaffer and George Krunz, and begged to differ when someone suggested they were connected with the Northfield robbers, whose presence in Minnesota, was known throughout the land. They said simply that they were "poor grasshopper sufferers, and had no money or work." Their few possessions, including a "fine silver-shooter," were confiscated. The men were held because they told "contradictory stories."[85] At some point the poor souls were released for they had no connection to the famous outlaws. Then, just like that, they were invisible again.

5

The Two That Escaped

> "The statement that the two who escaped carried away with them the money and the watches of the party is not true."
> —*The Faribault Democrat* in the *St. Paul Pioneer Weekly*, December 6, 1876

The two who escaped were Frank and Jesse James, and the story of their get-away, which is the principal theme of this book, is truly remarkable. They were far from home in unfamiliar country, Frank was suffering from a bullet wound, they had no food in their saddle bags, they had no saddle bags, and, quite often, no saddles. Anxious men by the hundreds were trying to capture or kill them, yet somehow they escaped through Minnesota, Dakota and Iowa, by stealing horses, convincing settlers to feed them both food and information, and finding safe places to get some sleep. They had every opportunity to kill any number of people while wandering over the frontier, but they didn't, perhaps because knew that a trail of dead bodies would provide clues as to their line of travel and increase the incentive for the outlaw hunters to mercilessly hunt them down.

Still, like so much of the written record about the outlaw exploits of the James boys, the story of the great escape is peppered with inaccuracies. But when someone has intentionally lived a life of hiding in the shadows, it is hard to introduce light and truth into the narrative, without tripping over rumor, speculation and falsehood. Nevertheless, many have tried. Several books and many motion pictures, in one way or another, chart the course of the Missouri outlaws into Minnesota where they made a daring raid on the bank at Northfield. Most books provide considerable detail about the shootout in Northfield, and the capture of the Youngers, but gun-toting saturation notwithstanding, the writers reveal very few details about the James brothers' incredible escape from Minnesota through Dakota, into Iowa, and then on to Missouri or other points south. The accounts are interesting and amusing but not at all convincing. Take your pick of the following.

5. The Two That Escaped

An Omaha newspaper, in 1881, summed up the "three week's chase" after the James brothers by simply stating that they escaped. The article provided no details except to say that along the way "they caused numerous of their enemies to bite the dust."¹ While they did exchange gunfire with their pursuers, they most certainly did not leave a trail of dead bodies.

James A. "Dick" Liddil, an outlaw who once rode with the James brothers, described their escape in a paragraph. After calling it one of the "most remarkable feats in all history," he simply said that they "obtained a wagon and team ... and drove down to Missouri." Calling this explanation "a fairy tale," journalist J. A. Derome wrote: "The James brothers could not have escaped that way, even in a covered wagon or as Will Rogers puts it, in two wagons, both covered."²

Another outlaw member of the James gang, the fearless Jim Cummins, noted in an interview about his memoir that "Frank and Jesse had a hard time getting away." An understatement to be sure, but Cummins was 69 years when he put forth his explanation and the old survivor should not be judged too harshly for his vagueness. He claimed that the brothers "rode in the covered wagon of a sewing machine man" and that they "returned home by a roundabout way," a journey that included such faraway places as the territories of Arizona and New Mexico. "They were nearly starved and ate raw rabbit and roots," but finally got back to Clay County, Missouri. The brothers may have eaten raw rabbit and roots, or something worse, but overall Cummins' sensational explanation reveals very little.³

Frank Triplett's book, *The Life, Times and Treacherous Death of Jesse James*, published in 1882, contains an account of the great escape that is hilariously inaccurate. He begins with the tearful and sad departure from the Younger brothers and Charlie Pitts, and then he places the James brothers in a heavily wooded area where they were able to hear their pursuers talking, discussing strategy. On foot the fugitives head east, steal a couple of chickens and cook them "on a fire that someone had built." Then after "a long sleep," they continued east. On their way they encounter a "Norwegian" and an "American," and just then Frank decides to put on an act. He speaks in broken English with a German accent and the strangers, suspecting nothing, leave them alone. Next they come across five riders and once again Frank's fractured use of the two languages convinces the riders that he is simply an idiot.

Triplett states that the brothers continued with this ruse until they come across a man with a team of "fair-looking horses." But instead of stealing them, they bargain with the man and end up with two purchased horses. They ride south into Iowa, and although they encounter many people along the way, Frank's awkward use of a mixture of German and English throws off all suspicion. At Fort Dodge, Iowa, they board a train for Chicago.[4] Readers of Triplett's book will find no footnotes, but it is his contention that information for the book was obtained from the widow and mother of Jesse James.

In 1883, a year after the death of Jesse, a man who described himself only as "One Who Dare Not Now Disclose His Identity" came forth with a bizarre and fanciful tale of the brothers' great escape. His pages reveal that the two were relentlessly pursued by determined men on horseback through a veritable purgatory, a haunted woodland that bordered a river bank. They were followed so close that the pursuers' voices were heard. They were shot at several times, and it was only through good luck and ingenuity that they were not captured. "They clung close to the bank, and silently reached a place they deemed safe, in a cave-like excavation made by the water under the roots of a great tree." The anonymous writer stated that the James boys could have easily shot their pursuers, but as they were low on ammunition, they held their fire.

It was only by wading for some distance in the river that they managed to avoid being arrested. Exhausted and hungry, they found a dry place and slept until morning. On foot all day, they came across "a man leading two horses, one of which was saddled." Strangely, they did not steal the horses, but rather they engaged in a discussion with the man for the purchase of the horses. A deal was reached and a sale was made: two horses and one saddle. The horsetrader confessed that "he did not own anything which he would not sell."

The secretive writer failed to mention any part of the Dakota sojourn, but he states that there was a fierce gun battle in western Iowa, where Frank "received a desperate wound." His narrative ends in Waco, Texas, where Frank's wounds were treated. Admitting his admiration of the outlaws, he declared in an applause line that "none other than men of very superior genius could have succeeded."[5]

On May 3, 1882, a Texas newspaper reported that Waco was the city where the robbers ultimately went after Northfield.[6] That may be true, but the anonymous book writer who dared not to "disclose his identity" failed to cite any sources that would corroborate the newspaper article. While it is known that the brothers did spend time in Texas, the unknown writer's account is out of step with others that reflect serious research and analysis, so *The Life and Tragic Death of Jesse James* should be branded historical fiction or simply as a mythmaking device.

Interestingly, the tales offered by Triplett and the anonymous writer are very similar to a story of the great escape that was included in a newspaper article in January of 1880.[7] Not only are all three stories similar but each one is vague and weak, and each fails to include dates, landmarks, direction of travel or name places. More strangely, however, is that dialogue is quoted, suggesting that Jesse and Frank were interviewed, for they were only two people who would have been in a position to remember any words spoken by their pursuers. And since both men steadfastly refused to talk about their experience on the prairie, the logical conclusion is that all three stories are false, or, to be charitable, very thin on facts.

A more recent writer claimed that they stole two horses, and then rode aimlessly south from Crystal Lake, Minnesota. At some point they split up, intending to meet in Fort Dodge, Iowa. Frank disappeared, presumably riding south, while Jesse "abandoned his horse and proceeded on foot" until he reached the Big Woods. Then, near the Des Moines River, he stopped at the farm of George B. Armes and convinced the farmer that he was looking to buy several farm properties, and asked if he could please stay for a few days. Armes was agreeable and the affable Jesse turned on the charm and won over the entire family. He even took a skinny dip in the Des Moines River with the three teenaged Armes boys. According to this writer, the James boys never went through Dakota Territory, but they did manage to find each other in Fort Dodge, and from there made their way to Missouri, with the aid of a shady but savvy Sioux City newspaper editor.[8]

This photograph shows the two children of Jesse and Zerelda James, Mary Susan and Jesse Edwards. Mary was born July 17, 1879, in Nashville, Tennessee. Since her outlaw father was hiding under an assumed name, Mary, and her brother as well, were both given false names. On March 6, 1901, she married Henry Lafayette Barr and was the mother of four children. Her brother, often referred to as "Jesse James, Jr.," was born August 31, 1875, in Nashville, Tennessee. Although he found success in business and as a lawyer, Jesse, the son, lived under the long, dark shadow of his famous father, whose daring and spectacular life of crime was the stuff of legends. Jesse the father became a star in a series of books, melodramas and finally motion pictures, all of which have either attempted to explain or have created a false narrative about the life of the Missouri outlaw (Library of Congress).

The foregoing accounts are not convincing, but other well-researched books and contemporary newspapers contain enough information so that the actual story of the great escape can be pieced together with reasonable clarity. After Thomas J. Dunning spread the word about his capture by the Missouri outlaws, there was "renewed excitement" in Mankato. A group of 38 men under the leadership of George N. Baxter, a lawyer, geared up for another search. Detective Mike Hoy, who had given up and returned to Minneapolis, quickly got his party together again, traveling to Mankato to join the others. Finally, the sheriffs of several counties including Rice, Waseca, Blue Earth, Winona and Faribault, headed a massive contingent of more than 500 men. "All the crossings of the Blue Earth River were picketed." Surely, this strategy and show of force would produce results.[9]

But once again, the outlaw hunters met with abject failure and bitter disappointment. On September 14, 1876, during the dead of night, the James and Youngers brothers made another daring and successful move. With Bob Younger leading the way, all six of the outlaws crossed the railroad bridge over the Blue Earth River, near Mankato, stepping cautiously on the railroad ties. They crossed safely, although Bob "had a very narrow escape from going through a hole."[10] Moreover, there was no attempt to stop them, because those men whose duty it was to guard the bridge "took to their heels."[11] To make matters worse, three "section hands armed with shot-guns were concealed in the bushes" and could have easily "picked off every one of them" as they crossed the bridge in single file. But like the pickets, they "dared not fire" and simply watched until "the robbers were out of sight."[12] The "Swede section hands" had another story; they chose not to shoot at the outlaws, claiming "they were insufficiently armed."[13]

The exasperated people of Mankato simply could not believe the luck of the outlaws. "All approaches to the river about and around the city of Mankato were well-guarded," and yet they were not stopped or even challenged.[14] The seemingly impossible escape sent the city spinning in a "ferment." Folks were sadly convinced that fate was aligned against the pursuers. After walking through Mankato, in the middle of the night, the fugitives moved toward the railroad bridge over the Blue Earth River. It was guarded just then by "two men and a boy." At 2:30 a. m., on September 14, six men were observed crossing the railroad bridge. "The boy wanted to shoot them," but they were overcome by fear, "and the pickets all ran."[15]

The failure of the guards or the railroad men to challenge or stop the robbers was seen as a serious loss of opportunity, for had just one man with good night vision showed some courage and shooting ability, he could have picked them off "one by one as they crept from timber to timber."[16] Since the route the robbers took to get to the railroad was directly through the heart of Mankato, it was thought they must have had help, and "parties suspected of aiding the villains" will be "closely watched."[17]

There was a report among the many rumors that "scouts near [the] Blue Earth River fired at two men, and the fire was returned." Tracks were found in the mud, "including the small heel and square toe" print that more than one tracker had found. It was taken as strong evidence that the pursuers were at least on the right trail.[18]

The morning after the Blue Earth bridge incident, the searchers, led by Mike Hoy, came upon a camp in a wooded area recently used by the outlaws near Minneopa Falls. They found abandoned coats and blankets and a "half cooked breakfast" of chicken and corn.[19] A frustrated newspaper reporter used the discovery of the vacated camp to vent his anger at Mike Hoy, the burly, belligerent and overbearing detective, a man clearly unpopular with the public and the press. Claiming that none of the robbers were sick, the reporter offered that the "puke" found at the site by Mike Hoy belonged to someone other than one of the robbers.[20]

Yet setting aside all snide remarks, some of the other clues at the site were useful. For although once again the bandits barely escaped, the discovery was viewed as encouraging, for the lawmen surmised that the escapees were on foot, hungry and exposed to the wet and chilly autumn elements. What the Minnesota riders of vengeance did not know is that they needed to take two lines of pursuit for the James brothers—whose names were unknown to the people in the remote, rural areas—were on the move without the Youngers. No longer burdened and slowed down by the wounded Younger brothers, Frank and Jesse struck out on their own hook.

Over the years a number of reasons for the separation have been put forth. One version concludes that despite the friction over what to do with Dunning, the men reasoned that if they continued in two groups, there was a chance that at least one group might escape.[21] Another explanation of the break up is that it "was purely accidental." The James boys left the camp to see if there was a way to get through the picket line set up by the lawmen, and they "got through, but did not return." The Youngers heard gunfire and "supposed the men might have been killed or captured."[22]

There is a third explanation. It says that the wounds of Bob and Jim Younger were so severe and their suffering slowed down the pace of the escape. Bob suggested that he be abandoned so that the more able-bodied men could successfully evade capture, but no one would hear of it. Years later Cole explained to Harry Hoffman that the night before the split up Jesse and Frank managed to steal two horses. They offered one to Bob but his suffering had increased immeasurably, so Cole told Jesse and Frank: "take the horses and go." According to Cole, the break up was done in the spirit of honor and loyalty. The James brothers rode off, taking with them many of the personal possessions of the four who stayed behind.[23]

Cole Younger was also heard saying, in one of his numerous jailhouse conversations with various listeners, "we parted in peace," and that the James brothers (whom he did not name) "left with the knowledge and consent of the remaining four."[24] In another interview Cole or Bob let it be known that the "two men who escaped" did so by chance; "it was purely accidental." Furthermore, the boys denied that the escaping parties took "their valuables," for they had very little among them to take.[25]

This writer takes the following position. The separation was purely by chance. After crossing the Blue Earth railroad bridge, a horse was captured and "it was agreed that the James brothers should go ahead and reconnoiter," in an attempt to locate the pickets. A large black horse was taken from the farm of John Vincent, located between Rush and Loon lakes, five miles east of the town of Lake Crystal.[26] About midnight, heading in a southwesterly direction, the two men on one stolen horse, attempted to cross a picket line on the road near the outlet of Loon Lake.[27] The area was well guarded but most of the guards had fallen asleep on some straw scattered along the road, leaving one young man, Richard Roberts, awake, alert, standing near the bridge. He was alert and when the horse quietly approached, and a shot in the dark by the Welsh native, spooked the horse.

The brothers suddenly found themselves on the ground with their horse running away. They landed, in a heap, on the soft sand. They could not get back to their companions without the risk of being shot, so after lying on the ground for a few minutes, they crawled away in the dark woods while their horse galloped away, attracting the attention of the aroused pickets. They were minus their transportation, and one man lost a "fine felt hat," but they had made it through the picket line and they did not linger or hide. After crossing the Crystal Lake road, they jumped over a fence and made their way west through a corn field.[28]

Once again, the James boys were the masters of the situation. Had they stayed on the horse, and continued toward the "fork of the road," they risked being shot. Instead they used the horse as a decoy, allowing it to "go forward a few jumps," after which they slid off its back and let the animal attract attention while they listened to discern the whereabouts of the pickets, and then they moved away safely in the dark. Instead of capturing or killing the fugitives, the pickets were left with a headless hat.[29]

While the felt hat was looked upon as a trophy of war, the incident was embarrassing to the proud people of Lake Crystal, and one citizen among them wrote a letter to the editor of the *Mankato Record*. The writer who identified himself only as "Z" praised young Richard Roberts of Mankato, who "did his duty like a *man*, but refused to mention the names of those who failed to do their duty." He explained that most of the "boys" left their posts for their warm beds because "they had so much faith in the men with the long needle guns." The rather tepid letter hinted that there would have been consequences had the negligent fellows been actual soldiers. But, he shrugged, "there is no use crying over spilt milk."[30]

On foot again, the two outlaws trudged on until they approached Garden City. Meanwhile, the large black horse that had lost its two riders made its way back home to its owner, John Vincent. It was wearing a bridle and the animal "showed signs of hard driving, and was very muddy."[31] It was the first of many horses that the James brothers would find, use, and then lose or reject in favor of fresh mounts during their long and epic journey home.

The townspeople of Garden City knew about the Northfield robbery and were in a state of excitement and alert. A posse was ready to mount up and ride out when two men walked into town rather boldly, but with sufficient nonchalance so as not to raise suspicion. Frank and Jesse James passed through town within listening distance of the posse, walking unhurriedly, not at all like wounded men. In the excitement, no one stopped them for questioning. Sometimes luck does favor the foolish and the bold; the pair figuratively dodged a bullet at Garden City.

The brothers were known for their luck, having participated in many successful robberies before the ill-fated Northfield affair. In March 1868, Frank and Jesse and their gang robbed a bank in Russellville, Kentucky, making off with a good haul. They escaped into Missouri after a long chase. Now flush with money, the brothers went west to a 30,000-acre California ranch known as the "La Panza Ranch" owned by their uncle Drury James. It was located about midway between Los Angeles and San Francisco on an old Spanish trail.[32] In addition to the massive ranch, Uncle Drury owned and operated a resort hotel and spa at Paso Robles.[33] Jesse had been suffering from the bullet wound to his lung that he received during the closing stages of the Civil War. The spa was known for its hot sulfur springs and over a three-week time, the spring water restored Jesse's health.[34]

Relaxation was not the only item on their agenda, and many years later, a story emerged about the brothers being stuck in the middle of an impromptu fight in a "gambling den." Knives and guns came out and were put to deadly purpose. "Lamps were overturned and friends fired on friends in the confusion." Jesse and Frank managed to get out unscathed but the toll from the melee was six dead, including a sheriff who had been playing poker when the excitement started. True or false, having had enough of California, the boys returned home to Missouri.[35]

Years later, wandering around in Minnesota, another lift from lady luck was probably on their minds. And once again good fortune was on their side, for although they were on foot, they came upon a farm, near Garden City, owned by a man named Seymour in whose stable were two fine gray horses. The team of mares was owned by a Methodist minister named George Rockwood often referred to as "Elder" Rockwood. He had brought his prized team of "iron" gray work horses to the Seymour farm and during the day the reverend assisted Seymour in putting up hay.

The James brothers arrived at 3 o'clock the following morning to find the minister in the barn with the horses, musket in hand. This precaution was in response to a notice to farmers to guard well their valuable livestock. One of the James boys eased, catlike, past the vigilant minister, "knocked the gun out of his hands, and pistol whipped him." Always thinking on their feet, and using whatever was at hand, the brothers created saddles out of sacks stuffed with hay, mounted up and rode away at great speed.[36]

After traveling about 20 miles west from the Seymour place,[37] they stopped at the house of "Mr. Jackson, two miles northwest of Madelia." It was about 6:30 a. m. and Jackson was away at the time. They spoke to Mrs. Jackson, asking for something to eat. The unsuspecting woman, seemingly eager to help, said "that breakfast was not ready." The brothers were not in the mood to stay, even though the woman "urged them to wait for breakfast." One of the brothers was hatless and he asked if she had an old hat she could spare. She informed him that she had just purchased a new one for her boy but was willing to sell it to the stranger who openly displayed "a roll of bills … as large as his arm," including "several $100.00 and $50.00 bills." The man with the big bucks paid $1.50 for hat and ten cents for a loaf of bread, and then he and his companion rode away on the gray mares.[38]

Horses were something both men understood, having spent so much time in the saddle while on their outlaw escapades. Jesse "had dealt in thoroughbred horses" under the guise of a respectable businessman using an assumed name, of course. It was said that he was a "wonderful horseman" and could ride "100 miles a day without any trouble."[39] The brothers were at home on the back of a horse, a skill that would prove very useful to them in their current situation.

They needed to move on, too, for after the Garden City men realized that the two strangers who passed through their town were in all likelihood the wanted robbers, they rode off well armed and ready for action. Coming to the farm where the James boys stole the gray horses, the Garden City posse called it quits. They did so because they were familiar with the speed of the gray mounts and they knew they would be out-distanced.[40]

The fleeing James brothers covered 75 miles after stealing the gray team, a long day's ride. That night they stopped at a point about five miles south of Lamberton, "a station on the Winona and St. Peter Railroad, seventy-five miles west of Mankato."[41] It was reported that they spent the night at the home of a German settler where the farmer's wife dressed the leg wound of one of the strangers. What she saw was Frank James' "flesh wound" that made "an ugly gash or furrow" from the hip to "near the knee."[42]

It was also learned from the visit at the "German" place that the riders had "five watches" and both wore rubber coats. They possessed a map of Minnesota and said that they had made "extensive inquiries about roads, rivers, etc." They told their host that they had been traveling in a wagon that broke down, injuring them both. They spent the night sleeping in their clothes and departed the next morning. The outlaws were watched as they started north for a short distance then turned at "the corner of a cornfield," heading south "across the prairie at full speed."[43]

Meanwhile groups of men under the leadership of Sheriff Barton of Faribault County and the indefatigable Mike Hoy had been within about ten miles of the James brothers, and Sheriff Dill of Winona County had been positioned 12 miles directly west of the robbers' line of travel. All this caused an exasperated reporter to write: "It is rather strange that he [Dill] did not encounter them."[44]

Outlaw sightings were a regular occurrence on the Minnesota prairie. Mid-afternoon on the 14th, "two men on grey mares" stopped at a farmhouse four miles north of the town of Mountain Lake, informing the resident that they were "in pursuit of horse-thieves from Garden City." The farmer, when asked, advised the riders to head to Leavenworth, because there was timber in that area. When authentic outlaw hunters arrived at the farm, the proprietor gave an accurate description of the two riders, noting that their horses looked tired and that one of them was sporting a nice new hat. This news set in motion another flurry of activity as it was surmised that the robbers were probably going to Lake Shetek, a place they most likely knew nothing about.

The two escapees were something more than outlaws running for their lives. They were suave, slick, well mannered and able to fit into any social situation with other gentlemen who would not suspect that they were in the company of killers. The brothers would need that same skill in order to deceive the unsuspecting homesteaders, men and women living in isolation in a time when a person could go for days or weeks without hearing another human voice. Utterly alone, there was the sound of nature but it was overwhelmed by the silent yet pounding voice of loneliness that threatened to drive people mad. Such was life on the frontier. Who but some anti-social hermit would not welcome strangers? This was something the James boys could exploit.

Acting out would prove to be an important part of their escape plan. Both had their own separate roles to play in accordance with their personalities. Frank was a quiet man, thoughtful, better read and more reserved than his brother. Jesse far more restless, inquisitive and extroverted and known "for his piercing eyes" that had the power to "look right through a person."[45]

The concern and excitement over the bank robbery, the casualties, the chase, and the prospect of reward was positively infectious. Every unfamiliar face suddenly became the front for a suspicious character, especially if he was wearing a linen duster, with or without a cape. On Saturday, September 16, it was reported that on the previous Tuesday, a man was arrested in Worthington, Minnesota, because he was a rough looking character. The man who said he was Thomas Thompson stepped off the train at Worthington and checked into a hotel with only a "sack containing a saddle, a blanket and a pair overalls," but no duster. He had no identification on him, no money, no gun and no one knew him, so he was arrested on the possibility that he might be one of the James boys or, more likely, Cole Younger. All this sent a wave of high excitement throughout the town of Worthington, as "dispatches were received urging the greatest vigilance." The unfortunate fellow was taken to Mankato where he was identified as Thomas Thompson from Marshall, Minnesota, and released.[46]

Mr. Thompson slipped from the spotlight back into anonymity rather quickly, having had his brush with fame. He was not a showy outlaw and he would not loom large on the pages of history. The real outlaws, the regal and historic James brothers, and their erstwhile companions, the Youngers, were the subject of an intense pursuit that promised to keep the spotlight on them while the presses were cranking out newspapers by the thousands. It was high drama, playing out in real time with a massive audience looking on, some cheering for the outlaws and some for the lawmen. As the James brothers moved steadily southwest, the pursuit shifted in that direction. Posses from Worthington and Luverne, in southwestern Minnesota, were in the field, looking for the last two, but they were looking in the wrong places. Someone revealed that the ubiquitous robbers were seen "south of Sleepy Eye."[47]

The brothers were well south of Sleepy Eye when they crossed the Des Moines River at "Swan's Ford," five miles south of Lake Shetek, the largest lake in southwestern Minnesota, in Murray County. Mr. Swan recalled that they "looked like brothers" and were "gentlemanly in their address." They had many questions about distances, roads and railroads, telling their host that they were from Rock County, Minnesota, and that they had bought the gray team on "account of their size and beauty." They did not dismount. They asked for food and were invited to come in but they refused the invitation. Instead some bread and milk was brought out of the house, and after taking some much needed nourishment, they departed in a southwesterly direction.[48]

Moving into the second week of the Northfield tragedy, the lack of success from among the hundreds of pursuers led to some angry finger pointing. The *St. Paul Weekly Dispatch* was among the impatient, bewildered and frustrated. In an editorial that newspaper let loose on Governor John S. Pillsbury for his failure to organize, mobilize and supply a force of men to "capture the ruffians, dead or alive." The *Dispatch* was sorry to pounce upon "so estimable a gentleman, but it is the fact." The head of state was accused of being asleep at the wheel when real, determined leadership was needed in order to do the job. Pillsbury was sharply criticized for his unwillingness to spend money and provide the needed provisions to those in the field. Meanwhile the leaderless, disorganized effort continued.[49]

Another Minnesota newspaper, *The Worthington Advance*, was also very critical of Pillsbury, while lamenting the fact that thus far, the six remaining outlaws had not been gathered in. In a thoughtful editorial, it was suggested that the posses from the various counties should have been organized under one qualified man, or, if "a company or two of cavalry" could have been placed in the field, the bandits could not have escaped. As it was, the eager but inept volunteers, amateurs who had to foot their own expenses, fumbled along while the governor was enjoying himself at the Centennial, in Philadelphia.[50]

The haphazard manner in which the great manhunt was conducted was bound to yield some monstrous mistakes that gave rise to zany memories and close calls. A posse led by John B. Bresette, a St. Paul detective and Civil War veteran, cornered "an unfortunate Swede" in "a clump of bushes." Someone fired "about thirty shots" in the bushes, none of which hit the terrified young Scandinavian. He managed to escape without a scratch but with a story to tell. The *Tribune* was unable to resist critical comment. It came out with a humorous article that said the incident "speaks volumes for the marksmanship of Bresette's squad."[51]

The mad saturation of men on the move searching for the James brothers had some unintended, but favorable, consequences. Two escapees from the Fort Dodge, Iowa, jail were apprehended near St. Peter, Minnesota, by men looking for two other absent men, meaning, of course, the James brothers. William and Bernard Rentz from Fort Dodge were the unlucky pair nabbed after two weeks on the run. At first it was thought that the Rentz brothers were "part of the Northfield gang," but the sheriff of Webster County, Iowa, put an end to that speculation when he identified them as fugitives from Fort Dodge.[52] They were brothers but not Frank and Jesse James.

But the James brothers were out there, on the broad prairie, riding toward Dakota. Two riders attracted the attention of a Worthington posse after they were seen north of that Nobles County town. The pair was "hunted and chased by Worthington men for nearly a week," and it was believed that they were the robbers on the run.[53] There was another report that the two were seen Saturday night, September 16, "ten miles west of Worthington," riding hard.[54]

Horses on the frontier were scarce, and in the 1870s, most farm work was done using oxen, and yet horses figured prominently in the outlaw odyssey across the Minnesota prairie. The James brothers were still riding the gray team of work horses taken near Lake Crystal, but even strong horses wear out and the fugitives would soon be looking for replacements.

One interesting horse story was told by Walter Converse who was a mail carrier between Worthington, Minnesota, and Dell Rapids, Dakota Territory, a story that found its way into print. While on his mail route one day, "probably" September 16, "about the time the outlaws were in his neighborhood," Converse came across "two farmers who were trying to hitch two horses to a wagon." He stopped to talk to them and was told that "two men had taken the farmers' horses and left those two in their place." The frustrated farmers were upset because they were having such a hard hitching the "two tired animals in order to get home." The story, like so many others, lacks confirmation and the thieves were not named or described in the narrative, but the timing of the event strongly suggests the larcenous intervention of the James brothers.[55]

6

A Ride for Life

"Their bravery ... and endurance on horseback for days and nights, wounded and almost starving, and without sleep, are without parallel in the history of crime."
—*The St. Louis Globe-Democrat*, December 5, 1876

After the James brothers left the Swan homestead near the Des Moines River, someone claimed to have seen the fast-moving outlaws at the Lutheran Church at Center, a town in Murray Township. From there they went southwest, riding hard through the night on the steel gray horses. They were still being pursued by lawmen who, based on some scraps of information, believed the two outlaws were heading for a strange place called the "Lost Timber," in Rock County. It was thought of as "a natural hiding place." A contingent of men searched the "famous" area during the night of September 16 and in the early morning hours of the 17th, but finding no clues, it was decided that the robbers had taken another route.[1]

The lawmen divided their forces and Sheriff William H. Dill of Winona County and two others went to Luverne, the county seat of Rock County, believing it would be easy to work up a large posse there, should it be needed. Luverne, a pleasant little village on the prairie, was first settled in 1867–68. It had been hit hard by the national depression and the grasshopper plague, but by 1876, with a population of about 300 people, its business places were showing signs of revival.[2] And if the people were still laboring under any semblance of lethargy, very suddenly, on a Sunday morning in September of 1876, they were about to be literally snapped to attention by the prospect of gunplay in their streets.

Sheriff Dill's instincts were right and his gut feeling placed the lawmen close to the runaway robbers. But he had no idea just how close they were to their quarry. Frank and Jesse James had entered Rock County in southwestern Minnesota on Sunday morning, the 17th of September. They had put many miles between themselves and the rest of the gang. They knew that men were still trying to find them so they needed to keep moving and yet they had to find time to rest and eat. Hunger has a way of directing human behavior. The James boys had been eating poorly and sporadically since they left Northfield. They needed food and were forced to take risks to find it.

They had heard about some mounds and rock formations in Rock County and thought these natural features would make a safe refuge. While in the area, they came upon the farm house of Charles B. Rolph and his family, about 12 miles north of Luverne, on the west bank of the Rock River. Originally from Pennsylvania, they came to Minnesota in 1872. It was a Sunday morning, Rolph was away, and it was his wife Sarah who spotted a pair of trail-worn, tired-looking men riding up on equally tired gray horses. They dismounted and rather nonchalantly asked for some food, promising to pay for it.³

They claimed they were looking for land and that they had been traveling in a wagon until it was destroyed in an accident. The weary travelers were served a meal by Mrs. Rolph. They consumed it in a very relaxed state of mind, with their backs to a wall, not the least bit nervous. According to historian Arthur P. Rose—who included an anecdote about the James brothers in a book about the history of Rock County—the Rolphs had seen pictures of the fugitives in newspapers. Mrs. Rolph was suspicious but wisely said nothing. The strangers asked questions about the location of the mounds and rock formations and

A sober-looking young Jesse James looks into the camera while holding what appears to be a cane or a walking stick. Most likely his outfit that day included a couple of revolvers and a well-stocked ammunition belt, items that were essential for the well-being of a highwayman. Jesse did not resemble one in this photograph, and while he and Frank were wandering through Dakota Territory, the nice business suits they wore during the Northfield bank robbery became torn, tattered and dirty. Still they were successful in convincing settlers that they were simply honest strangers in a strange land. While making their great escape, the brothers relied on their survival skills and the generosity of isolated people who were willing to share food, water and information (The State Historical Society of Missouri).

seemed especially interested in any large crevices and caves. They were falsely told that none existed, and apparently satisfied they finished eating and departed,[4] having first placed a silver dollar on the table.[5]

The Rolph encounter, and others involving the traveling James boys, inspired some investigative reporting, many years after the frontier era ended. In 1924, a Sioux Falls, South Dakota, newspaper, *The Daily Argus-Leader*, assigned a reporter named J. A. Derome to write a series of articles on the James brothers. Derome, also a minister, proceeded on the premise that Jesse and Frank James were not worthy of the adulation heaped on them by some local men and boys who believed the brothers were "robbing the rich to help the poor." Rather he concluded that the James boys were merely "plain thieves and murderers." But he admitted that the brothers' exploits were of worthy of a serious study, and their story was comparable to the sad and tragic fate of the legendary James Butler "Wild Bill" Hickok, murdered in the Black Hills[6] a few weeks before the Northfield bank robbery.

Derome went about his task with skill and determination, seeking the truth, and eager to tell the whole, unvarnished story, which by all accounts had become a mixture of myth and fact. He was dismayed at some of the literature on the James brothers, including an article in *Outdoor Life*. A writer for that Denver magazine, Chauncey Thomas, obviously a James admirer, wrote: "Jesse James may be alive today, and ... I for one would like to grasp his hand."

It was as if Thomas could not come to grips with a dead Jesse James, rather he preferred to think that the infamous outlaw was larger than life and thus able to cheat death or to successfully stage an assassination and his own funeral. Derome came up with a critical and satirically pure solution to the issues raised in the *Outdoor Life* story. "If he [Jesse James] is alive today, and reads this article, we hardly think he would like to grasp our hand, unless he thought ... we might be quicker on the draw."[7]

On the home front, the reverend turned reporter was forced to sort truth from fiction because of the "many stories, legends and contradictory statements about the passage of the outlaw brothers through Rock, Minnehaha and Lincoln counties."[8] To distinguish myth from fact, Derome visited the hinterlands and talked to people from Luverne, Minnesota, and Sioux Falls, Canton, Worthing and Valley Springs, South Dakota, who had some personal, or second-hand, knowledge of the James brothers' great escape.

He spoke to Judge Martin Webber who had lived in Luverne since 1870 and was familiar with the manhunt. The judge confidently remembered that the fleeing outlaws stopped at the Charles Rolph homestead. But Webber stated that Rolph, a Civil War veteran, had breakfast at his house with Frank and Jesse James the morning of September 17, 1876. Webber averred that the James brothers entered Rock County at the northeast corner and made their way, southwesterly, to the Rolph homestead.

Webber said that Rolph did not recognize the strangers, was not suspicious, and when they asked for food, was agreeable. His guests seated themselves at the table so as to be in a position to see anyone approaching. Rolph excused himself, saying that he had to milk his cows. One of the James boys objected, saying, "sit down and eat." Rolph said no, it was important that he milk the cows. But his guests refused to take no for an answer, and one of them demanded in a loud voice: "SIT DOWN." To reinforce the point, the man "laid a gun on the table." There was no further discussion; all ate and the strangers took their leave after dropping a silver dollar on the table. With their parting words, they hinted strongly that Rolph should not make note of the direction they took as they rode away.[9]

Webber's story is at odds with the report in the *Minneapolis Tribune*. On September 19, 1876, that newspaper reported that Rolph (spelled Rolfe) was away when the James brothers pulled up at his house. In speaking to Sarah Rolph, they claimed that they had been riding in a wagon that broke down. Sarah offered a friendly greeting to the road-weary strangers, asking "if they were sick." One of the outlaws replied that he "had rheumatism and his comrade had broken two ribs in falling from the wagon." Both men had difficulty getting off their horses and an even harder time getting back on after eating breakfast. She watched them ride off to the south, slowly, sitting on saddles made of "bags filled with straw"[10] and "old ropes looped for stirrups." To get back on their horses—that were "nearly fagged out"—they had to "climb up on the fence and slide on to their horses." Mrs. Rolph also noticed that one of the men "had fine boots with small heels and square toes."[11]

The road-weary James brothers were not tempted to tarry at the Rolph house; they departed the Rock County homestead having finished their meal and paid for the food. When Charles Rolph returned, he spoke to his wife then he whirled into action. He rode south to Luverne to alert the town and the authorities. Luverne erupted in excitement and the townspeople quickly prepared for the hunt.[12] It was said that "religious services were interrupted" and a Sunday school teacher dismissed his class to join the pursuit, putting down his Bible and picked up his gun.[13]

After they arrived in Luverne Sheriff Dill and his party, which included a reporter for a St. Paul newspaper, decided to take the night off and sleep in a hotel. Dill had experienced more than enough excitement over the past several days and wanted to relax for a bit. Dill was said to have been a likeable, genial, whole-souled fellow of great girth. He wanted to get cleaned up after ten days with no "change of linen." He located the nearest barbershop and got a shave, then went to a clothing store and bought "the largest shirt in town." Returning to the hotel, where he presumably took a bath, he attempted to put the shirt on but found he could only do so with great difficulty, if at all. Sheriff Dill needed help most urgently.

Pounding on the floor of his room in dire frustration, he summoned the reporter who came running upstairs to see what type of emergency was unfolding. He found Sheriff Dill in the throes of an intense struggle between flesh and fabric, a large man trying desperately to put on his shirt, "imprisoned half way into the stiffly starched garment." The newsman threw himself into the fray, and "after the most desperate efforts, the shirt was forced to its natural position, where it set tighter than the most fashionable female pull back." Dill pulled himself together, and as if overcome by hilarity of the valiant effort, stated rather boldly and with relief: "By God, my boy, I'm hide bound, sure as fate!"[14]

Armed with new clues, a posse of Luverne men consisting of Charles Rolph, Billy Patterson, Mike McCarthy, Jack Dement and others, including men from Worthington, set out to bring the chase to an end. The effort was unsuccessful and there are two explanations in the record. Arthur P. Rose wrote that the volunteer outlaw hunters went to nearby Larchwood, Iowa, and were informed that the wanted men were on the Big Sioux River at a place called "Uncle Dan's Ford." Members of the posses were then placed on both sides of the river. "Jack Dement came upon the outlaws who fired hitting the horse he was riding." The outlaws escaped before the rest of the party arrived at the scene of the shooting.[15]

J. A. Derome of the *Daily Argus-Leader* came up with another set of facts. The posse came across the brothers near the Split Rock River, a stream that flows out of Minnesota southwesterly into Dakota Territory. The pursuit ended abruptly, however, when one of the James boys fired and hit the neck of the mule ridden by Jack Dement, a member of the posse. The mule was not seriously hurt but the posse had seen enough gun action and the would-be captors went back to Luverne.[16]

Concerning the Luverne posse, it was also suggested that the volunteer lawmen simply got cold feet. "It is said that they often were within shooting distance of the outlaws but did not venture an opening fire on them." Rather than attack the seasoned outlaws they held back and "lost track of them near the Palisades," a large rock formation north of Valley Springs. This was the opinion of Perry E. Howe of Valley Springs, who was interviewed for an article by J. A. Derome.[17] This is also the view of the *Minneapolis Tribune*, for in an article on September 19, 1876, it was bluntly asserted that the posse men, who had rifles, "were afraid of them [the James boys] and are blamed for not shooting."[18]

A St. Paul newspaper was also critical of the posse, noting they "could have reached them with their rifles, but were afraid of them." The same article said that "this party followed [them] seven miles without attacking, and lost their trail after dark." They were an estimated three miles east of the Palisades, on the Split Rock River, when the trail went cold. The reporter left the impression that the posse missed a golden opportunity to kill or capture the last two Northfield robbers, who were "now in Dakota."[19] They were gone and "no grasshoppered man" in southwestern Minnesota would "share in the reward offered for their capture."[20]

Thus far the James brothers had done remarkably well in evading capture. Their success can be attributed, partially, to their survival skills. Lesser men would have given up or would have been apprehended. But from the beginning of the great chase, the lack of organization and poor management of resources was apparent, and that failure was the source of frustration for the public and for newsmen covering the manhunt. The effort was not lacking talent, for there were sheriffs, Civil War veterans, colonels, captains, detectives—even the mayor of Minneapolis—who "had a taste of outlaw hunting."[21] But it was complained that "everybody was an officer, and there was not a single soldier in the field." Southwestern Minnesota was called a "war zone," complete with determined men doing dangerous duty, but the war was not prosecuted in a military manner. As such "every night we think the morrow must bring down the game, and each day there is disappointment."[22]

The James boys' long ride in a southwesterly direction indicates that they were anxious to reach Dakota Territory. Getting out of the Minnesota deep woods and onto the open prairie might have given the boys a psychological boost, but they were still a long way from Missouri. Nevertheless they could breathe a small sigh of relief for they had so far evaded capture. Getting to Dakota did not guarantee a successful escape, but it would mean that they had come a great distance from Northfield.

The brothers might have reasoned that Dakota, as a territory rather than a state, was far less settled than Minnesota with less law enforcement and therefore less able to mount a pursuit. By reputation, Dakota was known throughout America as a faraway place, a bleak, wild land, famous for its blizzards and grasshoppers. It was thought of as a place that hosted bad men, many who deserved to hang, desperate men who sought out its borders to escape justice in the states. Gold had been discovered in the Black Hills two years before and the crazy rush for the riches included outlaws as well as honest men. Dakota, in all its primitive glory, was the bejeweled cornucopia on the minds of desperate dreamers and anxious men all over America; it would naturally attract men like Frank and Jesse James.

A Dakota newspaper featured an article that almost celebrated the outlaws' entrance into the territory, declaring rather boldly: "Minnesotans Turn the Northfield Robbers Over to Dakota and Go Home."[23] It was a gentle jab at the dedicated but futile Minnesota effort and a call for all brave Dakotans to take up the pursuit.

Minnesotans most certainly didn't feel as if they had simply quit, nor did know with certainty where the James brothers were after the Luverne posse gave up the chase. But it was believed that the "robbers wintered two years ago between Sioux City and Yankton," so it was surmised that their travel plans included a stop in that area.[24] All the authorities were alerted and "all crossings on the Missouri River, between here [Yankton, DT] and Fort Sully have been guarded."[25] Surely, many believed, this would be the trap that would at long last snare the elusive villains.

It seems as if the authorities in Missouri were hoping that the brothers would be snagged somewhere along the way. F. A. Rogers, sheriff of Cooper County, Missouri, expressed that sentiment in a letter dated September 21, 1876, to James King, the St. Paul chief of police. While he "placed no confidence" in the many reports of outlaw sightings, Rogers closed his letter with a wish, "Hope your authorities will succeed," and the hope that whole gang will get "their just deserts [sic]." Then, as an indication of a certain level of frustration, he wrote: "We have had trouble enough with them in our state."[26] Sheriff Rogers concluded that some of the Missouri friends of Jesse and Frank were resigned to the fact that they would never come home; they believed that the brothers had died from the wounds received in Minnesota.[27]

In November of 1876, a Missouri newspaper, the *Sedalia Bazoo,* came out with an article entitled "Interesting Story about the Escape of the James Brothers from Minnesota." The writer was clearly enamored with the brothers and his happy bias is reflected in the article that ended with the fugitives safely in Dakota Territory. His source of information was an unnamed man from Minnesota living near Madelia. The reporter—who clearly felt privileged to write about the outlaw luminaries—excitedly warned his readers that they were about to read some "interesting incidents connected with the escape" that were being reported for the first time. Those who read the article no doubt came away thinking that someone actually talked to the brothers, or at least spoke to someone who somehow had gained some critical and detailed information.

His starting point was Hanska Slough, near Madelia, where the six robbers were essentially "hemmed in a trap into which they unwittingly walked."

It was here, he breathlessly explained, that the James brothers made their bold charge for freedom, leaving their wounded companions behind. "While in the thicket, composed of sumach [sic] and prickly ash, where it was impossible to see a man teen feet, the James boys left the Youngers and proceeded to strike out on their own hook." So off they went, following a small creek for some distance.

Next he describes their arrival at Garden City where they found themselves in a "quandary." They had no choice but to stroll through town, hoping that they would not be stopped and questioned. They recognized their situation as dangerous, but gauged that it would be safer to proceed through on foot than it would be to suddenly turn around and go back. The reporter admiringly explained that somehow the brothers understood that James brothers had escaped the "thicket just in time to prevent being surrounded."

"And forward they went ... straight through the town while it was wild with excitement." They walked steadily, "with a defiant, easy nonchalance," passing by groups of armed men hastily preparing for the chase, "who little dreamed" that the outlaws they were after, the "famous Missouri bandit chiefs," were passing within hearing distance of "their conversations and plans." Frank screwed up his courage, concealing "the lameness caused by the ball in his leg," walking as if he were in perfect shape, "with all the elasticity of the step of a youth." Fortunately for the escapees, no one paid any attention to them, all so hurriedly making ready for the exciting hunt, perhaps savoring a taste of the reward money, or just the chance to shoot down one or both of the most famous outlaws in America.

At the outskirts of the village, "they drew a long breath of relief, and congratulated each other on their good fortune." At long last they were out of the thick woods, walking on a broad prairie where they could see for miles in each direction, thankful that they could not be "surrounded and shot down like dogs." Now if only they could find some horses, they could mount up and "bid defiance to the hosts who were on their trail."

This is, of course, the point in the story where the theft of the gray horses occurred. As luck would have it, the outlaws were rewarded for their bravery and boldness, for they spied "a pair of magnificent iron greys [sic]." The brothers had just enjoyed a meal at a farmhouse when they came upon the horses that the owner had carelessly failed to lock in a stable. It was explained by the happy writer that most of the horses in the area were either locked up or in use on the trail of the outlaws. But not the span of grays, and, as luck would have it, the horses were "beauties and the best horses in that part of the state, having taken the premium at the fair the year before." Their owner was said to have been away campaigning for office, telling a crowd of voters about the "expected capture of the robbers," when "two of their leaders were at that very moment appropriating his idolized horseflesh!" Then, revealing what was undoubtedly some key inside information, the giddy reporter states that the outlaws casually "entered the stable, took two empty sacks, filled they with hay," after which they slapped the makeshift saddles on the horses "and in the next instant were at home—in the saddle!"

The Missouri reporter was seemingly caught up in a rhapsodic spasm of pure joy that prevented him from making a detailed explanation of the robbers' route. He simply said that they "took the high road and pursued their course unmolested." They sped over the prairie "at an astonishing rate of speed" that put them far ahead of the would-be-captors.

Meanwhile, back in Garden City, the townspeople concluded that the pair of strangers, who had meandered through town only hours before, were indeed Frank and Jesse James. Thinking that they might still be on foot, they quickly mounted up and galloped in the direction taken by the strangers. When they came to the farm where the gray horses had been stolen, their spirits sank for they knew the character and speed of the horses. Realizing that they probably could not catch up, they quit the chase. The writer stopped his lofty narrative too, noting only, in one final, rousing salute to his outlaw heroes, "the gallant grays bore their riders to safety, and the reader knows the rest."[28]

But the reader did not know the rest of the story, and to this day many facts are missing. Still, those who sympathized with the James brothers naturally assumed that the story was true and that by November they were safely at home among friends and relatives. In Clay County, Missouri, the long-suffering robbers could hide, heal and rest while planning their next crime.

The *Bazoo* article was not without its critics. A man who claimed to be "one of a small, picked party who were in pursuit of the James boys from the time they crossed the river, at Mankato until they crossed the state line to Dakota Territory," said the *Bazoo* article was riddled with errors and he felt compelled to provide actual facts. For example, the bold and brazen walk through Garden City was "sensational" but false. The James brothers, he insisted, never got "within five miles of Garden City."[29]

Commenting on an editorial in the *St. Paul Pioneer and Press*, a Winona, Minnesota doctor, penned a letter, dated November 17, agreeing with the editor who said "the Bazoo story is a cock and bull yarn of the worst kind." Mocking the hapless "journalist" from the *Bazoo*, Dr. H. N. Avery boldly supplied some facts of his own in a response entitled: "The Truth of History about Their Exit from This State." "In the first place," he impatiently declared, "the James' were fired at [while] both [were] riding one horse, while passing the pickets at Luna Lake, two miles south of Crystal Lake." Dr. Avery claimed to have received his information from the guard who had fired at the brothers.

Moving on to the theft of the gray horses, Avery wrote that they were stolen about four miles west of Lake Luna, about 3 o'clock in the morning. He concluded by saying that if "you draw a line due west of Luna Lake, you will have their course until they struck Lake Shetek," after which the doctor insisted they set "a southwest course to Sioux Falls, Dakota."[30] As the years passed and work continued on tracking their trek, many other researchers and writers would find credibility in the doctor's bold assertion.

Lake Shetek area was thought of as a "notorious robbers roost," with an abundance of horses to steal. It was also reported that "one of the James brothers spent last winter between Yankton and Flandrau, [sic] Dakota Territory" and that "a James boy" was making haste for that area "from whence he undoubtedly came."[31] Like numerous other confusing reports and alleged sightings of riders wearing linen dusters, this one was false. But what was true is that the fugitive brothers had not separated. They were riding, together, southwesterly in the direction of Dakota Territory, a place where they may, or may not, have visited in the past.

There was a kind of hazy belief in the minds of some reporters, that having entered southeastern Dakota, the James brothers "were in familiar territory," referred to as the "Lost Timber of Dakota." Someone described the area as "full of knolls and ravines," a country "hard to hunt."[32] Right or wrong, the pursuit of the James brothers had entered a new phase.

7

Dakota and Devil's Gulch

> "To the north of the mill is what is known as the Devil's Gulch ... and [it] is a curiosity affording some most romantic scenery."
> —*The Dakota Pantagraph*, May 23, 1878

While all the clocks in America were rhythmically ticking in time, the James brothers crossed into Dakota Territory, although they probably were not aware of crossing the borderline. Dakotan Perry E. Howe believed that the outlaws were "coming west from Luverne,"[1] and it was about five miles north of the village of Valley Springs, in Minnehaha County, that Frank and Jesse James entered Dakota at long last, putting Minnesota behind them. But then there is the report that the Luverne posse, while fearfully following them at a safe distance, lost their trail near the Palisades, meaning the brothers were probably in Dakota, and if so they had crossed the state line a few more miles to the north on September 17, 1876.

At any rate, they were out of Minnesota, a hard, cold fact that weighed heavily on the minds of the worthy people of that state. The sting, the emotional anguish felt throughout the state is reflected in a tiny editorial piece in a St. Paul newspaper. The writer was constrained to say that the "slight hope" entertained toward bagging the James brothers had been extinguished, for it is "now quite certain that those two, at least, have escaped from the state." As for the others, their "whereabouts is at present a mystery and a matter of mere conjecture," but it was conceded that they too had put "a long distance between themselves and their determined though frustrated pursuers."[2] Truly, the decent and proud folks who fully expected a different outcome felt a sharp, insulting sense of injustice.

That all six outlaws had thus far avoided capture was a tribute to good luck, ingenuity, perseverance and ability to live off the land. It seems that their Civil War experience with the guerrilla Quantrill, much of it in the saddle, had served them well. Moving through unfamiliar country among strangers had long ago, become an essential part of their lives, traits they used to their advantage in their current crisis. No doubt the desperadoes, cold, hungry and with wounds left untreated, had earned some grudging admiration from the proud Minnesotans.

For the James brothers, a ramble through Dakota was probably not much different, if at all, from the terrain of southwestern Minnesota. It all looked very much the same. As they scanned the vast prairie landscape—where once buffalo roamed in great numbers—they saw an undulating terrain with few trees, tall prairie grass and nice fall colors. But there was deception in the sameness, for they were in a far more primitive and wilder land, and a much less settled area than Minnesota or their native Missouri. Nevertheless the Euro-Americans, who believed in a utilitarian approach to nature, had made a strong statement: the natural world was under assault. The last buffalo sighting in southeastern Dakota occurred in 1870, but evidence of their existence was everywhere in the form of thousands of bones.[3]

On the evening of September 17, a Sunday, two riders approached the sod-shanty of Andrew Nelson located about four miles west of Valley Springs, then a small, isolated village, in Dakota, situated close to the Minnesota state line. The village came into existence in 1872, when settlers erected a small building in a valley that was watered by a number of springs, hence its name. By 1876, Valley Springs had a post office and a school but little else.[4]

The Nelson family had arrived in Dakota in 1872 and claimed land along the Split Rock River, not far from the huge, dramatic rock formations known as the Palisades. They were one of the earliest families to settle in Minnehaha County. The Nelson sod house stood near the trail followed by the Worthington (Minnesota) and Sioux Falls stage line.[5] It was later replaced by a stone house that became a local landmark between Sioux Falls and Valley Springs.[6]

The James boys were tired and hungry, their horses worn out—the noble beasts' energy spent riding hard on the long trail. Both horses and riders needed rest, food and water. It was time to test their ability to convince another homesteader and his family that they were honest men who needed a break. But they had nothing to worry about because the Nelsons had no knowledge of wanted men accused of robbery and murder traveling in Dakota. Like others who lived on the frontier where isolation worked on the mind like slow death, when days or weeks could pass in utter loneliness, the Nelsons naturally welcomed the company of strangers.

Andrew Nelson had finished threshing the day before. He and his 13-year-old son Nels were outside standing by a smoky smudge pot they were burning to keep away the pesky mosquitoes. Between 6 and 8 o'clock that Sunday night, Frank and Jesse James halted their horses at the homestead, and in doing so, they became a link to the outside world. Nels recalled that they were mounted on white horses, and that their flanks bore the marks of sharp spurs. Being astride white horses would indicate that somewhere on their journey they had ditched the grays. But since it would have been difficult to distinguish color in the moonlight, or firelight, the gray horses may have looked as if they were white, especially if they were covered by foam.

The boy recalled that the two men were "finely dressed wearing even kid gloves." (Interestingly, the boy said nothing about small heeled boots with square toes.) Without introducing himself, of course, Jesse asked for a drink of water from the shallow well near the house. Only too happy to oblige, Andrew Nelson drew a pail of water from the well, but before Frank or Jesse could take a drink, a thirsty horse dipped into the pail. Nelson offered to get a fresh pail, but a parched Jesse drank from the first one, saying, "Never mind—I'd rather drink after a horse than some men."

Nels was a bright boy who as an adult would teach school and serve in the South Dakota state legislature. He closely observed the behavior and attitude of the two strangers, making mental notes. Nels later recalled that the two men seemed anxious and annoyed during the time they stood at the fire and talked. He reasoned that the wayfarers wanted to keep their travel plans a secret and were only waiting for the Nelsons to go inside. One of the men, probably Frank James, stayed on his horse, rubbing his leg as if it was causing him pain. The other man casually checked out the sod stable where a couple of horses were resting.[7]

Andrew Nelson lit his pipe and continued to talk, almost as if he desperately needed to converse with someone outside of his family. This annoyed his guests and one of the outlaws finally asked Nelson if he was "going to sit there all night."[8] Clearly, the brothers were anxious to get going, but they had something in mind to accomplish before they left.

At some point during the visit the conversation ended, the Nelsons went into their house, having "retired for the night," leaving the strangers alone. It was then that the attention of the James brothers was fully focused on the horses. It was unusual for settlers to have horses in those days as most of the field work was done by oxen. But the Nelsons did and the sight of the fresh horses was just too tempting. Their Minnesota horses were worn out, and after the Nelsons were asleep, the James boys departed but came back and stole the horses from an unlocked stable.

Of course, when someone decides to steal a horse in the dark of night, the thief doesn't always know what he is getting. In this instance the animals were work horses, not riding horses. Both were mares with colts at their sides. The mares looked good and strong but one mare was blind in one eye and the other blind in both. But off they rode on fresh horses, with the colts following along, into the night and in the direction of Sioux Falls. The next day one colt was found about 80 rods from the house and the other about five miles away; both had been tied up so that they could not follow their mothers nor could they return home.⁹

Everyone loves a horse story with a happy ending. Such is the fate of the gallant gray mares that the James brothers stole during the night near Garden City, Minnesota. The exhausted grays had been left at the Nelson place in Dakota, where the brothers ditched them in favor of the blind horses. They were taken to Luverne by the stagecoach driver. A man who saw them in Madelia said they were "some the worse for their journey" but looked as if

This is a striking picture of Devil's Gulch in winter, from a postcard with a 1914 postmark. A man is standing on the old wooden bridge, apparently looking down at two people below on the ice. Devil's Gulch is a quartzite rock chasm located in eastern Minnehaha County, South Dakota, close to the border with Minnesota. Native Americans called it Spirit Canyon, and many strange tales are associated with the scenic area. According to a legend started by an unknown person at an unknown date, a horse-bound Jesse James jumped across the 18-foot chasm while being hotly pursued by a posse. While it is possible for a horse to broad jump a distance of 18 feet, it would be impossible for a horse to make such a prodigious leap because of the rugged and rocky terrain. Nevertheless, the story lingers on and tourists gather every summer to view the majestic gulch in all its mythical glory (author's collection).

they would regain their strength and stamina. Eventually the prize animals were returned to their rightful owner, Elder Rockwood.[10]

It is at this point in the narrative that a slight change of direction is necessary because of the need to delve into and describe one of the most colorful Old West legends, a tale that seemingly came out of nowhere and attached itself to the dangerous saga of the James brothers. The story of their great escape would not be complete and indeed would be woefully less fascinating had this writer neglected to bring to light the mythical tale about an impossible jump over Devil's Gulch, horse and all. At the mere mention of jumping across Devil's Gulch, the reader knows that the alleged jumper was Jesse James, a larger-than-life daredevil of historic and unequaled proportions.

Devil's Gulch is a quartzite rock chasm located in eastern Minnehaha County, South Dakota, close to the border with Minnesota. Named after His Satanic Majesty, it exudes a dark, sinister intrigue, and yet Devil's Gulch is a place of intense, eye-opening scenic beauty, although to some eyes it might look like a strange freak of nature that suddenly burst through the dirt on the verdant, rolling prairie. A creek of the same name runs between the huge rock formations that are 60 to 70 feet high.

How is it, many have wondered, that the large outcropping of jagged quartzite rock that forms the deep gulch ever made its startling, seemingly noiseless appearance on the Dakota prairie? The easy answer, of course, is that quartzite exists, naturally, both under and on top of the ground from southwestern Minnesota and northwestern Iowa to central South Dakota. Back in the day when quartzite was used as building and paving stone, the supply was often described as inexhaustible and the structures created by it were magnificent and destined to stand strong indefinitely.

In its majestic and massive glory, quartzite—or jasper, as it is sometimes called—is also proudly on display in the City of Sioux Falls. There the Big Sioux River breaks into a series of cascades, culminating in a dramatic fall of splashing, laughing water that the Native Americans called "Minnehaha." The sprawling hunks of ancient rocks and the powerful falls of the Big Sioux River attracted the first town site speculators to the area in 1856 from Dubuque, Iowa. At this place of natural wonderment, the town of Sioux Falls was founded.

The Palisades proudly stand south of the town of Garretson, in Palisades Township, Minnehaha County. Just two miles from Devil's Gulch, the Palisades is another place of sheer enchantment where grand and high outcroppings of the hard, pinkish rock adorn the banks of the Split Rock Creek, a lovely stream that was once called Split Rock River.

The first settlers arrived in Palisades Township in 1873.[11] This date coincides with an article in an 1873 Sioux Falls newspaper informing its readers

This photograph, taken in winter, shows one of the many large quartzite rock formations in the scenic location long called the Palisades. Situated about two miles south of Devil's Gulch, the Palisades provides visitors with a splash of unusual beauty on the rolling Dakota prairie. The high and rugged outcroppings of rock form the banks of Split Rock Creek that gently flows toward its destination. Beginning in the early 1870s, Sioux Falls people would hitch up their wagons and carriages and take pleasure trips to the Palisades to enjoy a picnic lunch in the shade of the giant rocks. The first settlers arrived in the area in 1873, and by 1876, the small village called Palisades was created, later giving way to the town of Garretson. In the 1920s, booster groups proposed that the area be made into a park. They were successful and today Palisades State Park is among the many beautiful and scenic state parks in South Dakota (author's collection).

that on a balmy September day, a party of young girls, minus their boyfriends, hired a team and driver and visited the Palisades "to see the beauty of the place and enjoy the pleasure of the ride."[12] There was, however, no mention of Devil's Gulch.

Not long after, another article in the same newspaper told its readers of another excursion to the beautiful rock formations, based on the report from a couple of characters from nearby Valley Springs. They claimed to have ridden their "Indian ponies" across "Uncle Sam's" prairie until they came to the "opening in the rocks through which runs the Split Rock creek." The wiseacre who sent the story to the *Sioux Falls Independent* refused to describe the Palisades because that "might obviate the necessity of [others] going to see them."[13] Again, there was no mention of Devil's Gulch.

On the 4th of July 1874, a contingent of Sioux Falls people, including the editor of the *Independent*, decided to throw a patriotic get-together at the Palisades. On a very hot day, after a long, bumpy ride across the prairie, the beat-up, sweaty group arrived at the Palisades. For lack of trees, the only shade they could find was beneath one of the giant rock formations, and there they huddled to escape the hot Dakota sun. The place was deemed a "wonderful sight," but "to us who had been reared among New England's rocky steeps ... the sight was rather tame."[14] A Minnesota man who traveled with others from Beaver Creek into Dakota Territory in 1878 was very impressed with the rock formations at Palisades. In his eyes, the spectacular "pillars of rock" that rose to a height of 90 feet looked like "huge chimneys or buttresses."[15] They were a thing of beauty on their own so there was no need to compare or contrast them to what the East had to offer.

An enterprising mill operator from Union County, Dakota, also went to see the Palisades to check out their natural beauty, but more important, their utilitarian value. As it turned out, the area met with his complete approval, and in February of 1876, it was announced that Charles W. Patten from Elk Point, in the southeastern tip of the territory, "secured the water power on the Split Rock River ... and will at once proceed to erect a grist mill thereon."[16] Some of the timber from the old barracks building at Fort Dakota in Sioux Falls was used in building the mill.[17] This enterprise was instrumental in the founding of a village called Palisades near the mill.[18]

The titanic rocks at the Palisades—an area once called the Grand Canyon of South Dakota—very nicely complimented the rocks at Devil's Gulch, a place that unless legends die, or tourists lose interest, will forever be associated with Jesse James. How and when the word "Devil" was attached to the noted place is a mystery, but the gulch has all of the hellish and haunting qualities of a niche in Dante's Inferno.

It also has a history along with a mythology, due in part to the legendary James brothers. But the escaping Missouri bandits can't take all the credit for the lore, fame and mystery of Devil's Gulch. The Native Americans had long called it "Spirit Canyon." According to an old Indian legend, the canyon was created as a result of a tomahawk throwing contest between two warriors. One was a Yanktonais named Ha-Schootch-Ga and the other man was "the legendary spiritual personality and trickster," Untome. Ha-Schootch-Ga was the first to toss his tomahawk, and he threw it for a great distance, thinking that he would win. But Untome threw his much further and when it struck the ground there was thundering in the clouds. Suddenly the "earth trembled, the rocks split and the canyon appeared." Spirit Canyon became a holy place for the Indians, and for the white man, a place that the plow shall never touch.[19]

An old white settler, A. G. Risty, thought the inexplicable, natural pile of rocks was sacred too, and in April of 1924, he appointed himself "a committee of one" to change the name to something less devilish. In his name-change petition, Risty rhapsodized on the legendary appearance of "Longfellow's Hiawatha and Minnehaha" at Spirit Canyon. There "the noble Hiawatha" climbed atop "the giant stairway" and observed the "modest Minnehaha slumber dreamingly, in the bosom of the valley, weary from her long journey toward the Laughing Waters of the Big Sioux."[20] Nice, but Risty's petition never caught on with the public.

Other dramatic and tragic stories were associated with Devil's Gulch, the sculptural eruption of quartzite that offered the enchanted viewer an unforgettable look at "some most romantic scenery." In the mid-1870s, an "early settler" in a carriage or a similar conveyance got too close to the edge one night "in the dark winter." He was unfamiliar with the area and he "barely discovered the danger in time to save himself and his team," from a long drop off the rocky edge onto "sharp-pointed rocks below." A writer for a Sioux Falls newspaper in 1878 surmised that the anonymous traveler, while "looking down into the darkness," must have experienced a glimpse into "the infernal regions."[21]

Natural beauty can be deceptively threatening, and when man is matched up against the awful powers of nature, superstition sometimes enters the hazy equation and truth gets lost in the fog. Stories are told and passed on with embellishment. One such tale that survived is about a frontier family from eastern Wisconsin that "in the early days of the Dakotas" went west to find a new home. James Harding, his wife, son and daughter immigrated to Dakota. While camped on the bank of the Big Sioux River, a short distance from the Split Rock River, they were "attacked by a band of Indians led by a white renegade." All were killed except the girl, Nellie, who was taken captive. The three dead pioneers were later buried in unmarked graves, near the "old stage road" from Sioux Falls to Luverne, Minnesota, not far from Devil's Gulch.

Back in Wisconsin, on the very night of the massacre, Dick Willoughby, "the young girl's lover," suddenly woke up from a terrible nightmare. While dreaming he saw the attack and the killing of Harding and his wife and son. He had also seen that his lovely Nellie had been carried away by the white renegade. The dream was so vivid that he had no doubt as to the truth of it. Riding hard and well armed, he traveled west along the same route taken by his friends. In two weeks he arrived at Worthington, Minnesota, where he learned that the Harding family had passed through just the day before he experienced the terrible dream.

Willoughby rode on to Dakota, searching feverishly for the place where the killing of his friends had occurred. He had seen it in the dream so he knew he would find it if he kept searching. Finally, he did, and to his horror, he came upon the graves of the three murdered people, all friends that he had come to know in Wisconsin. The young man was determined, however, to find Nellie and would not rest until he took her away from the white renegade. He followed a trail along the Split Rock River left by the party of killers; that trail led him to Devil's Gulch. He spotted a fire burning on a "shelving rock" and saw a group of about six Indians and the white man. Creeping closer, Willoughby aimed his rifle and fired, killing one of the Indians. He had them trapped on the rock and took advantage of his position, firing again and killing another man. "Consternation seized the Indians" as the rifle sent its leaden contents into their ranks. Those who were not shot "threw themselves into the depths below."

The only one left standing was the white renegade. In his desperation, he grabbed Nellie. There was a scream and a pistol shot: Nellie was dead. Dick Willoughby, who had come so far with such determination and purpose, failed to save her. But there was still work to do: he could avenge her death. The white renegade made a mad dash for his horse and the chase was on. After about five miles, the renegade's horse stumbled, losing its rider. Willoughby took advantage of the accident, shooting and killing his enemy, the evil man that murdered his lover. But Dick was shot too, and though badly wounded, he crawled back to Nellie and died a romantic, Shakespearian death, with his arms around her.[22]

In the 1880s, Devil's Gulch was thought to be an extension of the Palisades, although they are now in two separate parks, about three miles apart. A reporter for the *Sioux Falls Daily Press* was drawn to the area in 1886, when it was believed that a rich deposit of silver had been discovered in quartzite rock formations. It was a bogus claim, but for a short period of time, it caused excited men to swarm all over the scenic area with picks, shovels and dynamite. The *Press* reporter called Devil's Gulch the "Palisades' greatest attraction," reminding him of the "canons of Colorado."[23]

What is fascinating about the foregoing reports is that there is no mention of the James brothers, even though it was believed and reported in newspapers that the Northfield fugitives were seen near the huge rock formations. There also were stories about a cave in the rocky west bank of the Split Rock River where the brothers supposedly hid for several days. It was named, fittingly, Jesse James Cave, and it became a tourist attraction because some people will believe anything.[24]

Interestingly, it was Frank James who "quashed a legend" when he was asked about a legendary cave. Without confessing the location of the cave, Frank, with a wink and a nod, told a listener that "we never went into any place we couldn't leave by the back door."[25] It is unfortunate that Frank was unwilling to talk in more detail, because if he had he might have revealed and explained the incredible story about Jesse James jumping across Devil's Gulch, on horseback, in a desperate attempt to put distance between him and a posse.

The fact that news of the prodigious 18-foot leap emerged in 1922 is most curious. It was then that the editor of the *Wentworth News*, a Lake County, South Dakota, newspaper, wrote that he had been given a tour of Devil's Gulch by someone (unnamed) who "showed us the place where Jesse James jumped the channel riding horseback."[26] After that a series of articles appeared in 1923 that are equally vague as to the origin of the tale, the wild story that strangely emerged in the public mind many years after 1876. Why, when and how the leap legend surfaced at all are three questions that have plagued historians and history buffs for a long, long time.

While most writers tend to dismiss the jump as myth, not worthy of mention, Carl W. Breihan, in 1974, came out with a book entitled *The Escapades of Frank and Jesse James*. In it he states that a gunfight took place at Devil's Gulch and Frank suffered a severe arm wound. He also states that a man riding with the posse informed a reporter that he saw a horse-bound Jesse jump across a "rocky gorge, a distance of fifteen feet," all the while belting out "his old battle cry." While Jesse was jumping and yelling, Frank was leading his horse down the nearby "Devil's Stairway."[27]

Breihan was a respected expert on the James brothers and other outlaws, and he has written extensively on the Old West, but his decision not to cite his sources is puzzling and raises questions. What posse man from what posse told what reporter? And when did all this take place? The story of the great escape begs for names, times and places, more certainty and less ambiguity.

Since 1974, other books and articles have dealt with the notorious brothers and for the most part the writers take a negative position on the legendary jump. Most people, especially those who know something about horses, also conclude that a jump of about 18 feet would be impossible, if only because of the presence of jagged rocks. While it might be possible for a horse to broad jump 18 feet, it seems impossible for a horse, even a fresh, fast one, to get up the necessary speed because of problems presented by the rocky surface. And yet in 1924, W. W. Sanders, then an editor of a Garretson newspaper, wrote: "It was across the Devil's Gulch—as the legend has it, that Jesse James jumped."[28]

The quote was published in *The Daily Argus-Leader*, a Sioux Falls newspaper, and a legend was born—one that has found a permanent home at

Devil's Gulch on the north edge of Garretson, South Dakota. Calling it a "pedigree legend," J. A. Derome wrote, "it is probably true that Jesse and Frank James had to jump across some chasm there, as there were no bridges of any kind," and they were being chased by a Luverne posse.[29]

Editor Sanders was in love with the area, as was the Garretson Booster Club. In the summer of 1923, Sanders invited a group of southeastern South Dakota newspaper editors to visit the scenic spot. He gave them a tour of the Palisades and Devil's Gulch that included a bit of storytelling. Taking the group across the footbridge over the Gulch, he told them they were walking where, years ago in the past, "Jesse James jumped across the Gulch."[30]

In an article entitled "Jesse James' Big Jump," Sanders launched an explanation that showed a lack of knowledge about the outlaw and his background, and a terrible misunderstanding of the laws of physics: "As we get the story, it was when Jesse James was hurrying south to his old home in Missouri after one of his raids in Minnesota. Perhaps it was after the hold-up at Northfield. Anyway, he was closely pursued and his faithful horse had all he could do to keep ahead of the officers of the law, who had fresher mounts. Coming to the Devil's Gulch, he was so closely pressed that he did not have time to go around—that would have probably meant capture. Preferring death, if need be, to capture, Jesse spurred his horse on to the jump. They rose in the air in a mighty leap. They just made it, some of the rock being broken off as the horse's feet struck the opposite edge and falling down fifty or sixty feet to the water below."[31]

In this simple, incredulous recitation, Sanders revealed to the reading public his story, or repeated the story of someone else, about a great jump, or the "Leap," as it was also called. And he left at that; there was no explanation of who claimed to have seen the alleged jump, no naming of sources or explanation of what Frank was doing at the time, preferring to let people speculate. There must have been some head-scratching among his readers and fellow editors.

Some months later, while promoting the Gulch as a tourist attraction, Sanders again made mention of the jump. Noting that the preservation of the legend and lore lingering among the "great rocks and gulches" was important, Sanders wrote that "Jesse James leaped a certain 18-foot chasm on horseback while pursued." Once again his article lacks specifics. He didn't delve into or explain the origins of the story, nor did he name or otherwise identify the person or persons who may have had first-knowledge of the Leap.[32] For Sanders, it all just seemed to come out of nowhere. Although he was a newspaperman, trained to probe, question and investigate, his lack of curiosity about actual facts is most curious.

In his massive and detailed *History of Minnehaha County, South Dakota*, published in 1899, Dana R. Bailey, described Devil's Gulch and included a photograph of it, but he made no mention of Jesse James or a jump across it.[33] This suggests that the legend had not yet taken flight or that Bailey, who evidently spent considerable time at Devil's Gulch, knew about it but dismissed it as false, not even worth a line or two. There was a tendency among historians of that era to write little or nothing about outlaw characters. Jesse who?

While the story of the jump fails the tests of history and logistics, it is possible that the brothers were at or near Devil's Gulch, or the Palisades, where the Split Rock River passes between huge, high chunks of quartzite, thus seemingly "splitting the rock." Had they traveled in a westerly direction from the Rolph farm, 12 miles north of Luverne, they would have crossed into Dakota Territory close to Devil's Gulch, with lawmen and others in pursuit.

Although some books about the escaping brothers state that their border crossing occurred about five miles north of Valley Springs, it seems that if their line of travel was due west of the Rolph farm, they would have crossed further to the north, near the scenic gulch or the Palisades. It was reported that a Luverne posse lost their trail "three miles east of the Palisades on the Split Rock River in Dakota," thus putting the riders in the area of Devil's Gulch.[34] But this report is not entirely reliable because the Split Rock River runs through the Palisades, not three miles to the east. Of course the witness could have meant to say the trail was lost three miles upriver or three miles downriver from the Palisades.

However, if the two men rode southwest from the Rolph place, toward Luverne, they would have by-passed the infamous Devil's Gulch, crossed into Dakota near Valley Springs and stopped at the Nelson homestead, thus shooting down the legend of the "Great Leap." The time sequence is important too, for they had breakfast at the Rolphs' on the morning of September 17 and pulled up at the Nelson's that same evening. Was there even time for Jesse and Frank to visit Devil's Gulch?

In 1948, an old man who claimed he was Jesse James (one of many), insisted that he did indeed make the magical jump and wanted to make sure that people knew about it. The secretary of the Sioux Falls Chamber of Commerce received a mysterious letter dated March 18, 1948, from a Texan named Orvus L. Howk. He was writing on behalf of a very old man named Frank Dalton from Lawton, Oklahoma. The ancient one was really Jesse James and Frank Dalton was an alias, for he had faked his death in 1882, a lie believed by many people. The letter asked: "Do you have any place called Devil's Gulch, a deep canyon north of Sioux Falls? It is near a little town called Garretson, I think. There is an old man here past 90 years old who says he once jumped across a place when it appeared that canyon walls were about 15 feet apart and a sheer drop below. He says he was in a hurry back in 1876—I wonder if such a place exists. In every respect the old mystery man's memory seems good."

The letter writer described the old man as nearly six feet tall with a "square face and red complexion." His body bore evidence of a life of violence in that he had scars that looked like bullet wounds and a rope burn on his neck. Dalton was reputed to be a "good shot," even though he was nearly 100 years old.[35]

Frank Dalton was not only phony who tried to slip into the life and reputation of the famous outlaw Jesse James for they had been popping up regularly, but he was one of the most persistent. His claim fails because by 1948 the legend of Devil's Gulch had made its way around the country and access to stories about the jump was available to the public. The Howk letter could easily have been concocted from information in the public domain. Frank Dalton was no Jesse James; he was an impostor.

But Charles E. Mason was Jesse's great grandson, or so he claimed. In a letter to the Garretson Chamber of Commerce, dated July 12, 1966, Mason attempted to lay to rest all doubt about the legendary Leap. Writing from St. Joseph, Missouri, he angrily insisted that he got the truth from none other than great grandpa Jesse himself. It was in 1928 that Jesse told Charles, "I was riding toward Sioux Falls, South Dakota with a posse ... right behind me when I came to the gulch, a 25 foot chasm." The outlaw quickly estimated the distance, spurred his horse and "sailed across." According to Mason, Jesse rejoined Frank and Cole Younger and the three men rode to Valentine, Nebraska, passing through Sioux Falls.[36]

In addition to insisting the story of the Leap was true, Mason also declared that the story of the Jesse James Cave was also a fact. And since facts matter, his letter can be dismissed as a fabrication. Mason may have believed with all his heart that Jesse James did incredible things during a remarkable escape from Northfield, after which he faked his death. But to believe Mason one must ignore the important fact that Cole Younger was still in Minnesota and therefore did not ride to Nebraska with his outlaw mates. Including Cole in his letter shows how little Mason knew about the Northfield incident. Cole Younger did not escape. He went to prison. He would not leave Minnesota until 1903.

And yet the legend and lore of Jesse James' improbable but magnificent Leap across Devil's Gulch lives on, drawing new life from people like Mason and Dalton and other death deniers. It is a legend with a long life and it is an integral part of the story of the great escape by the James brothers. There is no point in trying to drive a stake through it, because it can't be killed. Somewhere out there someone might find an answer, a rational explanation for an issue that seems to be pleading for closure, but then again, maybe not. Maybe, just maybe, the romance of history has a legitimate place in this outlaw narrative alongside plain, dull facts.

In the heat of the moment or under stress caused by fear, anxiety or uncertainty, people sometimes see what they want or need to see in order to stay steady and make sense of their situation. It is known that the Jameses were pursued by many men, and in the course of the pursuit, more likely than not, one of the brothers jumped across a rocky creek bed or something similar. The jump takes almost less than a couple of heartbeats and is witnessed by one or more men. It is mentioned in conversation, repeated over the years, changed slightly each time, until the insignificant puddle-hop becomes a legendary Leap, a gargantuan feat by a larger-than-life desperado. One wonders if the story would have come to the fore had the lawmen been chasing ordinary horse thieves through the rocky region.

It is doubtful, however, for only heroes are able to clear tall buildings with a single bound, or ride and coax a tired horse across a rocky, deadly chasm. Neither Jesse nor Frank ever uttered or wrote a word about their dangerous Dakota sojourn. But had Jesse made the jump, and considering his penchant for self-promotion, why would he not have bragged about it? He said nothing, not even after they had successfully returned to their home in Missouri, where they were reasonably safe and free to talk. How could he not have been tempted to rub it in a bit and enhance his already mysterious reputation? Instead it is reasonable to believe that Jesse, who would die in 1882, never knew just how important he would become to South Dakota tourism.

But wait, for there came before the public gaze a newspaper report that Frank and Jesse James were not at Northfield, did not participate in the historic robbery, never set foot in Dakota, and therefore could not have been the subject of such a massive manhunt. It was two other guys, nameless, nondescript fellows, neither of which had the audacity or ability to attempt a jump across Devil's Gulch, something only a Jesse James could do. The faceless outlaws, without a reputation, simply meandered through Dakota and, because of pure, dumb luck, disappeared from the record, believing, of course, that it is better to stay anonymous than claim their rightful place in one of America's greatest criminal enterprises and subsequent manhunts.

It was the editor of *The Faribault Democrat* that broke the surprising news several weeks after other newspapers had reported that the two men on the run were Frank and Jesse James. The editor was relying on the insistence of Cole Younger that the James boys did not ride with the Younger boys in Minnesota, and, furthermore, that he had not talked to the James brothers in the last six years. Cole added that if he ever again had a discussion with Jesse, it would begin and end with a revolver.

The editor also noted that "the two robbers who escaped do not in the least resemble the James boys. They are larger, coarser and much heavier men." They had long beards that they braided and tucked inside their vests before participating in the robbery, and after they left the bank, they unbraided their beards. If anyone was looking for a reason to dismiss the editorial, the outlandish claim about the braided beards was more than sufficient.

But there was more so-called proof. The editor claimed to have spoken with Fanny C. Twyman, who averred that her nephews, the Younger brothers, would have nothing to do with Frank and Jesse because a "deadly feud exists between them." For further evidence, the editor claimed that existing photographs of "the James brothers do not bear the slightest resemblance to the men who escaped." The editor concluded that, most likely, the "rascals who got away" were "ordinary horse thieves enlisted for the raid."[37]

The editor carried on as if he had written the article on behalf of Cole Younger, the good friend of Frank James, and a man who wanted above all else, over the long haul, to keep secret the identity of the two who escaped. It has been said that there is no honor among thieves. That may be true among common culprits, but if the thieves had forged the bonds of friendship during the bloody Civil War, when death and chaos ravaged their home state, turning them into killers, then honor—stubborn Southern pride—was the reason for the silence.

8

A Wild State of Excitement

"[T]he general impression seems to be that the robbers are members of the famous Younger and James gangs."
—*Daily Press and Dakotaian* (Yankton, DT),
September 9, 1876

Long before the James brothers actually entered Dakota Territory, its leading newspaper, and the only daily, on the 9th of September alerted its readers that the Northfield bank had been robbed and blame for the crime was credited to the notorious Missouri bandits. Ten days later, there was more big news: the Northfield robbers had invaded Dakota, and the authorities were quick to react to the reports. Two men believed to be the fugitives had been seen near Sioux Falls, causing "considerable excitement in Yankton," and "several parties have gone out well-armed."[1] Yankton, the capital city of Dakota Territory, had experienced some shootings and had seen its share of villainous men, but none with a reputation to match the James brothers.

While picking their way toward Sioux Falls, the brothers entered a more primitive patch of prairie, when compared to the much more developed Missouri counties. As frontier communities were rated, Sioux Falls, a relatively new and peaceful town, was the county seat of Minnehaha County. In 1874 its population was listed as 560 people.[2] Sioux Falls was fairly prosperous despite the sluggish national economy and the grasshopper visitation during the summer months that damaged crops. It was a promising town, in a beautiful setting, including the high bluffs and hills that framed the falls of the Big Sioux River.

While the wondrous falls were known throughout the Great Northwest and were considered a must-see destination, Sioux Falls was in 1876 an unincorporated entity governed by Minnehaha County. It had no telegraph and wouldn't have one until November of 1876. It had a bank, but the brothers were not in a position to conduct another holdup. Sioux Falls had no jail, so had the James brothers been apprehended, they would have been taken to Yankton.³ There were some established wagon roads, no railroads and few, if any, bridges that crossed the many streams of Minnehaha County, so travel was not easy for man or horse.

Families lived in sod houses, dugouts and log cabins, although some buildings made out of lumber were starting to appear in the rural areas and small towns, all roughly tied together by the trails used by settlers to get from place to place or to a market center such as Sioux Falls. Like any two strangers approaching Sioux Falls, the James brothers trudged on, learning as they progressed. If only we could know what impressed them and what they disliked. One thing is certain: had the James boys been making their escape in the spring, when streams were swollen or flooded, their chances for success would have been much less.

Other than ride hard, steal horses, ask for food, and sleep when they could, what did they do, those two brothers, lost, hurt, threatened and so far from home? A man who claimed that he was acquainted with the James and Youngers, in an interview by a reporter for the *New York Sun*, took that question and boldly offered an answer. "Sometimes Jesse left Frank in a thicket," then feeling his brother was safe, Jesse went to a nearby town "and bought medicine." Then returning to his "sick" brother Frank, Jesse "ministered to him and at night they resumed their ride." This routine was kept up until the brothers reached Kansas City, where a doctor took charge of Frank and brought him back to health.⁴

If there is a kernel of truth to the story, it's a very small one, for it is unlikely that they were separated for long, if at all, as they worked their way through Dakota. While the record of their progress is sketchy, it appears that they spent most of their time in the saddle and at a gallop. That they made it to Dakota within ten days following the Northfield robbery and shootout indicates they put their time to good use, made wise decisions, and were the recipients of more than a little luck.

Their next stop after visiting the Nelsons was at the log house of John and Anna Samuelson along Beaver Creek, in Split Rock Township, a mere two miles from the Nelson place and six miles southwest of Valley Springs. The Swedish immigrants had settled there in 1869, making them the first settlers in Split Rock Township.⁵ It was their lucky day because the visitors didn't steal any horses; they simply asked for directions to Sioux Falls. If the information they got was accurate, the James brothers knew they were getting closer to Sioux Falls, a place about which they knew little or nothing.⁶ It wouldn't be too long before Sioux Falls knew something about them, and then armed and mounted men would exit the town to hunt for the outlaws who were out there, somewhere.

An indignant Andrew Nelson wanted very much to go after the two men who stole his horses. He went to a neighbor, Madison Webster, who lived on a homestead about ten miles east of Sioux Falls, asking to borrow a horse for that purpose. Webster wisely refused the loan of a horse, sensing that the angry Nelson was risking too much, that his life would be in danger should he find and confront the thieves by himself.[7]

Meanwhile the horse thieves were getting closer to the Big Sioux River, a stream they would have to cross in order to get to Sioux Falls. It was said that they stopped at the farm of Abraham Banning whose homestead bordered on the Big Sioux River, approximately eight miles southeast of Sioux Falls.[8] Banning's Crossing was a local landmark, where the Sibley, Iowa, stagecoach crossed regularly before a bridge was built at that site. It would have been an ideal place to ford the river.

But more likely they crossed Big Sioux River further north, for it was reported that they stole "a fine pair of gray geldings" from a settler named Burgeson,[9] about five miles north of Sioux Falls. A reckless young man who wanted to get the stolen horses back was turned away after one of the outlaws fired a bullet into the neck of the boy's horse.[10] The neck shot had worked before and it worked again.

Working their way south, in the wee small hours of the morning on the 18th, near Sioux Falls, the brothers came upon the Yankton stagecoach. They hailed the driver and asked where he was taking the rig and were told that Yankton was the destination. The brothers immediately took off in "a northwesterly direction, and, as expected, the driver turned [the stagecoach] around and aroused the people of Sioux Falls." Suddenly armed men were off toward the northwest, doing exactly what the James brothers expected them to do. If it was a ploy, it worked; the outlaws turned toward the south and again came upon the Yankton stagecoach. Seeing the bewildered driver, they could not resist a little jab, asking him "if he was not doing a d—d sight of running around."

The driver was not amused but he was very much afraid. In a panic, he "put his whip to the horses and dashed down the half-mile hill in a mad gallop." The hill was said to be very steep like "the roof of a house." The steep terrain and the reckless speed of the horses, under the control of a man frightened out of his wits, was almost too much for the only passenger inside the coach who "thought his end had come." As for the James boys, they "walked their horses through the streets of Sioux Falls with reckless bravado" as the day dawned.[11]

Later on September 18, Sioux Falls was again thrown into a state of wild excitement after a group of outlaw hunters arrived, including Tom McDermott who came all the way from Faribault, Minnesota.[12] Other riders from Rock and Nobles counties in Minnesota stirred up the locals with news that two of the Northfield bank robbers were on their way to Sioux Falls, so people get ready for some serious shooting. It was believed that the outlaws would strike out in the direction of the Black Hills. The Minnesota men were of the opinion that the robbers would cross the Big Sioux River about ten miles north of Sioux Falls, so in order to cut them off, a line of men was stationed on the west bank of the Big Sioux River in a north/south line that stretched for about 15 miles.[13]

In Yankton, "considerable excitement erupted" when the townspeople were informed that the Northfield robbers were on the run and "coming in our direction." The stagecoach driver also informed his anxious listeners that the new group of "pursuers came in sight of the robbers near the point where the stage was stopped." But for unknown reasons, they turned around went back toward Sioux Falls. Once again, the minions of the law seemed to have experienced "cold feet."

Sheriff Milliard A. Baker of Yankton County, along with U.S. Marshall Leeper and Deputy Sheriff Dr. Hurd from Northfield, organized yet another posse. Baker was an experienced, hard-working lawman who was never known to shirk his duty. He and his men were about to head west along the Missouri River to Springfield "when fresh information" caused them to change their strategy. About 10 o'clock that night, John W. Callender, the sheriff of Minnehaha County, arrived with other Sioux Falls men, including hotelman Harry Corson. These men believed, and convinced their Yankton counterparts, that the robbers went south from Sioux Falls, not west. They reasoned that the two men on the run were making their way toward the Clay County town of Vermillion on the Missouri River. After midnight, the posse, led by Dr. Hurd and Sheriff Baker, rode toward the Missouri River, "intending to cut off the robbers, if possible."[14]

This determined body of men traveled all night, and by 5 a.m., they arrived at the town of Gayville, east of Yankton, and from that point, they rode on to the Missouri River. They followed the "Big Muddy" to Vermillion, while along the way they warned settlers and ferrymen. Everyone knew that the Missouri River was too wide and too deep and dangerous to cross without assistance.

At a Norwegian church near the Lincoln post office, a group of about 40 men, including the preacher, had gathered and were ready to join the pursuit. Dr. Hurd made a speech to the men, urging them to be on the alert and to make certain the Missouri River was well guarded. The preacher and "his flock promised to spread the news," and satisfied with that, the Yankton posse left for Vermillion, arriving about 2 p.m. on the 19th.

By this time, Sheriff John McDonald from Sioux City, Iowa, had 12 men in the field looking for the fugitives. They had covered the area known as "Sioux Point" up to the town of Elk Point in Union County, Dakota. This force was augmented by another from Clay County that reportedly had gone as far southeast as Ponca, Nebraska, thus having covered the area between Ponca and Sioux City. It was a valiant effort, but unproductive, and the Yankton posse called a halt to the chase. They pulled into the capital city, empty-handed and "very much worn out and very wet."[15]

On the 20th, a postal card from Sioux Falls was received in Yankton dated September 18, 1876. It was appended *verbatim*, on the 20th, to an article in the *Daily Press and Dakotaian*: "Two of the Northfield bank robbers have been scouting around in this county for the last twenty-four hours. They have changed horses three times to-day. They have thus far eluded their pursuers by changing their course every few miles. The whole country is in arms. The robbers when last seen [were] about two miles northeast of Valley Springs traveling north-westerly. The presumption is that they will attempt to reach the Missouri River at a point north of Yankton."[16]

The message on the postal card reveals the high level of interest in southeastern Dakota on the subject of capturing or killing the two Northfield robbers. But the "presumption" was incorrect for the James brothers were not planning on crossing the Missouri River above Yankton, and they were one day's ride from Valley Springs on the on September 18.

A successful pursuit is one in which the pursuers adopt the thinking of those they are searching for. That did not happen in southeastern Dakota, in the balmy September days of 1876. A Yankton newspaper informed its readers that "during the past week, everyone who had a little leisure time, have been out scouring the country for the Northfield bank robbers … but [they] have up to this writing eluded the many officers and citizens in pursuit of them."[17] This is a nice way of saying that the pursuit had been bungled. The makeshift posses were on the wrong trail, meaning a lot of horses got more than their share of exercise. The route the wily brothers had taken was to follow, or stay close to, the Big Sioux River, continue going south, and at some convenient point cross into Iowa, and thence to the Missouri River.

Apparently the Yankton authorities felt the same. And if the robbers were going in the direction of Sioux City, they would find themselves trapped between the Big Sioux and Missouri rivers, where the streams come together at Sioux City. Then, with a "band of avengers in the rear," capture would be inevitable.[18]

8. A Wild State of Excitement

But things changed very quickly even in an age when information passed slowly from source to source. Two Yankton men, Charles F. Rossteuscher, a brewer, and Deputy Marshall Wood, had just completed a tour in the opposite direction. They raced north up the James River, "where they warned all the people." They reported that the "Jim" River was high and that the only likely place to ford it was at the town of Olivet in Hutchinson County, well north of Yankton.[19]

The next day, the 21st, a Vermillion newspaper reported that Sheriff McDonald from Sioux City and a posse of eight "arrived here last night and left in the direction of Olivet, as the robbers were last reported to be northwest of Finlay," another small frontier town in Turner County on the bank of the Vermillion River. The reporter excitedly noted: "They change horses with farmers on their route every day." So many men, "most of them strangers to each other," were out looking for the "famous" James brothers, that "we would not be surprised at any time to hear of them firing into each other."[20] That never happened, of course, and it is doubtful that the James brothers roamed around Finlay or Olivet, nor did they venture toward Vermillion.

Working their way further south, after having chatted with the stagecoach driver, they decided it was time to get something to eat so they stopped at the home of Peter Lommen and his wife in northeastern Lincoln County, about two miles east of where the town of Shindlar would one day be platted. They told Lommen that they were lawmen looking for the James brothers and then asked for a meal. Lommen greeted the two men in the spirit of friendship. He was apparently happy to have some company, and without the slightest hint that he was a player in of one of the greatest escapes in American history, he freely answered their questions, telling them, among other things, that Sioux Falls had no telegraph and no railroad.[21]

Mrs. Lommen was a good cook and their affable guests were well fed. But their hosts took note and remembered that, as they leisurely ate their food, they were careful to sit facing the door. The strangers and Mr. Lommen freely indulged in a bit of storytelling—about horses, of course. One of the riders mentioned something about seeing a horse race at a fair in Minnesota.[22] Lommen was also treated to "many interesting tales of their work as peace officers." It was a friendly exchange, but when Lommen explained that he knew a thing or two about firearms, and asked if he could take a look at their guns, the smiles vanished and the request of the curious settler was sternly denied. Still, the brothers left the Lommen homestead in good spirits, having paid for the food that had been prepared for them.[23] They could have killed him but they didn't.

After leaving Mr. and Mrs. Lommen, the two men, with miles to go and secrets to keep, stayed close to the Big Sioux River where they had trees, hills and ravines for cover, and if they were interested, the colors of autumn. At some point they crossed the river into Iowa. Tucked away in the extreme northwest corner of Iowa is the village of Granite. It did not exist in 1876, but the town was a point of reference in a 1924 account that has them riding along the Big Sioux River south of Granite, until they came to the crossing at the Amos Syverson place. There they crossed the river into Dakota and followed an established, well-wooded trail going south that travelers took to get to Canton, the county seat of Lincoln County. The timber and the rough terrain provided good cover for James brothers.[24]

Early in the evening on September 18, about five miles northeast of the town of Canton, Dayton Township, Lincoln County, Dakota, they stopped at the homestead of Ole Rongstad and his wife.[25] Their house was situated on the west bank of the Big Sioux River. After they told the Rongstads that they were hunters in need of food and shelter for the night, Frank and Jesse James were welcomed into the rough cabin and were given food. They told their hosts that they would be up and on their way early the next morning, and after placing a dollar on the table, they asked Mrs. Rongstad to leave breakfast for them in morning.

Tired out and feeling relatively safe, the brothers climbed the ladder to the garret in the small cabin. Later that night, one of the men came down and asked for some tools to pry open a window that they found had been nailed shut. As the stranger returned up the ladder, Mrs. Rongstad saw "a shining revolver under his coat," but she was unconcerned; they were simply hunters and she and her husband were just following the golden rule.[26] Ole Rongstad surmised that one of the men was wounded, and that "one would sleep for a time while the other would sit up and watch."[27]

Early the next morning, having spent the night in a bed, as opposed to on the hard ground, the brothers got up and started out on foot, carrying their saddles, for they had left their tired horses behind. This suggests that the brothers learned of the location of the nearest farm while talking to the Rongstads. It was raining when they arrived at the farm belonging to Albert Larson, near the bank of the Big Sioux River, a few miles northeast of Canton. When they arrived, "farm hands Peter Wahl and Andrew Shulson were going to the barn."

The situation was ripe for another ruse. One of the strangers yelled: "Get your horses boys, and catch some horse thieves!" An unexpected adrenaline rush surged through the boys, and they mindlessly did as they were told, suddenly caught up in the excitement of the moment. Wahl called out that he had the fastest horse, and as soon as he mounted the steed, Jesse, with a gun in one hand and other on the bridle, ordered Wahl off.[28] Then, with Frank on Shulson's horse, the outlaws were galloping toward the Big Sioux River, after forcefully boasting that "there were not enough men in this part of the country to take them."[29]

About this time Ole Rongstad's young son pulled up at the Larson place after discovering two horses belonging to the overnight guests in his father's barn. Although Peter had been warned not to follow the James brothers, he and Rongstad did just that. The boys caught up with the fleeing brothers just as they were crossing the river. Suddenly a shot was heard and the neck of Rongstad's horse was hit, causing him to give up the pursuit, but he wasn't about to merely go home. Rongstad raced toward Canton on his bleeding horse to the sound the alarm while Wahl rode after the James boys. He was unarmed and bareheaded so he kept a safe distance, and after riding all day, he lost the outlaws in the hills east of the tiny Dakota town of Fairview, situated along the Big Sioux River.[30]

While Wahl was trailing the James brothers, the sleepy town of Canton was riled up and agitated as never before. On an otherwise mundane Monday afternoon, September 19, the town was thrown into a "state of wild excitement" by the sudden appearance of eight men from Luverne and Worthington, Minnesota. They had come down the Big Sioux River on the Iowa side and crossed the river near Beloit, Iowa, just a short distance south of Canton. The Minnesota men explained to those gathered that they had tracked the Northfield robbers to the point where the Split Rock River emptied into the Big Sioux River, east of Sioux Falls. It was at this intersection of two major streams that the tracks of the robbers were lost.[31]

The wounded horse ridden by the Rongstad boy was the immediate center of attraction, "as it stood in mute witness to the marksmanship of the freebooters." It was reported that "a hundred or more Cantonites examined the horse and felt the bullet" that was pressing against the skin, for it had not completely passed through the animal's neck. The Rongstad boy was described as "cool and brave" when he calmly explained the theft of the horses at the Larson place and that he and Peter Wahl had followed the outlaws. He told his eager listeners that he "was climbing the Iowa bluffs" when one of the outlaws "dismounted, and, taking careful aim," fired the shot that was lodged in the neck of his horse.

After hearing all this, the Canton street crowd was suddenly caught up in a frenzy of excitement "as never witnessed before or since." It was the unanimous consensus that the "the James boys must be killed," for it was "war, bloody war." The men gathered their guns and ammo and prepared to go on the attack. Among them was Harvey Stafford, a sharp-shooting merchant with "two revolvers and a double barreled shotgun." "Dan Hawn had a rifle, Jim and George Kellar had shot guns, Duke Rudolph had a rifle, and he was a fine shot." They wanted to intercept the fugitives before they reached the Rock River, well south of Canton.[32]

While they were preparing, Andrew Shulson arrived in Canton to tell his story about the robbers who took horses from him and from Peter Wahl and were heading for Iowa with their four-legged contraband. Nothing more was needed and soon a large group of well-armed men rode out of Canton, going south, armed with their own guns or weapons and ammunition they purchased from the hardware store owned by O. A. Rudolph. Although it was raining hard, the aforementioned group, along with three of the Minnesota men, rode south along the Big Sioux River, hoping to catch up with the robbers, who were presumed to be the James brothers. The next morning, the rest of the Minnesota contingent rode back to Sioux Falls.

The Canton group of outlaw hunters was augmented by a number of men from Beloit and a band from Sioux Falls that also joined the manhunt. Among them were John D. Cameron, Melvin Grigsby and Billy Holt, all three prominent Sioux Falls citizens, sporting fellows and always open to adventure and risk taking. Although the chase was merely a footnote in their successful careers, their names are forever linked to the notorious James brothers and their improbable escape. They were looking for two men who were described as about six feet tall with light complexions and sandy colored whiskers. Both of the outlaws wore long rubber coats that covered up their guns.[33]

In total, about 30 well-armed and well-equipped men on horseback were in the hunt, minus the Minnesotans whose horses were "played out." Local newspapers were all into the Northfield robbery so the impromptu posse was aware of the reward money that had the potential to make a man rich. They all, of course, ultimately returned to their homes disappointed.[34]

Actually it seems as if the wild enthusiasm was short-lived and that same night a few of the pursuers trickled back into Canton. In hindsight, some men thought that it was for the best that they were unable to catch up with the James boys, for had there been an encounter, "some of the Canton hunters would have been killed, as their guns and marksmanship were no match for the outlaws." There was also the fear that some of the outlaw hunters could have been killed by "friendly fire," for "every stranger" was presumed to be one of the James boys and some of the "hunters were for firing on any man traveling on horseback or in a buggy." It was the loosely held belief that shooting a man before asking him questions was the best strategy because "it was death to try and take the bandits alive."[35]

It is generally believed that a man on the frontier was well armed and experienced in the use of firearms. While there was a great proliferation of guns due to technological advances following the end of the Civil War, the belief that gunslingers were everywhere is false. For during the outlaw emergency, time and time again, the lack of guns and experienced shooters stood in the way of killing or capturing the James brothers. Perhaps a frustrated Minnesota newspaper editor expressed it best: "the fact is we lack the arms." While the editor was not casting aspersions on people of the frontier, or questioning their courage, they simply could not compete with high caliber outlaws who outmatched citizen posses, armed with shotguns and birdshot.[36]

Once again the James brothers were successful in avoiding fatal contact with the minions of the law. And as a nice coda to the outlaws' Dakota adventure, the handicapped horses stolen from Andrew Nelson had been recovered and were in the custody of Clay Parke, a Canton area homesteader.[37] The blind horse was found on a sandbar in the Big Sioux River, about 12 miles southwest of the Nelson's homestead, and the horse with one good eye was recovered about eight miles northwest of Canton.[38] The horses taken from Shulson and Wahl were later found near East Orange, Iowa.[39]

While all the excitement in the Canton area was going full throttle, a pair of men on horseback on the Greenwood Indian Reservation in Charles Mix County, west of Yankton, were thought to be the seemingly ubiquitous James brothers. This fed into the belief that the outlaws were heading west into Indian Country. But on September 22, Sheriff Baker sent disappointing news back to Yankton that the suspects were merely "half breeds," not the full-blooded outlaws. That same day a report from Council Bluffs, Iowa, informed Dakotans that the "two remaining members of the gang are between Sioux City and Council Bluffs" with a posse in "hot pursuit."[40]

Another report in circulation in late September was that Sheriff John McDonald from Sioux City, with his posse, had confronted the "two robbers down on the Missouri in Dakota, near what is known as Texas," and when the smoke cleared, one of the James boys was dead and the other was in custody. This report spread through Sioux City "like wildfire," but it was a fire with a short life for it was "disproved by noon." Sheriff McDonald was on the job but not in Dakota.[41] The same report was given a bit of space in the *Minneapolis Tribune* with the caveat "How true it is I cannot say."[42] Well, we can now say it was not at all true.

The members of the press did their best to provide up to date and accurate reports of the exciting search that Americans were anxiously following in their newspapers, but the accuracy of some reports was questionable. To their credit, when a report was known to be false, the newspapers were quick to correct it. For example, when it was reported that Sheriff John McDonald had killed one of the fugitives and captured the other, a correction was forthcoming. The next day, by a "Special to the Pioneer-Press and Tribune," the public was informed that there was no killing or capture of the outlaws.[43]

The James brothers were still very much alive although they were no longer on Dakota Territory soil. The great Dakota manhunt was history and it left the editor of the *Swan Lake Era* of Turner County feeling melancholy. "Since the Northfield robbers have exited Dakota soil, excitement has died away and dullness reigns supreme once more."[44] But the story of the great escape that was playing out in real time, almost as if it was being viewed by an actual audience of spectators, had lost none of its intensity.

The fugitive brothers, whose cup of luck truly did runneth over, were most definitely somewhere in Iowa, beyond the reach of the Dakota authorities, but it seems that Dakotans were not ready to let them go. The excitement the brothers inspired was slow to subside. In fact, the mere presence of the brothers created several lasting memories about how close some people (allegedly) got to the famous bad guys. As the years progressed, stories were circulated by Dakota "old-timers" who explained with dash and relish how, where and when they came in contact with the larger-than-life Missouri desperadoes.

Martin Axlund, who had lived near the Yankton County town of Volin, was a man who shook the hand of Jesse James. Axlund liked to tell people how, as a small boy, he and a little sister were visited by two strangers in a wagon while their parents were in Vermillion. According to Axlund the men were Frank and Jesse James. Curiously, he insisted that they were traveling salesmen, not robbers on the run, for they asked the youngster if he was interested in buying any "calico or gingham." The brothers chatted with the boy and sister for a time, and before they left Jesse "shook hands" with young Martin.

Another Yankton pioneer claimed to have eaten dinner with the James brothers. Zack T. Sutley wrote a memoir entitled *The Last Frontier* and included a short essay about how he allegedly met the notorious brothers. Sutley claimed that he had been in Northfield on September 7, 1876, and witnessed the gunfire that erupted in the Division Street. Sometime later, he and a few companions were back in Dakota, camped along the Vermillion River when two men came into their camp riding on farm horses. The strangers asked for and food to eat, and later everyone sat around the campfire, engaged in friendly conversation.

While the men were eating, it was suggested by one of the strangers that Sutley and the boys should engage in target practice. Sutley recalled that "the farmers made a fine showing" with shooting that was far superior to the others. They then returned to eating, and when the last morsel had been swallowed, the strangers mounted up. As they said their goodbyes, one of them called out: "Boys, if you see anyone looking for Frank and Jesse James, you can tell them you ate dinner with them."

Sutley wrote that the elusive brothers made their way south along the Vermillion River, stealing horses along the way. After they reached the Missouri River near the town of Vermillion, they crossed into Nebraska, and made their way back home to Missouri. Sutley claimed that many years later, he actually met Frank James and the two of them talked about the time of the chance meeting on the Dakota prairie that followed the Northfield bank robbery.[45]

The Last Frontier was published by a reputable, big-name New York publisher and was no doubt well circulated, so Sutley probably had a leg to stand on when the book came out. But the business about meeting, talking, shooting and eating with the James brothers has all the makings of a made-up yarn in an otherwise well-written and useful book about life on the frontier.

Other claims about meeting the brothers were just as weak. A Yankton man, B. L. Burgess, claimed that when was a boy, he met the brothers when they stopped at his family's homestead north of Vermillion. Another Yankton resident, Theodore Gigge, said he saw the James brothers near "the water tank that used to stand along the James River east of Yankton, where the trains used to stop and take water." Gigge's claim to fame is that once while the train was stopped, he saw two men rush "out of a shelter of nearby bushes" and jump aboard the train. According to Gigge, the men who rode without tickets were the James brothers. Then there was Dan Morey, who at the time of all the excitement lived south of Gayville. The story he told was similar to the others: Frank and Jesse James "called" at his family's home and "stopped for some time."[46]

A man who might be expected to have actual knowledge of the James brothers' appearance in Dakota Territory was historian and pioneer newspaperman George W. Kingsbury of Yankton. He wrote a massive history about the Dakota frontier and the people, both good and bad, that were connected to it. But in 1923, he was a very old man, and when asked if he had any recollection of the great manhunt for the James boys, the man who came to Dakota in 1861 could only say, "I distinctly remember the James party being reported in the Territory and it seems to me now to say that they went up to Firesteel Creek," near the present day city of Mitchell, some 70 miles west of Sioux Falls. Kingsbury went on to state that from the Firesteel Creek, the pair went even further west to the Crow Creek region to an Indian reservation, because "horseflesh was quite abundant" and white people were scarce.[47]

Kingsbury's faulty memory could be attributed to his old age, but it places him in the same category as those who made up simple yarns and tall tales about the James brothers, stories without any foundation in factual history that were then told to both the curious and the skeptic. No one ever seemed to get enough of the spicy gruel concocted from a blending of myth and fact. The desperadoes were on the mind of everyone who in some way participated in or remembered the great manhunt. Impressions and memories were formed and shaped into mini-dramas that, like all folklore, were handed off to listeners in whose excited minds the stories could be and sometimes were reshaped and retold.

It is almost as if there was no door that was unacquainted with the brothers' knuckles, no farmer's wife that refused to feed them, no barn between Northfield and Clay County, Missouri, that they did not sleep in and no campfire that did not provide some measure of comfort in the night. Whenever two strangers were spotted on horseback, they were Frank and Jesse. The elusive brothers were seemingly everywhere at once, riding, shooting, eating, sleeping, talking or doing all sorts of remarkable deeds. But of course in order to become immortal, one must first become ubiquitous and the James brothers effortlessly fleshed out their starring roles in the grand Western drama. And they didn't have to act; they were naturals and the audience—with its insatiable need to be connected to the outlaws—would always cry out for more.

9

Northfield Avenged
*The Capture of the Youngers
and the Killing of Charlie Pitts*

> "The four missing robbers show themselves at a farm house in search of bread and butter."
> —*Minneapolis Tribune*, September 22, 1876

September 21, 1876, was a day that would live long in the memory of 19th century Minnesotans. First of all, a report from Sheriff John McDonald in Sioux City, Iowa, via the telegraph, alerted the public to the "probable capture" of "the two that stole the grey [sic] horses of Elder Rockwood." The alert proved to be untrue; "the two" were not captured.[1]

But the next telegram was for real and it set all of Minnesota cheering. For it was on the 21st day of September 1876 that a righteous vengeance was taken against the four Northfield bank robbers who were unable to get out of the state. And with the James brothers out of the picture, and therefore two fewer guns to face, the avenging men closed in on Charlie Pitts and the Younger brothers. Wantonwan County Sheriff James Glispin sent the following dispatch to St. Paul: "Madelia, Sept 21—Have four robbers surrounded in a slough about six miles from here. We want some men and some long guns. Have them come on the first train sure."

The telegram sent the city of St. Paul into a "spasm of the most extraordinary excitement." The startling news was received with great joy after two weeks of dogged searching amid wet, cold weather and precious time spent sorting through countless rumors and false leads. It was one effort after another, all futile, all ending in disappointment. The people had long been laboring under the distinct possibility, that the four cornered bandits had, like the James brothers, escaped and were miles away. Now the villains were trapped and ready to be bagged.[2]

Up until the time of the happy telegram, it was feared that the Youngers and Pitts were beyond the reach of the law. But because of the instincts and tenacity of young Axle Oscar Sorbel, the outlaws were located and surrounded in the brush at Hanska Slough northwest of Madelia, Watonwan County, by Sheriff James Glispin and about 40 excited volunteers. Just one hour after being informed of the outlaws' location, the hard-charging 28-year-old sheriff and his men found them.

Thomas J. Dunning had made a "solemn vow," a most vigorous, life-sustaining vow, that he would not utter a word about having encountered the Northfield bank robbers, but he broke the vow at the earliest opportunity. Still other sources contend that it was a 17-year-old farm boy who provided the most useful intelligence on the gang after the hapless attempts to capture them had become "the joke of the season."[3] The *St. Paul Weekly Dispatch* identified the lad as Oscar Oleson Sanborn, who was living with his family in Riverdale Township just eight and a half miles from Madelia.[4] The name was wrong but the substance of the story was right.

In 1924, a respected veterinary surgeon living in Webster, South Dakota, Dr. Axle Oscar Sorbel, stepped up to provide the desired clarity. Dr. Sorbel, usually referred to in the newspapers as Oscar, insisted he was the 17-year-old boy that was responsible for locating four of the Northfield robbers. He had not—as was suggested—dropped off the face of the earth, nor did he, according rumors, exhibit "himself in a dime museum."[5] In fact his life had been one of honor and success, and he revealed that he had adopted the name Oscar Sanborn to protect himself from possible reprisals from other gang members or Missouri friends of the outlaws.[6] His narrative published in the Sioux Falls *Daily Argus-Leader,* is consistent with the 1876 report in the St. Paul newspaper and, more importantly, it provides additional information. While there is some confusion in the record about the spelling of his name, there has never been any doubt about the significance of the role he played in the capture of the four outlaws.

In a letter to the Sioux Falls newspaper, Dr. Sorbel related his "experience in the capture of the Younger boys," thus adding a fascinating chapter to the story of the great manhunt. On September 21, 1876, he rose early, "just after sunrise," to assist his father in milking the cows. Two weeks of steady rain and drizzle had turned dirt into mud, but the cows needed to be milked so he dutifully went to the barn with his milk pail. In doing so, he noticed two men that he called Jim Younger and Charlie Pitts walking alongside his father. Seemingly in a cheerful mood, they said, "Good morning" and playfully "stroked the cow's back." Oscar Sorbel stood by the gate until the two men had gone far enough so that they could not hear what he had to say. Then he said to his father, "They were the two robbers." His father quickly dismissed the suggestion, saying that men he met on the road were too courteous to be outlaws.

But the young man, dubbed a "modern Paul Revere," was persistent; he trusted his gut. As proof he pointed out to his father that the toe prints from their boots in the mud indicated that they were walking in worn-out footwear. Rain meant mud and mud meant footprints, but his father was still unconvinced and ordered him to continue with his milking chores. Oscar milked one cow, set the pail inside the fence and started "after them." About "60 rods west of our place, I saw where they had walked into the timber." Cautiously Oscar backtracked so as not be seen and then hurried off to the farm of Anton and Mads Owen and told them about seeing two of the escapees.

He went on to warn other farmers in the area, although they scoffed at his warnings or were too busy with farm work to get involved. Determined not let the outlaws "steal a march," he walked to the top of "a big hill" where he could see the three roads, "one to New Ulm, one to Madelia, and the other to Lockstock." He was convinced that the outlaws had not left the timber by way of any of the roads. The plucky Oscar recruited three men to climb up the big hill and watch the roads for signs of the robbers, then returned to his home with the intent to ride on to Madelia, the county seat of Watonwan County, 25 miles west of Mankato.

At home he learned that two other men had stopped by the house and purchased bread and butter. With this intelligence, Oscar concluded that there were four men in the timber and he sent his sister Mary to the hill to advise the three men standing guard that four outlaws had been located. The future veterinarian then took off for Madelia, covering the eight miles as fast as his horse could run.[7] The horse and rider fell in the mud, but that did nothing to dampen Sorbel's enthusiastic effort to organize a force to capture the outlaws. Covered in mud "from head to foot," he finally convinced someone that he was trustworthy and soon "the whole people of Madelia were in the road."[8]

The trustworthy source was the sheriff of Watonwan County, James Glipsin, the worthy foe of any bad man. When Oscar described the four men and mentioned that one of them had a wounded arm, the sheriff was certain that they were the robbers. Very quickly, the sheriff and a handful of men sprang into action for this was the break they were hoping for. "Stores were shut up, and nearly all the male population started on horseback, in teams and on foot," for the woods in search of the outlaws.[9]

Sorbel recalled that "we got to the timber about three miles from St. James, just as the robbers got there."[10] It had been reasoned by the four outlaws that the pursuers would be more likely to follow the two men on horseback, the James boys, leaving the others alone, thus allowing them to continue on foot, unmolested. Time and circumstances would reveal that their decision was fatally incorrect.

The unfolding of critical events on the afternoon of the 21st would lead to the discovery of Cole Younger, his brothers, and Charlie Pitts. The advance unit came upon the fugitives about five miles west of Madelia as they were crossing the slough. Horses could not pass through the slough so the sheriff and men had to stop at water's edge and watch as the robbers commenced running. The command was given to surrender, but it was ignored by the bandits. Both sides opened fire and a short skirmish took place but no one on either side was hit. The only victim of gunfire was the horse of one of the pursuers.

The robbers went in and came out of a thicket of plum brush and willows and walked up toward the house of Andrew Anderson. There they came upon Horace Thompson, the president of the First National Bank of St. Paul, who was "out on the prairie gunning" with his son and some ladies. While Thompson and his son were innocently hunting, the sheriff and his men had crossed the Watonwan River and were closing in on the fugitives who were just then well hidden in the dense cover.

Horace Thompson was later interviewed by a St. Paul newspaperman, and, as a result, the banker and his son emerged as the accidental heroes. They just happened to be out hunting prairie chickens when, by pure chance, they came upon the skulking outlaws. Thompson told the reporter that he and his son, four ladies and two children were "on a hunting excursion in the vicinity of Madelia." They were riding in two conveyances, each one drawn by a pair of horses. It was the four horses that attracted the attention of the four horseless men.

Leaving the women and kids in the buggies, Thompson and his son proceeded across the prairie, looking for birds to shoot. Suddenly, they spotted three or four horsemen at a gallop, going west. Thompson thought it was odd to see men hunting on horseback when there was no elk or other big game in the area. Their curiosity aroused, the two men hurried to a high ridge so they could get a better look at the riders. When they reached high ground, they saw another group of men riding hard in the direction of the first group. Knowing that the Northfield robbers were, or had been, in the area, they concluded that what they just witnessed was a posse in pursuit of the long sought outlaws.

Thompson and his son hurried back to their buggies and got their teams moving in the direction of the men they believed were chasing the fugitives from justice. "This extraordinary race was kept up for some time," until "the distance between Mr. Thompson's party" and the other group had substantially decreased. Suddenly, they saw that the "pursuers were seen gathering from all directions, and gradually closing in upon the robbers." The Thompsons stopped their buggies near a house on the bank of the Watonwan River. While waiting for further developments and some possible gunplay, "a woman emerged ... from the house and with shrieks and exclamations" made sure that everyone within hearing distance knew that "the robbers were coming!"

About the time her screams ceased, "the four footpads were seen coming on foot from the brush" near the house that later was revealed to be the home of Andrew Anderson and his wife. The four men then began approaching the Thompsons and their wagons. The father and son quickly concluded that "prompt action was required" and they both "loaded their guns with wire cartridges." Leaving the carriages, they "boldly marched out to meet their assailants ... who evidently had an eye to the four fine horses" hitched to the fancy carriages. Tension was building as the distance two erstwhile prairie chicken hunters and the horse-hunting robbers grew shorter.

Thompson told the reporter that he "scanned the landscape in every direction and not a human being was visible anywhere," with the exception of the frantic farmer's wife; she and her equally frightened husband were running away as fast as their legs could propel them. At the same time "the terrified ladies in the wagon" stood up on the seats and "waved their handkerchiefs for assistance." Thompson and his son did not falter but kept walking toward the Younger brothers and Charlie Pitts, coming four abreast.

When they were within reasonable firing distance, the four men stopped. Just then Thompson realized that "he never saw four more robust and powerful looking men," and then, when he believed that the shooting was about to start, the four men, "one by one, crouched and disappeared among some tall weeds."[11] The steely nerved Thompson and his equally gutsy son were given due credit for standing up to the outlaws, another example of the strong mettle of Minnesota pioneers. In the face-off, although it was four against two, it was the outlaws who stopped, blinked and then turned away.

The bold face-off set the stage for what happened next. About 2 o'clock in the afternoon a large number of Madelia area men were at Hanska Slough all prepared for deadly duty. These men, about 20 in number, were posted in a manner that surrounded the outlaws. The sheriff, sensing imminent danger, asked for volunteers from among the others to "enter the brush and find the robbers." The ordinary men gathered by the slough that day faced a terrible moment of truth. It was understood that the concealed outlaws, now very desperate, were at an advantage and anyone approaching their lair might be killed. It was a real test of leadership and courage but six men volunteered to join the sheriff in the dangerous task. Each man would thereafter be known as "one of the seven."

The cadre of brave men consisted of Captain W. W. Murphy, Benjamin M. Rice, George Bradford, Charles Pomeroy, Sheriff James Glispin, T. L. Vought and S. J. Severson. They advanced in a skirmish formation and conducted a thorough search for the robbers, walking near the bank of the Watonwan River. Suddenly, one of the robbers stood up and pointed a gun at the sheriff. The sheriff was ready and both men fired at about the same time. It was a bullet from the sheriff's gun that hit its mark.

Then the shooting in Hanska Slough started in earnest. "In five minutes over thirty shots had been fired by the robbers," but with little effect. Captain

The seven brave men, who volunteered to form a squad, work their way into the brush and shoot it out with the Younger brothers and Charlie Pitts, became known as the "Madelia Seven." The ordinary but magnificent men, who put duty above personal safety, are shown here from left to right: George A. Bradford, James Glispin, W.W. Murphey, Charles A. Pomeroy, Benjamin M. Rice, S. J. Severson, Thomas L. Vought. Knowing that the outlaws were desperate and would put up a good fight, they faced a terrible moment of truth. But they all advanced with their odd collection of firearms that included rifles, pistols and fowling pieces, in a true test of leadership and courage. When the shooting stopped, Pitts was dead, and the Younger brothers, all badly wounded, were taken into custody (Northfield Historical Society, Northfield, Minnesota).

Murphy suffered a relatively minor wound from a bullet that struck his "large rosewood pipe in his vest pocket." The well-placed pipe saved him from death or serious injury. George Bradford had a slight wound on his wrist. For the outlaws the outcome was much worse, and when a cease-fire was ordered, Pitts was dead and the Younger brothers, having taken more bullets, were unable to continue the fight.[12]

When interviewed by the *Argus-Leader* in 1924, a much older Axle Oscar Sorbel recalled that Bob Younger, who had been shot through the lung, raised his one good hand, his left, expressing the universal gesture of surrender, while saying that "the others were shot to pieces."[13] Bob also called out: "don't shoot me, take me south and I am worth a pile of money to you."[14]

But standing in the brush with a fresh bullet wound, Bob Younger was as far south as he would ever be. The others were on the ground. While Pitts breathed his last, Cole seen "was resting his head on his elbow" and was otherwise badly wounded, having taken bullets in the shoulder, back, left side and in the left leg, plus a "wound of buckshot or bullet which entered near the bottom of the left ear." Other than that, Cole was described as "a strong, well-built man," bald but with a full beard. "Another, who calls himself Jim Younger, was lying on the ground, apparently senseless, with a ghastly shot in his lips and mouth."[15] The doctor who attended him thought that the "ball was spent on the bone" of the upper jaw "and that he spit it out."[16]

The tragic, macabre sight was a stark reminder of the wages of sin, and it was the final scene in the outlaw career of the Younger brothers. The robbery, the chase and finally the capture of the outlaws was, in total, an experience without "parallel ... since the thrilling days of the war of the rebellion." The wild bells of celebration had good cause to ring out. It was time for cheering, hugging and the happy grasping of hands. It was time for popping corks and sharing drinks of happiness and success. And yet there were many in St. Paul, the capital city, who could scarcely believe the truth of the good news about "the victory over the Missouri cut-throats ... so complete and decisive."[17]

Years later while in prison, Jim Younger told a visitor that he and the rest of the gang had been relentlessly pursued by detectives, some of whom came from New York and Chicago, "in droves to capture us." But the boys always escaped—until a "crowd of farmers with muskets and pitchforks, finally brought them down.[18]

The Youngers were badly shot up and would soon be locked up. And yet a defiant Cole Younger was not ready to accept defeat at the hands of men from the North. He wanted no part of quitting, although when he was sprawled out on the cold ground, he had more lead in him than before the shooting started. Oscar Sorbel recalled that he "offered to fight two of our best men at once. He said he had been dogged for two weeks in the rain, with nothing to eat," and yet he projected an intense anger and energy at the thought of being made a prisoner. But the long-suffering Bob urged Cole to give up lest they be hanged on the spot. The elder Younger brother said that "he did not care, and that he would just as soon hang today as tomorrow."[19]

Cole may have had some fight in him, if we are to believe an article in a Sioux City, Iowa, newspaper. The reporter claimed to have spoken with "Judge Younger," allegedly an uncle of the outlaw brothers, and the "Judge" said that Cole could have killed "twenty of his pursuers." The "Judge" reasoned that none were killed because of Bob's wounds. The gang would at some point have to abandon him, and thereafter when he fell into the hands of the posse, he would be tortured. For that reason, the "Judge" surmised, Cole didn't wipe out the pursuers.[20]

It was an outrageous assertion and utterly false. There was really no other choice but to surrender because there was no fight left in Bob, or Cole, or, for that matter, Jim, who "was shot in the mouth and five of his teeth had been knocked out."[21] It was all over for the Youngers; they were prisoners who might die on the gallows, if they were not first lynched by their captors or later by a mob. Bob Younger said it best: they had "tried a desperate game and lost." They were rough boys, used to rough work, "and must abide by the consequences."[22]

As the three brothers were placed under arrest, the 17-year-old farm boy who played such a prominent role in their capture assisted the others in loading the body of Pitts into a wagon. The authorities, of course, did not know the identity of the dead man, and the Youngers refused to name him, nor would they name the two who got away. Therefore, it was speculated that the dead man was one of the James brothers.[23] But within a few hours, the dead outlaw was, in fact, recognized as Charlie Pitts, an alias for Sam Wells.[24]

While yet in the field, some "excited citizens were in favor of shooting the prisoners" but Sheriff Glispin stifled that notion by threatening to shoot "the first man that laid his hands in violence upon them." All such talk ceased immediately.[25] The Youngers were his prisoners and their fate would be determined in accordance with the law.

Pitts' body was turned over to a doctor who wanted a pickled corpse to dissect and a skeleton to display. That doctor was John H. Murphy. He took possession of and embalmed Pitt's body, and after it was photographed, he and his medical students dissected it. Dr. Murphy then instructed that the body be taken to a lake where it would remain until it had completely decomposed, after which the skeleton would be retrieved and put on display in the state capitol.[26]

But before the dead outlaw could be sliced and deboned, the public would be permitted to take a last look. The embalmed body of the handsome man "with thick short feet" was viewed by a steady stream of the morbidly curious people of St. Paul and those that came in from the surrounding areas. Pitts "occupied a table in the side room in the rear wing of the statehouse," almost as if the body was lying in state. An estimated 2,000 people, including women and children, "took a glance at the repulsive face of the dead villain."[27]

More than two years later, in December of 1878, a ghastly discovery was made in Como Lake in the form of a bag of bones. This minor mystery set off a flurry of activity that ended when Dr. Murphy came forth to claim the bones, insisting they were the skeletal remains of Charlie Pitts. When the coroner told Dr. Murphy that the bones would be buried after an inquest, the physician sternly replied: "No, you will not." He went on to tell the coroner: "I own these bones and I intend to have them to decorate my office with."[28] The outlaw episode in Minnesota had, indeed, taken on a macabre aspect as it marched into history along with a battalion of other unforgettable memories.

After the shooting ended in the Watonwan County thicket, it

A dead Charlie Pitts, killed in the gunfight in the brush near Madelia, shares a photograph with Bill Chadwell and Clell Miller, both of whom were shot and killed during the botched bank robbery at Northfield. While the surviving Younger brothers refused to identify the three men, their remains were positively identified by a party of men from Missouri. The disposition of their remains is somewhat of a mystery and the record is unsettled. It was said that Pitts' bones became the proud possession of a St. Paul doctor who decorated his office with the skeleton of the outlaw. It is believed that Chadwell's skeleton also, rather mysteriously, turned up on display at a doctor's office, while Miller's embalmed body was displayed in various places in Minnesota until his family claimed and buried the remains in Clay County, Missouri (Minnesota Historical Society).

was time to load up and take the wounded men into town for much needed medical treatment. Axle felt some pity for the outlaws, and when Bob Younger was placed in a wagon, he asked for some tobacco to chew. The future animal doctor got a "10-cent plug" from Oke Wisty and gave it Bob over the objection of the older men. Bob bit off a big chunk and then handed back to Axle. He told Bob to keep it.[29]

As an old man, Dr. Sorbel, a veterinarian in Webster, South Dakota, falsely claimed to be one of the "Madelia Seven" who "went into the timber." That he received a share of the reward in the amount of $225 was probably true, for he was widely recognized in the press and in the public mind for his contribution.[30] He was also given one of the revolvers taken from the outlaws.[31]

If the outlaw hunters were expecting money from other obvious sources, they were disappointed. No one received "one penny of the $50,000 offered by Missouri and the express companies."[32] Furthermore, if the men were expecting a nice payday from the state of Missouri, they were sorely disappointed because the state had not offered rewards for the Younger brothers.[33] Nevertheless, had Sorbel and the others been pressed, each one would no doubt have said that he did what he did for Minnesota and the victims of the Northfield raid.

Telegraphs aplenty were sent back and forth between Missouri and Minnesota, among them a terse invitation to the governor of Missouri to "send up somebody to recognize and properly label" the men snidely described as "four of his constituents." Detailed descriptions of all four were sent south. James McDonough, the St. Louis chief of police, sent a dispatch to St. Paul: "I will leave tonight with a party to identify all the robbers. Don't bury the dead, if any, until I come."[34]

The badly wounded brothers were taken to Madelia and put up in the Flanders Hotel, owned by T. L. Vought, a member of the party that brought down the outlaws. At the hotel doctors treated them for exposure and multiple bullet wounds. Cole had been hit 11 times, some of it buckshot, Jim five, including a devastating face wound, and Bob had a damaged lung to compliment his shattered elbow that had plagued him the past two weeks. Despite their pain and suffering, the Younger brothers kept their pledge not to reveal the names of the other gang members, be they dead or alive and on the run.[35] They did not, however, deny participating in the Northfield bank robbery.

A reporter from the *St. Paul Dispatch* was apparently one of the first newsmen to see and talk to the wounded robbers at Madelia. He approached Bob Younger whom he described as "the finest looking man of the whole gang," tall and brawny with a "thick neck" and otherwise "well defined" features and a "singularly toned voice." When the reporter asked Bob to identify himself, he replied, "George Huddleston," but when pressed he gave his true name, saying, "Yes, we are all brothers; we are all brothers, sir."[36]

One of them, most likely Bob, talked about their experiences in the days leading up to their capture. The night they crossed the railroad bridge over the Blue Earth River, "they walked right across not seeing any guards." Once across the river, they followed the tracks until they came to General Matthews' melon patch and helped themselves, after which they robbed a chicken coop of four birds and went into camp near the town of Minneopa Falls. To ease the savage pinch of hunger, they had subsisted on "corn, potatoes, sorghum and acorns." The chicken would have been a nice change, but they were forced to quickly abandon the camp because of the approach of Detective Mike Hoy and his squad.[37] Bob—who was reflecting, sadly, on his first bank robbing experience—added that "if he had had the use of both arms, he would have carried off the chickens, for they were dreadfully hungry."[38]

The presence of the badly wounded Younger brothers was the cause of great excitement in Madelia, suddenly a town of heroes. There was some talk in the streets about lynching the prisoners, but that was soon replaced by another form of attention. People flocked into town on the trains and by horse-powered vehicles to see them in the flesh. Long lines of the curious passed by the wounded and weary Youngers, young and old, men and women, many of whom were in tears or were otherwise sympathetic to the outlaws. Some even brought gifts and begged for autographs.

The mother of Axle Sorbel—the boy who provided the information on the whereabouts of the outlaws—was pathetic and persistent in her attempts to apologize to the outlaws. With tears flowing from her eyes, she pleaded and begged, over and over again, to be forgiven. One of the caged men said: "I have nothing to blame you for, madam."[39]

Cole and Jim were in such bad shape that the doctors thought they might die from their wounds. Jim's facial wound was so severe that he was forced to stay silent. Cole showed a little moxie, despite his condition, when he requested a cigar, saying he wanted to smoke it and "look like President Grant."[40]

Bob was seen by the doctors as having the best chance at survival. In the slough fight, he took a flesh wound in the rib cage, and he had somehow managed to withstand the pain and loss of blood due to the shattering of his right elbow during the Northfield affray. He was still in pain but that didn't stop him from talking freely, admitting that he was one of the three men who entered the Northfield bank on the 7th of September. Bob Younger did try to hammer home one other major point: it was Pitts who killed Heywood during bank robbery.⁴¹ It was a convenient but untrue statement, rendered plausible in the minds of the authorities because Pitts wasn't around to offer a rebuttal.

The seductive Bob, who was described as polite and mild-mannered, was carrying on in manner that suggested that he wanted and needed to talk. He was apparently proud of his athletic appearance and claimed to be a baseball player. While regaling his newfound fans, he recalled that while he and his friends were in St. Paul, to buy horses, the local team, the Red Caps left for Winona to play the Clippers. Although he was a fan of the game, he said that he "made no bets on the game."⁴²

Another point of contention for the authorities and the press was the positive identification of the "two who escaped on the gray horses." The talkative Bob gave no clue, but based on comments made by Cole, everyone concerned with the mystery tended to believe that they were the James brothers, although "nothing has been definitely stated."⁴³ But the boys kept talking freely, and once again Cole hinted that the escapees were the James brothers, and, further, he "knowingly remarked," they "are where they [the authorities] won't get them now."⁴⁴ When Cole was shown two pictures of the James brothers taken some years ago, he recognized them immediately but said that they had changed so much over the years.⁴⁵

A reporter for the *St. Paul Weekly Dispatch* tried trickery telling Cole and his brothers that "the two James brothers had been caught, one killed and the other captured." The follow-up question from Cole was "Which one was killed, the smaller or the larger?" Then he quickly said, "Mind, I don't say they are the James boys." The reporter told the Youngers that the James boys "acknowledged they were" Frank and Jesse James. Cole then asked, "Did they say anything of us?" After hearing from the reporter that nothing was said about them, the Cole stated with obvious satisfaction, "Good boys to the last!" With that outburst, Cole all but gave it away; he all but said that the two escapees were the James brothers.⁴⁶

While the Younger brothers remained smug and secretive about the James brothers, neither confirming nor denying their presence in Northfield, they did express deep regret for not having killed Thomas Jefferson Dunning, the man they happened upon when he was out looking for cows; it was their great "mistake." They also were upset over the poor judgment they exercised when they encountered Horace Thompson and his hunting party. For had they known that Thompson and his son were armed only with scatter guns, Cole and his allies would have "advanced and coolly shot him down."⁴⁷ To another reporter Cole said that it was "Thompson [who] took flight with his team" at the approach of Cole and the others.⁴⁸

Cole also boasted that he and his brothers were "dead shots" and could have killed many men during the Northfield shootout, but killing people was not their purpose, adding that he "had never killed a man in cold blood." When an interviewer accused Cole of shooting the "Norwegian" (meaning Nicolas Gustavson, the Swede) at Northfield, the outlaw changed the subject.[49]

After two days in Madelia, the outlaws were transported to Faribault, thus heaping great disappointment on the swarms of people gathered in St. Paul, all very eager and excited because they fully expected that the wounded men, "the Missouri land pirates," would be transported to the capital city for identification and for viewing by wide-eyed citizens of the Twin Cities.[50] Sheriff Glispin was urgently requested, even ordered in the name of the governor, to ship the prisoners to the state capital, it being necessary for proper identification. But he ignored their pleas and contacted Rice County sheriff Ara Barton, saying the prisoners were ready to be taken to Faribault, the county seat.[51]

There were other reasons for not taking them to St. Paul. The wounds of the Younger boys, especially Jim, were so severe that the doctors urged that they not be moved, thus tossing a wet blanket on people who were reveling in "the greatest sensation ever experienced in our state's history." The body of Pitts, however, was sent to St. Paul where it was embalmed and made presentable for officials from Missouri who were expected to positively identify the deceased outlaw.

Getting to Faribault—city with a population of about 4,000 people—with the three wounded men was anything but a routine train ride. The doctors who wanted the men to stay put were overruled and the journey began. Rice County sheriff Barton deemed it his duty to get the prisoners to the county seat, where they would be jailed and tried for their crimes. At each stop along the way, huge crowds of morbidly curious people, whose "necks were stretched to their utmost length," gathered at the train stations. At Mankato, where it was necessary to take the prisoners several blocks to a place where "breakfast was taken," large mob-like groups of anxious people had gathered at the town's two depots. Others "ran after the carriages in which the wounded robbers" and lawmen were riding. When the party of men reached their destination, the prisoners were loaded in an omnibus that "hurried through the streets" with a mob in hot pursuit.

The prisoners, who remained calm amid the madness, were somehow escorted to their jail cells, but that failed to cool the ardor of the mass of frantic people, jostling, pushing and shoving, so entertainment-starved and seemingly ready to kill in order to get a good look at an outlaw. Sheriff Barton and his deputy had to literally beat them back, denying admission to anyone to the small, stone-built Rice County jail in Faribault.[52] It was estimated that on the Sunday after their arrival, a "little less than 4000 people of all ages" turned out to take a look at the sullen and suffering prisoners.[53]

The excessive showering of attention on the criminals shocked and outraged some members of the press who shamed the people for their "silly or stupid sentimentality." Cole Younger, his condition improving, took the queue and in pious manner expounded religiously, asking for the prayers of people of Faribault. When asked about the shooting of Heywood, Younger said that "90 out of 100 men would have opened the safe," and, further, that Heywood was "shot in self-defense" because it appeared he was about to get a gun out of his desk.[54] It was an outrageous statement that was contradicted by the evidence against prisoners, all locked up and awaiting further legal proceedings.

Further proceedings, to most people, meant a triple hanging was in the offing. And yet a reporter for the *Minneapolis Tribune* pondered over the matter of proving that one of them killed Heywood at Northfield, noting that it would "be a difficult matter." After considering the possibilities, the reporter eliminated Pitts, but blamed him for shooting and wounding Bunker, a claim that Wilcox, the bank clerk, supported. The reporter then concluded that since "Bob Younger did not shoot in the bank. Jesse James was the man that killed Heywood."[55] One of the Younger brothers said that "they would not have done anything in Minnesota," but for the St. Paul gamblers that took their money, "they made the raid to get even."[56]

Statements from the bold and mouthy outlaws, coupled with the angry and emotional newspaper articles, were bound to inspire some pushback. It came in the form of letters containing threats against people in Northfield, with special emphasis at taking the lives of Henry Wheeler and Anslem R. Manning, the two men shot and killed Clell Miller and Bill Chadwell. For example, in a letter to Wheeler, the anonymous writer declared: "you are a doomed man from this hour. A dagger or bullet will find your heart." Another such missive chillingly reminded people in Northfield "three men have got to fall for every man of our company that was killed at your place!"[57]

Northfield responded to the threats by watching and even questioning all strangers who appeared on the streets. "The plucky little town" was in no mood to tolerate wild threats. All suspicious looking persons in town were immediately confronted, even roughly so, and "compelled to establish who and what he is."[58] As it turned out, however, there was very little to fear. In many cases, the vile and violently worded letters were just a matter of letting off steam, and, over time, there would be no retaliation.

One of those who might have felt uncomfortable upon reading the threatening letters was Alonzo E. Bunker, slowly on the mend but able and willing to talk about his brush with lasting notoriety. He spoke in St. Paul within hearing distance of a newspaperman, thus adding further confusion to a tale that was unraveling because of the lack of clarity. Bunker said it was Pitts, not Bob Younger, who shot him in the shoulder as he was running away. After he viewed the body of Pitts in St. Paul, he knew that he was staring at the lifeless form of the man who had shot him. Since he was out of the bank when Heywood was killed, he offered no opinion as to the trigger man in that crime.[59]

Overall, the Minnesota people felt proud of their success in killing or capturing six out of the eight outlaws that rode into Northfield. Then suddenly, a challenge to their success was launched from the South. It came from *The Kansas City Times* in the form of a sharply worded editorial that called into question the accuracy of reports that the Younger brothers were captured. Although the brothers had freely admitted their parts in the crime, the *Times* stated that their identification as participants in the Northfield bank robbery was merely "surmise." The "Minnesota people" were so thoroughly caught up in the excitement of having hauled in four celebrated outlaws and therefore they fabricated facts to suit their wishes. These people were claiming more credit than they deserved. The editorial suggested that there was a pronounced and obvious hypocrisy in it all. The proud Minnesotans were prancing publicly, boasting of having brought down four hardened criminals, when it was the expectation of enrichment that was foremost in their minds. Like little people scrambling for crumbs during a depression, "they think more of getting the [reward] money than of anything else. "[60]

It was a hollow and mean argument that barely put a dent in the pride felt by ordinary men who bravely risked their lives in order to take down members of a Missouri gang that robbed a bank and killed two innocent people. The victorious Minnesotans had done what the Missourians had failed to do, and it was that failure, coupled with the success of the Northerners, that riled up the *Times* editor. By simply doing the right thing, the Minnesotans had inflicted a wound on Southern pride.

The argument by the *Times* editor was countered in a letter from *The St. Louis Globe-Democrat* that heaped praise on brave Minnesota, just the tonic needed to calm nerves and assign credit where credit was due. Minnesota was mightily thanked for doing "what Missouri could have done—but to her shame, did not do." All of America was called on to acknowledge "the extraordinary spirit displayed in pursuing the perpetrators" who robbed the bank at Northfield. "Breaking up this powerful and dangerous gang of outlaws is the most important event which has happened in the criminal history of the country."[61] The letter was a powerful endorsement of the character and courage of the people of Minnesota.

10

Missouri Outlaws Face Minnesota Justice

"Minnesota has shown the Governor and people of Missouri what to do with highwaymen."
—*The Faribault Republican* (Faribault, MN), October 11, 1876

James McDonough, the chief of police for the city of St. Louis, Officer Russell, a St. Louis policeman, and C. B. Hunn, the assistant superintendent for the United States Express Company, came to Faribault to identify the prisoners as well as the three outlaws who had been killed. The Missouri men held court at the Barron House in Faribault, regaling the Minnesota men with tales about the outlaw exploits of the James–Younger gang, while displaying photographs of the gang members. Local authorities were warned to be vigilant and careful, for it was known that the gang had "many confederates" who would risk life and limb to affect an escape.[1]

McDonough would later be dismissed by a Minnesota newspaper editor as a "wind bag" who grossly overstated the danger of a jailbreak while boasting about how his presence and superior knowledge of the outlaws convinced people that the prisoners were not worthy of their sympathy. His published comments about the many people who came to the jail to have a look at the famous outlaws were thought to be "a libel on our people," out of line and unworthy of a visiting police chief.[2]

But the St. Louis chief of police and the others were in Faribault on official business, and after examining the body of Pitts, McDonough, Hunn and Russell unhesitatingly recognized him as the outlaw Charlie Pitts. They were shown photographs of the dead Clell Miller and Bill Chadwell, and they recognized them as well. When taken to the jail, they identified two of the sullen men behind bars as Cole and Bob Younger and the third man as "Al Carter, a notorious desperado from Texas." The St. Louis men insisted the man in jail with the messed-up face was not Jim Younger. Furthermore, they insisted that Jim did not go to Minnesota, rather he was in Texas, and "he was so badly wounded not long ago and could not have recovered" in time to participate in the raid. Jim Younger's picture in the *Minneapolis Tribune* is labeled "Cal Carter, in Jail."[3]

This was a mistake, of course, for the third man was Jim Younger. And no one knew that better than James Hardin Younger himself, the reluctant bandit who almost sold his horse and left the gang.[4] Having been seriously wounded in the mouth, he was unable to speak. But when he was misidentified, he "shook his head in denial." His brothers chimed in too. They were clearly aggravated that they could not convince the St. Louis crowd that the wounded man was not Al or Cal Carter, but their brother. It was as if Jim was suffering anonymously, and, moreover, he had been denied his claim to fame in favor of another.

There was at least one Northfield man who objected to the misidentification of Jim Younger. That man was Miles Church, who claimed to have purchased a horse from Jim Younger and had a bill of sale to prove it. Rice County officials disagreed with Church and the disagreement led to a spat that in turn became a lawsuit. When it was over, the horse that allegedly had been owned by Jim Younger became the property of Miles Church. *The Faribault Democrat* crowed that a bill of sale from Jim Younger is just as valid as one from Sheriff Barton.[5]

While it seems unlikely that Jim Younger would have exposed his identity in a legal document, his personal concerns at the time did not include a dispute over the ownership of a horse. Based on those who were close to him, it was felt that Jim Younger was getting weaker and would not survive his wounds, and if brother Bob lived he would have to do so without a right arm, for it was believed that it would have to be amputated. But the boys responded well to treatment, rest and nourishment, and the *Minneapolis Tribune* was compelled to concede that they would survive. It did so in a spurt of sarcasm: "The physicians have no other hopes than that the Younger brothers will not die from their wounds."[6] A St. Paul doctor, eager to ignore his Hippocratic Oath, was overheard saying that the wounded men would live "unless he doctors them."[7] Minnesota newspapers had no sympathy for the outlaws and a sharply worded editorial in the *Tribune* ridiculed those who fell for the pleas of the Younger brothers, calling it all "namby pamby."[8]

Also, as time passed, Cal Carter gradually morphed into Jim Younger as, one by one, knowing men offered convincing evidence, and the family resemblance came through as Jim improved. Under a doctor's care, Jim regained his ability to speak and stated his name for all to hear. Still, there was reluctance to believe him until his younger sister, Henrietta "Retta" Younger, arrived and after a prelude of shrieking and screaming, she stated, sadly, but with conviction, that the man thought to be Al or Cal Carter was indeed her beloved brother Jim Younger.[9] Retta was allowed to enter Jim's cell where the distraught girl "proceeded to pair his nails and bestow some womanly attention upon his toilet." After this moving and emotional display of sisterly love, there was no longer any doubt as to the identification of the outlaw.[10]

A Cincinnati detective, Larry M. Hazen, a man who had long been in pursuit of the James–Younger gang, reached the same conclusion as Retta. Hazen had come to Minnesota to satisfy his own curiosity and, after seeing their faces, he "identified the robbers" as the Younger brothers, the men he had been hunting. Hazen also named Frank and Jesse James as members of the gang, thus giving the Minnesota officials some additional insight into the two men who had escaped.[11]

The visiting officials were asked if "they could prove anything against the Youngers in Missouri and the reply was always, nothing." They acknowledged that Cole, a man "hunted like a tiger," was an outlaw but his brothers Bob and Jim were not. While the James brothers "were cold-blooded and deliberate murderers," the Youngers, on the other hand, were best known for having hunted down and killed the "Kansas Jayhawkers" who murdered their father, Henry Washington Younger. They only resorted to vengeance because the authorities were slow to act.[12]

The Youngers' aunt, Fanny C. Twyman, the wife of a doctor but nevertheless described as "on the shady side of life," also tried her hand at softening the image of her wayward nephews.[13] While some men called them cutthroats and killers who deserved to be hung, she asked that her relatives be shown at least a modicum of respect. Mrs. Twyman sent a letter from Blue Mills, Missouri, to the editor of the *St. Peter Tribune* thanking the "Christian charity" of the people of Minnesota, and while acknowledging that her nephews broke the law, she hinted that forces beyond their control steered them in the direction of crime. "You can take almost any man and accuse him of crimes of which he knows he is innocent, and persecute that man until he becomes almost a demon." She begged that Minnesotans would try to understand "how those poor persecuted boys have been treated." With unfeigned humility, Fanny asked that Cole, Jim and Bob be allowed legal counsel and given a fair trial.[14]

After the Youngers were identified to the satisfaction of all, a St. Paul newspaper took an informal poll, asking interested folks their opinion on the appropriate punishment for the soon to be convicted felons. Seventy-one people voted for hanging all three, six people voted not to hang them, three were undecided, and a one woman favored hanging—except for Bob whom she wanted to be spared the death penalty.[15] A Minneapolis paper suggested that should they "escape the legalized noose," no one should be surprised if the people were to ignore the verdict and "string the boys up."[16] Another newspaper not only declared that they must be hanged, but added that "they serve to die a thousand times."[17]

But as time went on the appetite for mob violence diminished. On the 26th, Judge Samuel Lord "held court in the Rice county jail," a procedure that was known to very few in the community. It was a short hearing in which the warrant charging the Younger brothers with the murder of Joseph Lee Heywood was read to the prisoners. Cole waived preliminary examinations apparently on behalf of his brothers and himself and the hearing was over.[18]

The Youngers were incarcerated in a tiny, one-story jail made out of stone, attached to a small house, that "looked as though it might be easily knocked to pieces."[19] While it was not impressive to look at, it was built well enough to keep its occupants inside, as opposed a the rude, ramshackle jail, or calaboose, commonly found on the Plains of Dakota, Wyoming or Montana, where jail breaks were frequent and mob-inspired executions were a constant threat to the orderly judicial process. The people of Minnesota had the maturity and good sense to allow justice and fair play to rule the day, meaning the Youngers, inside a secure jail, would not succumb to mob violence. After all, as was proudly stated in a St. Paul newspaper: "Minnesota was not Missouri."[20]

And yet there was concern, almost an alarm sounded, over the large number of people who randomly and causally went in and out of the jail with the apparent consent of the sheriff who said or did nothing. Most people were simply satisfying their curiosity but there was always the possibility that some visitors would arrive with unlawful intentions. An editorial in a St. Paul newspaper pleaded, "Guard Them Well," for in all likelihood, the prisoners have secret confederates who might appear and slip a weapon or two through the bars. The sheriff and other jail personnel were reminded of their solemn responsibility to be ever vigilant and take no chances, for an escape of the culprits would not only endanger the people, but would prove to be a terrible insult those brave men who captured them.[21]

The failure of the St. Paul men to secure the attendance of the Younger brothers in that city, created a minor newspaper disturbance that led to a mean-spirited critique of the Faribault jail. A reporter for the *St. Paul Dispatch* jumped into the fray, calling the jail a joke with walls so weak that "a strong man could with his shoulder prostrate them from the inside." *The Faribault*

Republican was up to the challenge, however, and sprang forth to defend both Sheriff Barton and the jail. With walls of limestone it was "one of the newest and strongest in the state." The *Republican* editorial declared that the St. Paul critics were simply smarting over their inability to display the "Younger desperadoes," and "their disappointment is evidently the foundation of such petty flings."[22]

But wasn't only the St. Paul newspapers that leveled blasts at Faribault. Sheriff Barton was gently jabbed by the editor of the *Mankato Record* for his jail visitation policy. The editor reminded the sheriff that he had publicly declared that he was not a showman, and for that reason he would not ship the prisoners off to St. Paul where they would be put on exhibit and viewed by thousands. And yet to all appearances, Barton was "a greater showman" than P. T. Barnum, and the sheriff had, in fact, turned the Rice County jail into a "sort of reception room for the prisoners" and their guests "the curious that flock to the jail for a peep at the notorious villains confined therein."[23]

Stung by the criticism, Sheriff Barton fired back at his critics, but not everyone was satisfied. There was some lingering concern that even if the brothers did not escape from the Rice County jail, the state prison would not hold them, for "they will break out in less than a year, and will be more bloodthirsty and revengeful than ever."[24]

None of that ever came to pass, but unfortunately, a tragic incident occurred outside the Faribault jail as a direct result of the distinguished company lodged therein. Jail personnel were given strict orders to shoot anyone who approached the jail and failed to provide proper identification. Early one morning, Henry Kapernick, a Faribault police officer, walked up to a guard, and when asked to stop and identify himself, he replied: "Don't you know I am a policeman?" He kept walking, and as he uttered those words, he reached for his breast pocket and was then and there shot dead through the heart.[25]

Kapernick was in fact wearing his star, his badge of office, "on the lapel of his coat," but it was buttoned up and when he reached into his coat to reveal his badge and show that he was a police officer, "the guard mistook" the motion "for an attempt to draw a revolver." He had been a member of the Faribault police department for only two weeks.[26]

The contrite shooter was Frank Glazier, from Dundas, who had recently been hired as a guard. At the inquest, Glazier testified that, in the early morning darkness, he could only see the outline of the man, and that the victim "put his hand to his breast" as if he was about draw a revolver. And since Kapernick twice failed to stop when commanded to, Glazier raised his gun and pulled the trigger, thus adding to the death toll of the Northfield incident.[27]

Most likely Henry Kapernick was buried rather quietly, since he was not an outlaw and therefore not the subject of intense public interest and scrutiny. There was no hunger to view the remains of lawman whose tragic death could have been easily prevented had he simply halted as ordered.

In Northfield the photographer was raking in money selling photographs of the dead bandits, "having already sold over 50,000 pictures." It is doubtful that Kapernick's body was photographed but it was reported that the photographer offered Henrietta "Retta" Younger $500 for her photograph. She promptly refused the offer, for she clearly did not want to be put on display like her poor brothers.[28] Still it would have been nice to have a picture of a young Retta for this book, even if it showed her with a sad face.

Then there is anecdote about "one of the sisters of the Younger brothers," no doubt Retta, who secretly and stealthily took a sack full of something back to Missouri. As the story goes, "about two weeks after the capture, a woman came to Madelia." She hired a "livery rig," and in the company of the wife of T. L. Vought, owner of the Flanders Hotel and one of the "Madelia Seven," drove out to "where the capture took place." With Mrs. Vought sitting in the conveyance, the young woman went into the thicket, and several hours later, she returned with a heavy sack. According to Mrs. Vought, the young woman wanted the incident kept secret, and it was until 1930, when the story broke. The inference is that during her talks with her brothers, one or more of them told her about personal items that were concealed by the outlaws who were subsequently shot up and taken in to custody. Did she go out there "for valuables left at a certain place, or was it for sentiment? Who knows?"[29] No one, of course, knew the answer.

The pending trial of the Younger brothers was expected to be long, tedious and hard fought, taking at least three weeks' time. The brothers did have good legal counsel. They retained T. S. Buckham and George W. Batchelder from Faribault and Thomas Rutledge from Madelia, all of them experienced and able attorneys.[30] The man who would preside over the trial, Judge Samuel Lord was described as a "tall, stooped-shouldered man" in poor health, and with a soft voice that was likely to be interrupted regularly by a persistent cough. His "delicate health" and slow, faint speech meant that rulings from the bench would test the patience and endurance of all others in the courtroom.[31]

When the Youngers had their day in court, their sister Henrietta and aunt Fannie C. Twyman—both heavily veiled—were present for moral support and to cry tears of anguish and familial love. The Youngers, handcuffed together, with Cole, "fat and hearty,"[32] in the middle, all looked well and were "neatly dressed." Except for Bob, who had his right arm broken and set again,[33] their wounds and suffering were relegated to the past, even though their future was gloomy. Jim had been writing letters regularly while Cole tried his hand at penning poetry. Bob was said to be acting defiant.

In court they appeared to be completely at ease, talking to newsmen in the moments leading up to hearing the charges against them, filed by George N. Baxter, the young prosecuting attorney. Baxter earned praise for his leadership of the posse that "marched through the brush" near Mankato, searching for robbers he was now prosecuting. His reputation was soaring.[34]

Cole, the fledging poet and seemingly never at loss for words, disliked the wording of the indictments. He complained that the charges against them, as printed in a newspaper article, contained "typographical errors."[35] Truly, Cole Younger was a man who would never be satisfied with the truth if it had a negative effect on him.

All three men were under indictment for the murder of Joseph Lee Heywood, the murder of Nicolas Gustavson, the assault on Alonzo E. Bunker and the robbery of the Bank of Northfield.[36] Their lawyers announced that each man was prepared to plead, and, when asked, each man uttered, "I plead guilty," in a loud clear voice that betrayed no evidence of fear. It was all over. There would be no trial, no public spectacle and no national news media feeding frenzy, and perhaps most significant of all, no hangings.

By pleading guilty, they avoided the death penalty. According to a law passed by the Minnesota legislature in 1868, a person charged with murder in the first degree could plead guilty and, instead of death by hanging, be sentenced to life in prison. All of a sudden the leniency in the law was apparent and exceedingly unpopular; murderers could cheat the gallows. This was unthinkable in the 19th century where the overwhelming majority believed in the death penalty for murder. But it was automatic; the judge had no choice but to sentence the guilty parties to prison for life.[37]

And that's what happened on November 22, 1876. Judge Samuel Lord sentenced each man "to hard labor at the state's prison at Stillwater for the remainder of their natural lives." While the brothers exhibited no emotion, their sister and aunt wept openly. The convicted felons were ushered back to jail under orders to be taken to "Stillwater at the earliest possible moment." The weekly *St. Paul Pioneer* closed its report with an appropriate coda: "And so for the present ends the most exciting criminal drama ever enacted on Minnesota soil."[38]

Cole Younger seemed resigned to his fate, life behind bars. After the court proceedings were over, he was heard to say to a reporter: "I have seen nearly all the world and am ready to retire."[39]

On November 29, 1876, the people of Faribault got one last look at the

Youngers as they exited the jail and were taken to a train station. Among those bidding good-bye to the prisoners were the fawning, "vealy" reporters who had spent some weeks writing about the convicts, spinning stories about "shrewdness, personal courage [and] desperate daring." The editor of *The Pioneer Press*, however, declared that it was time to see the three men for what they really were: "vulgar and brutal ruffians, every one of whom deserves a gibbet."[40]

Upon their arrival at the state prison in Stillwater, a reporter asked them about the identity of the two who escaped and was met with a "point blank" refusal from Cole and Jim. Bob did, however, have a pointed and terse answer. "If this cell door was opened now, and I was taken out to be hung, I would not reveal their names." And then anticipating what the next question might be, he said: "but they are not the James brothers."[41] At long last, a denial, and so it came to pass that with a lie that would confound and tantalize historians for generations to come, the brothers began serving their life sentences.

Stubborn and loyal to the end, they may have deserved death because of the sum and substance of their outlaw careers. But when the curtain closed on the drama, the Younger brothers emerged as celebrities, much more popular than newspaper editors and writers whose job it was to tell their story, and far better remembered than the upright men that brought them to justice. A New York reporter spoke the truth when he wrote: "The names of the James boys and the Younger brothers are familiar to the whole country."[42]

That same reporter attributed their long record of success to mistakes made by the news media and law enforcement. One of the biggest mistakes was blaming the Jameses and Youngers for all the robberies and murders committed in Missouri and elsewhere, forgetting that other outlaws were out there robbing and killing. By tossing out a blanket accusation, the Jameses and Youngers were able to establish perfect alibis for many of crimes they were accused of doing. This tended to invite and incite sympathy for them from many people across Missouri and other parts of the country. Another major mistake was the mixed and confusing personal descriptions of the men given out in the press and by word of mouth, all of which created more uncertainty that worked to the outlaws' advantage.[43] And yet in the end it was the mistakes made by the outlaws that led to their defeat.

The two sets of brothers were defeated, battered and tarnished, and would forever bear the curse of their crimes, but as time went on, something strange and unaccounted for happened. They emerged as celebrities because like the stars on the stage, they were exciting, they took desperate chances, and were therefore very entertaining. Moreover, they had the wounds and scars as proof, and oh, the stories they could tell. They gave ordinary people a dose of excitement, blasting them out of the monotonous and grinding dullness of mindless hard work. It was like a dime novel plot, played out in real time. They were daring, hard-riding desperadoes, men who lived by the gun. In a towering defiance of the law, in the purest form of unfettered freedom, they spoke to the anarchist in every man.

They were bad but they were brave, and more than that, they were gallant, and in America, gallantry in every form must always be revered and never diminished or scorned. The law distinguished right from wrong but it failed to interfere with theatrics of gallantry, especially when gunfire was in the picture. That was another matter altogether. After all, they were not torturing people, nor were they killing little children or small animals. On the other hand, they became role models for young, impressionable boys who, when at play, most eagerly wanted to be an outlaw, always the boldest actor of the cast. The outlaw had power, terrible, romantic power to cause fear, and in America where toughness and strength are exulted, fear is sometimes more important than respect.

So without a single blush of shame, the epic, lawless adventure of America's most popular outlaw gang became a story for the ages, and nothing would ever alter their

A casual glance at the photograph of "Retta" Younger and her brothers would give the viewer the impression that he or she was looking at a happy, well-adjusted family. Not true, of course, for it was crime and punishment that brought the four of them together on September 5,1889, for a formal photograph—in the Minnesota state prison. A stranger looking at Bob Younger (left) would not know of the suffering he had experienced because of the bullet that shattered his right elbow, at the Northfield shootout. Cole Younger (right), with a look of grim determination, had been generously peppered with bird shot in the brush near Madelia, when he and his brothers were captured. And finally, Jim Younger, who had long suffered from a devastating mouth wound, could thank prison officials for allowing him to grow a bushy mustache that concealed an ugly scar. While it was not a happy occasion, it was timely, for Bob was suffering from tuberculosis and had but a short time to live (Library of Congress).

exalted status in the public mind. A criminal who acted with dash, boldness and style performed an act of chivalry, and the theatrics eclipsed the crime and the evil-doer was, by some inexplicable transformation, made worthy of respect. The Youngers had been shot all to hell, convicted and sent off to prison, and had they been hanged, they would still have been admired.

The Youngers, and their erstwhile friends, the James boys, and other former Rebels-turned-outlaws as well, were clothed in a form of immunity and invincibility that cannot be rationalized or fully understood, but it doesn't matter. What matters is that they shot something of lasting importance into the dark, empty and hungry space that lies in wait in the collective mind of man.

11

The James Brothers Go In and Out of Iowa

"There is at least one man in Sioux City who can say that he has seen a couple of the notorious Northfield robbers."
—*The Daily Journal* (Sioux City, IA), September 22, 1876

On September 23, 1876, the engineer in charge of a train on the Dakota Southern Railroad saw what many other men had been seeing: two men riding together on the open prairie. They were on horseback approximately seven miles west of Sioux City when he spotted them. Of course he thought that he had located the James brothers and they appeared to be headed in the direction of Elk Point, thus placing the escapees in southeastern Dakota Territory. Dutifully, he notified the authorities.[1]

Another Jesse James sighting, a few days before, allegedly occurred at a fair in Pleasant Hill, Kansas. It seems that a man named John Budd encountered both Jesse and Cole Younger at the fair. Conversation ensued and Budd recognized, in a crowd, a face that belonged to the most wanted outlaw in America. The wanted man said that Clell Miller and Chadwell were probably "killed in Minnesota." He (Jesse) didn't know for certain, but they "might have been there." Mr. Budd was mistaken or lying. Finding Jesse James in Kansas on September 18 was impossible for he and his brother Frank were in Dakota Territory.[2]

By the 23rd, the James brothers were most likely in Iowa, having crossed the Big Sioux River. They crossed near Beloit, two miles south of Canton, if there is any credence in the claim of A. D. Krogness, whose father was the Rev. S. N. Krogness, a circuit-riding Lutheran pastor. Their farm was one and a half miles northeast of Beloit, and it just so happened that the James brothers "crossed the river and landed on our farm." Krogness' narrative does not mention a date, but it must have been the evening of September 19, 1876, when the outlaws "came face to face" with "my father who was very much surprised to see them appear above the bluff."

They asked permission to stay the night. "In those days hospitality was freely given," so the two trail-worn strangers were given supper and lodging. "They were well-armed but looked very much fatigued and played out." The Krogness family was aware of the Northfield robbery and knew that the two robbers were on the run. "We knew at once who they were," but out of concern for their safety, they pretended not to know. The next morning, after breakfast, the brothers departed, thanking their hosts and then they took a horse, saying, "We are sorry but we will have to take this horse." With that, they saddled up and rode off.

The mother of A. D. Krogness noticed bloodstains on the sheets of the bed that the outlaws slept in, "which she attributed to their forced riding." Rev. Krogness went to Beloit to notify the authorities, while his son followed the robbers on his pony. A posse was organized, but like all the others, it was unsuccessful. A. D. Krogness found the stolen horse near the town of Calliope, a river town that was 47 miles north of Sioux City, Iowa.[3]

The Krogness story is not without credibility and could explain why the James brothers were not found by the 30-man posse that galloped out of Canton. While the would-be robber catchers were traversing through the woods and over hills, the James boys were in bed, all tucked in, getting some much-needed rest.

Win Braley, whose family lived east of Beloit at the time of the great escape, had a Frank and Jesse James story in his past that he was most eager to reveal. While relating his story to a Sioux Falls newspaper, Braley recollected that word of the robbery in Northfield had "traveled ahead of the outlaws in spite of the crude methods of conveying information," back in 1876. Years later, in 1913, with notable advances in transportation and communication at his disposal, he talked about his connection to the outlaw adventure. Braley stated that his family was informed of the robbery and the two fugitives, and that was enough for him and three others to strike out and find the two men that an entire region was looking for.

Armed with a couple of old muzzle loading shotguns and a .22 caliber pistol, they hit the trail. Luckily, they came across signs of horse traffic early in the day, and although it started raining hard, by noon, the plucky lads were able to follow it. Braley claimed that he and his friends got close enough to Jesse and Frank and heard their voices. But darkness fell upon the land, and the quartet of hunters gave up and went back home without actually seeing the bandits. The boys and their guns were rain soaked to the extent that the firearms were worthless. But they considered themselves lucky to have had the experience. They came away wiser men, because they did not approach the brothers who may have "plugged them when they first drew their blunderblusses with the idea of firing."[4]

One may wonder how many times Win Braley told his Jesse James story before the year 1913, when it finally found itself in print. Of course one may also wonder how it was that Braley and his friends knew they were actually on the trail of the fugitives when they had only heard voices. Perhaps the best answer is that they heard what they wanted to hear.

What is accurate about the Braley yarn is that the robbers did indeed enter Iowa. It was reported that they were seen in Doon, Iowa, and later in East Orange, where the horses stolen from Wahl and Shulson were released in exchange for fresh mounts, also stolen.[5]

Then from East Orange came the report that a party of pursuers arrived in that town with news that "the two robbers" were seen "at the Big Sioux River, six and a half miles above Yankton, DT, where they had stayed all night Tuesday." In the same report it was stated that on "Tuesday morning at six o'clock they [the outlaws] were on foot, and when discovered, made for a stable and took out a pair of horses" and then dashed toward the river with a posse in hot pursuit. When the robbers reached the "top of the bluff on the opposite side of the river," they stopped and fired shots at the posse, hitting "the neck of one of the horses." While the posse did not simply retreat, they lost the trail of the fugitives in the timber.[6]

A similar report, equally breathless, in a Kansas City newspaper states that the two robbers who "were chased into Dakota, were overtaken by a citizens posse, six miles above Yankton, today," meaning September 21. When they were sighted, the robbers opened fire, wounding a horse, after which they "took to the woods," once again making an escape.[7]

The problem with these reports is that Yankton is on the Missouri River, not on the Big Sioux River. Had the outlaws been six and a half miles above Yankton, they would have been close to the James River. But to place them anywhere above Yankton would be inaccurate. Most likely, the James brothers stayed close to the Big Sioux River, possibly crossing it one or more times between Iowa and Dakota Territory. In all likelihood, the reported sighting was accurate, but the location was not.

It seems that news was coming in so hot and fast that it was difficult to tell information from misinformation. According to a report from Portlandville, a town on the Iowa side of the Big Sioux River in Plymouth County, the robbers were seen riding in a southeasterly direction. Dan McDonald, brother to Sheriff John McDonald, was at the head of a posse that was riding after them. But again, the pursuit was in the wrong direction, for after having breakfast six miles north of Le Mars, the James boys rode off in a southwesterly direction.[8] The date was September 21, 1876,[9] the same day that the brothers were reportedly seen in Dakota, and the same day Younger brothers and Charlie Pitts were shot up near Madelia, Minnesota.

As for the far more fortunate James brothers, another piece of luck had fallen into their hands in the form of a doctor on his way to a house call. But his patient would only wait in disappointment for the doctor never called. Instead, on September 21, an exhausted and tired Dr. Sidney Mosher trudged into Sioux City on foot, and within minutes of his arrival, the city erupted in excitement and anger. Dr. Mosher, whose office was located in Sioux City, had been kidnapped and held for four hours by the two men that had for two weeks been the subject of an intense search: Jesse and Frank James. "Our citizens were almost wild with excitement" was the mood of the people after hearing the tale of terror related by the respected doctor.

Dr. Mosher had "procured a bay saddle horse of R. A. Broadbent," and then set out on a medical errand, having been summoned to attend to a patient living northeast of Sioux City on the Little Sioux River. He had traveled about eight miles "northeast of the James station, and not far from the Big Whisky," when he saw two men riding slowly toward him, in the direction of Sioux City. Dr. Mosher decided to intercept the men in order to ascertain whether he was on the right trail. He approached them rapidly only to see the wayfarers whip out from under their coats "two navy revolvers."

With both guns leveled at him, the stunned doctor cried out, "Don't shoot," adding that he was not an outlaw nor was he an outlaw hunter. His first impression of the armed men was that they were lawmen searching for the robbers, and it didn't occur to him that he was facing the actual robbers. In that state of mind, Dr. Mosher pleaded with them to hold their fire for he could prove his identity. He could have told them that he was listed in a Sioux City newspaper as a "physician and accoucheur," specializing in chronic diseases.[10]

To his utter shock, "the strangers then dropped the muzzles of their navies and informed the doctor in plain English that they were the robbers," and furthermore they suspected that the man covered by their guns was indeed an outlaw hunter. One of the men "covered the doctor with his shooting iron," while the other rode off to a farmhouse a short distance away, where he "inquired concerning the doctor." Not long after, the man returned convinced that he and his partner had commandeered a doctor, out on a mission of mercy, meaning that Dr. Mosher would remain a prisoner until such time as they decided on his fate.

It was about 4 o'clock in the afternoon, and the traveling physician was informed that he would be held at least until dark, meaning he could expect to be a prisoner for about four hours. At that point, the three horsemen leisurely and slowly rode in "almost the direction that he desired to go."

Being a doctor and trained to make careful observations, he thoughtfully studied his captors, noting the appearance and behavior of the two men. He described them to the towns' people as follows: one man was tall and thin with a "sandy complexion and wearing a thin growth of whiskers." The other he described as "a short man, dark complexion, with whiskers evidently clipped quite close." He said that both men were "roughly dressed and rode sorrel and gray horses." They continued on their way until they came to a farmhouse where one man dismounted, went in and "procured some victuals."

They rode away from the farmhouse and stopped to eat, the James brothers dividing their lunch with the doctor. The taller of the two men told Dr. Mosher that he would have to give up "some of his wearing apparel." Then the tall man, Frank, took "the doctor's pants, coat, drawers and socks, leaving the latter with a pair of pants and a short-coat." As the doctor put on the pants he noticed "a large rent on the outside of the right leg." He also noticed that the tall "robber's leg was bandaged and that he appeared very lame."

Dr. Mosher didn't have to ask how he became injured for to his surprise the taller of the two robbers said that he had been "shot in the leg in the street in Northfield during the attempted bank robbery." The short robber tried to convince his wounded companion to let the doctor dress the wound, but the wounded man refused, contending there wasn't time to do so.

As they remounted the wounded man had to be helped on to his horse. They rode out on the prairie until it was nearly dark, when they spotted another Iowa farmhouse. One of the men rode up to house and it was later revealed that he told the people at the house that he needed a saddle for Dr. Mosher, who was on his way to treat a patient on the Little Sioux River. He returned with the saddle but it was not, of course, to be used by the doctor, rather it was put on the gray horse. Then they informed the doctor that he was about to be released, but first they wanted his horse and saddle.

A much-relieved Dr. Mosher was only too willing to give up his horse and saddle in exchange for being released. After all, the sorrel horse "was badly worn from hard usage," and it made sense to him that they would take his rented horse. So the doctor dismounted and one of the brigands took charge of his horse, but before they moved on, they warned Dr. Sidney Mosher that he was not tell anyone about his encounter with the two of most wanted men in America. As the men rode off, they ordered the doctor to walk toward a light two miles distant and not to look back at them "on the peril of his life." Then they rode away, taking the tired-out sorrel horse with them.

The doctor later stated that he had felt like a "freshly caged bird" and yet "comparatively safe in their hands." He only feared for his life when it came time for them to part company. And when he was released—wearing Frank's rubber coat that had been damaged by gunfire at Lake Crystal in Minnesota—he looked straight ahead, as ordered, and simply walked away in the darkness, all alone, but lucky to be unharmed.[11]

He walked for about an hour and then he stopped at a farmhouse where he spent the rest of the night. The next day he was taken to Sioux City by the farmer who gave him a place to stay. Along the way, they found the abandoned sorrel horse. They took the worn out animal to Sioux City where Dr. Mosher gave it to the liveryman to replace the horse stolen by the James brothers.

Of course everyone in Sioux City, a town "almost wild with excitement," wanted to ask Dr. Mosher questions about his four hours in captivity. The relieved doctor seemed most eager to be interviewed, and in bold strokes he addressed the crowd. Although he did not name his kidnappers while he was interviewed, he said the outlaws declared they might be caught but they would never be taken alive. Rather, they would go down guns a-blazing. They would fight "to the bitter end and sell their lives as dearly as possible." But the doctor related more bravado that he got from the notorious desperadoes, and it came in a dire warning to the banks of Sioux City. In the event that the brothers returned to rob the banks, the bankers "would do well to give up the vault keys peaceably, and thus avoid making martyrs of themselves." This was clearly a reference to the shooting of Heywood at Northfield.

After delivering the threats, Dr. Mosher obtained another team of horses from the liveryman and headed out to see his patient on the Little Sioux River. Mr. Broadbent, however, mentioned to the good doctor that "he should make a better trade next time, in case he was called upon to exchange animals." In the midst of the serious excitement, some humor found its way into the discussion.[12]

As time progressed, a "continuous stream of reports concerning the robbers" flowed into town, much of it false and outlandish. For example, the James brothers had actually been in Sioux City; they stopped for a beer at the "Greenville House" across from the Floyd River, and someone had spotted them at Sergeant Bluff, a local landmark. Casting aside all such intelligence, the hard-working sheriff reasoned that the two men on the run were moving southeast and would soon be approaching the town of Dennison, which is where Sheriff McDonald and his men would continue the pursuit.[13]

On September 23, more conflicting reports came in to Sioux City, but they revealed nothing that was helpful. The report that two men thought to be the brothers, having breakfast at the Greenville House, "across the Floyd," was wrong. The two men were a couple of herders who were actually herding cattle. There was an equally false sighting of the coveted outlaws in Sioux City by a character named C. R. Marks. While Marks was walking down Third Street "on business," he "happened to cast his eyes over on to a vacant lot on the corner," when he spotted what he thought were two men "in the tall weeds." Thinking he had discovered the infamous James brothers, Marks carefully crept closer to get a better look. Then to his horror, he saw what he believed was a gun in the hand of one of the two figures he was watching. This was too much for Marks and he hastened away to seek reinforcements. After he and several assistants arrived and surrounded the vacant lot, they were greeted with extreme disappointment for the two figures thought to be the outlaws were "an Indian and his squaw."[14]

Dr. Mosher, the one man who actually saw the James brothers up close, made a medical observation when was traveling with the Missourians. One of the outlaws, Frank James, was wounded, having been shot above the right knee. The doctor believed that the serious injury would at some point prove to be so severe as to prevent further travel on horseback. This gave rise to the thought that the brothers might try to board a train, and that therefore they were probably trying to reach the Chicago and Northwestern Railroad.[15]

But another observer, August Pruist, who had witnessed Dr. Mosher riding with the outlaws, claimed that after they parted with the doctor the two men returned to the Floyd River and crossed it at the Hungerford farm, in Plymouth County, and from there, they went west. Pruist's theory was bolstered by reports coming in from people who believed they had seen the escapees on the Broken Kettle Creek, "among the bluffs, not many miles north of Sioux City." Acting on this intelligence, Sheriff McDonald divided his forces, sending some to scout the Broken Kettle bluffs, while others were ordered to go east toward the town of Smithland.

Dr. Hurd of Faribault, a dedicated man who rode all the way to Yankton in pursuit of the James brothers, had retired from the chase, and when he reached Fairbault he reassured people that Sheriff McDonald was "still in command of a well-organized party of determined men and is not disposed to give up the hunt." The sheriff was searching in the Big Kettle country, and he was confident of success: "every outlet is believed to be guarded," "it is just a matter of time."[16]

A party of three men pulled up in Sioux City on the evening of the 22nd, with "reliable news of the robbers." They had stopped at the farm of J. C. Thompson, a short way from Le Mars, about 11 o'clock in the morning, one man riding a gray horse and the other on a dark bay horse. The strangers told Thompson that they were chasing "the damned robbers," and that their horses "were badly worn out from the chase." They convinced Thompson to lend them a team and buggy, for which service he would be well paid—later. The tired horses were put in a stable, a team was hitched to a buggy and the two strangers drove off, promising they would return the same evening. They, of course, did not and worse yet a despondent Thompson had no idea which direction they took when they left his place. He just knew that he had lost a team of horses to the smooth-talking James brothers. Sheriff McDonald was equally gloomy, having returned to town from the Broken Kettle Creek area with "no tidings."[17]

As an example of how an incident got reported in more ways than one, a Kansas City newspaper offered another version of the Thompson story. In this version, the James brothers arrived at the Thompson place in the middle of the night, roused him from his slumbers and "either compelled him or hired him to hitch his horses to a buggy and drive them to the Broken Kettle." Thompson's younger brother was present and overheard the James boys barking driving and direction orders to his older brother, and off they went.[18]

On September 29, James McDonough, the chief of police for St. Louis, wrote a letter to Missouri governor C. H. Hardin, explaining that the Youngers had been captured and identified, that Pitts, Miller and Chadwell were all dead, and most important, that "the James boys were of the party." But, he was constrained to explain, that after separating from their comrades near Mankato, they had escaped. McDonough assured the governor that the James brothers would be captured for he had a large force of men in the northwestern part of Missouri, covering "their crossings and haunts." Based on "information received" the chief of police was certain that they would return to Missouri, "after making a very circuitous route, and doubling on the pursuers."[19]

This letter pre-supposes McDonough's belief that the James brothers were still in Iowa, ahead of the lawmen, but not so far that they couldn't be caught. In fact, the Missouri authorities were cheering on the Iowans, hoping for success. Woodbury County sheriff John McDonald was still very much in the hunt, determined to catch the runaways and walk away with unprecedented laurels. History would be more than kind to him. Then news broke that he arrested a wounded man near Sioux City and the sheriff thought he had, at long last, reined in one of the Northfield outlaws. But the suspect was merely a farm hand who was injured in a threshing accident, and he was, of course, released.[20]

About this same time, "Ames the painter" drove a wagon into Sioux City with a prisoner on board, a "man believed to be one of the James brothers." The "excitement was intense" as the wagon passed along Fourth Street the prisoner was surrounded by "guards with pistols covering the presumed to be robber." The prisoner was dumped into a jail cell and "in less than ten minutes two or three hundred men had taken a hasty glance at him."

Dr. Mosher was brought to the jail, but after scrutinizing the sullen prisoner, he declared that he had never seen the man before. Three other sheriffs, all of whom were caught up in the pursuit of the James brothers, checked the man too, who was said to have had "a very piercing eye." The luckless man, experiencing his only brush with fame, said his name was William C. McFarland and he was out looking for work when he was arrested. When he was questioned, McFarland, a Civil War veteran from Iowa, said he had heard of the James brothers but he had not seen them. For certain, he was not Jesse or Frank James, and as a result Mr. McFarland sank back into anonymity.[21]

Another silly instance of a so-called sighting of the James brothers occurred north of Correctionville, in northeast corner of Woodbury County. Two men were spotted by someone claiming to be a deputy sheriff of Woodbury County, one of whom was "limping along as if suffering from a painful wound." The excited deputy—who was riding with another man—declared that he was certain that the James brothers were at long last discovered in a position to be taken or killed. The two men rode up a high bluff where they came upon a farmer "on his way for a load of hay." The deputy directed the farmer to ride fast to Correctionville and bring a "hundred or two well armed men" for the purpose of capturing the outlaws.

Before long a veritable army of 150 men were standing in battle array on the bluff. The deputy made a speech meant to steel their nerves, telling the men that if the robbers "offered any resistance" they were to be shot down. This seemed to have the desired effect for in an instant, the mass of men was in motion, blazing toward the men thought to be the James brothers. But before there was any shooting, the farmer yelled out, demanding that no one pull their trigger. The two suspected fugitives from Northfield were none other than the farmer's two "little boys who [were] out herding cattle."[22] The great manhunt had spawned another ridiculous story that somehow made it into a Sioux City newspaper.

Despite printing some stories that were clearly concocted for sensationalism, the newspapers of Minnesota, Dakota and Iowa did a respectable job, for it is only because of the frontier journalists that we have any record at all about the progress of the great manhunt. But it has been claimed that a certain Sioux City newspaper editor used his high social status to aid the James brothers, whom he admired, in their flight back to Missouri. G. W. Hunt, the editor of the *Sioux City Democrat*, came forth to say that he misdirected a posse, sending it in a false direction. Then he located the brothers and essentially joined them in their escape, having provided them with a "skiff" at the junction of the Little Sioux and Missouri rivers that the boys used to make their way down river to St. Joseph and safety.[23]

If Editor Hunt gave assistance to felons seeking to avoid capture, then he committed a crime, and if he publicly admitted or boasted of helping his new friends, the James brothers, all those who listened and learned were not convinced that he was a true outlaw helper. It was simply another tall tale, a made-up yarn, designed to tie him to the legend of the James boys.

And he had some company, for a fellow editor, an all-around plunger and seeker of excitement, Charley Collins, who once edited the Sioux City *Journal*, made a similar boast in 1877, when he was about to launch a newspaper venture in Deadwood, a wild, frontier town that was both reveling and suffering in the throes of a gold rush. The colorful, foul-mouthed Collins, often accompanied by his dog "Typo," was a frontier character of the highest order. He once bragged that he had intervened and assisted the James brothers in their escape in exchange for "information from their own lips as to the daring deeds of the robbery; but was sworn to secrecy except under circumstances which have not yet risen."[24]

It is probably safe to say that the "circumstances" for the dramatic revelation failed to rise to the proper level. At any rate, the Iowa authorities were criticized for not pouring more resources into the chase. It was said that "aside from the work of Sheriff McDonald, there appears to have been no effort in this state [Iowa] to affect the capture of these outlaws."[25] And the brothers, for whom luck never seemed to run out, continued their long journey home.

It was believed by some in the news media that the journey home included a stop in Nebraska, where it was known that the James boys had good friends. It was thought that they crossed the Missouri River into Nebraska, somewhere between Sioux City and Springfield, Dakota. If this was true, then at some point they left Iowa and returned to Dakota, a theory put forth by the Sioux Falls journalist J. A. Derome.

In 1924, when Sioux Falls *Daily Argus Leader* was involved in a journalistic investigation into the great escape, a man named F. M. Larson sent a letter to Derome revealing his family's encounter with the outlaws at the tiny Union County village of Spink, located in the far southeastern tip of Dakota. His father, John Larson, was the postmaster at Spink when the James brothers showed up and spent the night.

But it wasn't until the next day, after the strangers left and mail arrived, that Larson had a clue as to the identity of his guests, for the mail contained information about the robbers and the reward. The story lacks credibility because it was claimed that when the James brothers arrived at the Spink post office, they were driving "different rigs with several heavy suitcases." They even "had a stick of candy for us kids."[26] The well-dressed strangers were most certainly not the James brothers, the two weary travelers whose clothes were being steadily reduced to dirty rags.

In early October of 1876, a man called "one of the very highest officials in Jasper County," Missouri, rushed in the door of the St. Louis office of Chief of Police James McDonough. The man breathlessly exclaimed that none other than Jesse James, traveling alone, passed through Jasper County, and he "could prove beyond a shadow of a doubt" that the man was "the bandit leader." The beleaguered McDonough—who had heard so many crazy stories, and followed so many false leads—abruptly ordered the anxious citizen out of his office, roughly and rudely declaring that the man "did not know what he was talking about."[27]

But McDonough was a knowledgeable man and would not quit. On October 13, 1876, the St. Louis chief of police wrote another hopeful letter to Governor Hardin. The chief seemed earnest and confident when he wrote that he had "received information from a reliable source, locating the wounded James, and his partner." Acting on intelligence indicating that the James brothers were back in Missouri, he had sent a well-armed force of men "for the north-western part of the state," where, according to an informant, "the parties [Frank and Jesse] are under cover, well-guarded day and night by four Texas desparadoes [sic]" who were likely to fight off fiercely any attempt to make an arrest of the men they were guarding. McDonough asked that more money be appropriated for his use and assured the governor "that the object of our long search was near at hand, and every precaution was being taken to make the raid a success."[28]

Two days later, on the 15th, a headline in a St. Louis newspaper crowed rather boldly that Frank James had been caught and was confined to "the St. Louis Calaboose."[29] Frank and Jesse had, indeed, made it back to Missouri and were in the Jackson County, or so it was believed. When caught, the man believed to be Frank James was hiding in the home of Dr. William W. Noland, and at the same time, Jesse was thought to be in the nearby home of Dick Talley.

McDonough assigned Sergeant Morgan Boland and his men to make the arrest. Boland and eight other officers had been in search of the James brothers in the weeks following the Northfield raid. They went south until they reached the border of Texas and then turned back when they received word that a wounded Frank James was in Missouri, holed up at the house of a physician.[30]

The night before the wounded man was seized, a St. Louis police officer showed up at Dr. Noland's place, and after "prowling about, under the guise of a retired Black Hills miner," he asked if he could spend the night in the barn. The request was denied by the doctor who instead invited the officer to sleep in the house. Hearing that, the "fellow sneaked off at the first chance" and was not seen again until the actual raid.[31]

Boland and his party first raided the home of a Mrs. Dearing, near Independence, bursting in at 2 a.m. with guns a-blazing.[32] Sorry, wrong house. Not finding their man, they rushed over to the house they should have gone to in the first place: the home of Dr. Noland. There, after breaking in the door, they found a wounded man believed to be Frank James lying in bed. At about 5 o'clock in the afternoon of October 13, 1876, he was roughly nabbed. A frantic Mrs. Noland begged them not to take the wounded man, insisting that he was not Frank James, but rather John Goodwin (also spelled Goodin) from Louisiana. The lawmen would have none of it and hauled off to jail the man believed to be Frank James; they also arrested the doctor's son. The Talley house was also raided but there was no sign of Jesse James in the house.[33]

An article in *The Daily Journal* of Sioux City, Iowa, did not mention his name, but it revealed in detail facts about the man thought to be the dangerous Frank James. The gamesmanship started with his arrest. Lawmen burst into the Noland house where the prisoner and two women were the only occupants. One of the arresting officers said: "How are you Frank?" to which the man replied: "My name is not Frank." Not satisfied with the answer, the wounded arrestee was carried out on a mattress and taken to Kansas City and from there to St. Louis. All the while, "the prisoner did not utter a word of protest but took the matter with singular coolness."

In Kansas City, the suspect was questioned about his identity in a time when a man was identified only by his appearance, any papers on his person, and the word of others. The man believed to be Frank James claimed that he had served in the Confederate army out of Louisiana and was transferred to a Missouri unit. When he was told that "he had been arrested for a James, he remarked that was alright." The authorities thought it was all right too, for at that point, they believed they had their man, "having reliable information that he came direct from eighty miles north of Sioux City within a short time."[34]

The *Minneapolis Tribune* was happy about the arrest of "THE SEVENTH" man who had participated in the Northfield robbery, that man being Frank James. In a celebratory article, the *Tribune* boldly declared that the man claiming to be someone else was really Frank James, and if he "is not

Frank James the police authorities" expressed confidence that he was the mysterious Cal Carter. But be he Cal Carter or Frank James, "he is one of the Northfield bank robbers beyond a doubt."[35]

In a St. Louis jail, the prisoner spoke freely about his life, and claimed that he got his leg wound due to an accidental firing of his gun, "while riding in a wagon." Owing to the fact that he was arrested as Frank James, he was carefully observed in his cell. He was described as having eyes that were "deep blue and very clear, without any ruffian look in them." He seemed very comfortable in jail, this man of a "backwoods appearance," with small, soft hands and "black hair which is inclined to stick straight up." He looked as though he had "been about the world enough to be at home wherever he drops down." In short, he was beginning to look more like an ordinary drifter, hoping to get a free meal and a warm bed, and less and less like Frank James with every glance of his tired eyes and every vapid word that came out of his mouth.[36]

This incident shows how little the keepers of the jail knew about the real Frank James. While the elder James brother lacked a formal college education, he was an intelligent, introspective man who liked the classics and frequently quoted Shakespeare, one of his favorite writers. Unlike his hotheaded younger brother, the philosophical Frank was not impulsive or over emotional; he was a thoughtful, mature man who was interested in American politics and world affairs. He came to believe that women should have the right to vote, a position that put him far ahead of most men of his time.[37] Yes, the lowly, disinterested fellow in the St. Louis jail was a far cry from the real Frank James.

And yet the authorities were still working as if they had Frank James in their clutches. They called in two respected men that knew both James brothers well and asked if they could identify the prisoner as Frank James. They could not. The frustrated authorities knew full well that there were dozens—maybe hundreds—of people in the area who could say whether or not the man behind bars was in fact Frank James. Unfortunately, from among this mass of people, the James brothers could count as friends loyalists who would not identify them under any circumstances.[38]

Dr. Sidney Mosher in Sioux City was telegraphed, asked to come to St. Louis to identify the man believed to be the infamous outlaw and escapee from the Northfield crime scene. The doctor was extremely reluctant, however, having been fully acquainted with the James brothers after a chance meeting while on the Iowa prairie. But it was a postal card bearing a dark warning that was more than sufficient to keep the weak-kneed physician in Sioux City. It stark message was "If you consider your Damned Neck with a

11. The James Brothers Go In and Out of Iowa

cent you had better keep away from St. Louis." It was signed "One of the Boys."[39]

It was the former Confederate soldier's connection with Dr. Noland, however, that convinced the authorities that they had the wrong man, so there would be no need for Dr. Mosher to risk his life. The suspect told his listeners that the Dr. Noland had treated him since he was a boy, and for that reason, he traveled from Louisiana to Missouri, because there was no one else he trusted. It was also known that Dr. Noland was well acquainted with members of the James and Younger gangs. He would therefore certainly be in a position to say whether or not the Missouri authorities had captured the right man. In due course, after a short time in the national spotlight, and having been likened to a great outlaw, John Goodwin was released from custody and simply allowed resume his life such as it was.[40]

The incident, however, sparked a round of criticism from some newspapers. Among them, *The St. Louis Globe-Democrat* mocked the authorities for their bungling amateurism, actions that only served to provide "ample room for Carter and the Jameses and their friends to laugh at the expense of the people and the papers."[41]

After he was released, Goodwin "got off some pretty good jokes" of his own at the expense of his captors, the bumbling detectives. He also told others that he knew nothing "of the James boys or Cal Carter," but he admitted that he was at one time in Hunt County, Texas, "to help hunt for Carter" who had been actively stealing horses. But the hunt was a failure for the outlaw got away to "Indian Territory."[42]

Some years after the arrest of Goodwin, it was learned that he had sued Boland for false imprisonment, but for reasons unknown, he failed to pursue the matter through the court system. Goodwin disappeared and "has never been heard of since." Apparently there were those who believed that Goodwin was actually Frank James. In April of 1882, a Missouri newspaper, *The Sedalia Weekly Bazoo*, resurrected the old matter and concluded that "all the evidence" points to Frank James.[43] At least one reporter believed that one of America's most wanted men had hoodwinked the authorities. But he was dead wrong, for the doctors who examined Goodwin after he was released noted that his wound was at least four months old, meaning he was injured in June of 1876. The real Frank James was wounded during the Northfield fracas that September.[44]

To close the book on the John Goodwin incident, a telegram was sent to Dr. Mosher telling him there was no need to come to St. Louis.[45] No doubt the doctor was more than satisfied, for having been in the company of the James brothers for four hours, he learned a thing or two. During that time they could have easily killed him but they chose not to do so. Having been allowed to live, Dr. Mosher was probably not looking forward to going to Missouri, into a lion's den, so to speak, especially after having received the postal card with the dire and deadly warning to stay home. The card could have been a prank, but that possibility was outweighed by the prospect of being killed so far from home.

The man the Dr. Mosher was to have identified was not Frank James; the *Bazoo* reporter was wrong. Had the doctor come face to face with Goodwin, in all likelihood he too would have denied that he was looking at Frank James. Nevertheless, it is doubtful that the James brothers or their friends would have extended any tender treatment to the doctor who, with fear and trepidation, was preparing to cooperate with the authorities.

But a brother-in-law of the Younger brothers, Richard S. Hall, from Lee's Summit, Missouri, claimed to have "fell in with the old doctor whom the James boys pressed into their service." According to Hall—who was said to be "plain and unvarnished in his statements"—the doctor dressed the wounds of both men, Jesse having been wounded "just above the heel" and Frank had a "severe wound just above the knee."[46] Hall did not name the "old doctor," but in all likelihood he was referring to Dr. Sidney Mosher, the only doctor known to have encountered the James brothers during their great escape, and further proof as to the identity of two that got away.

12

The Dark River

> "The career of the James brothers has been a remarkable one, and its most startling development consists in the proof it affords of the prevalence, upon the border, of a spirit of lawlessness which does not yield to time."
> —*Sacramento Daily Record-Union*, April 5, 1882

The year 1876 was one of thrills, surprises and nervous excitement, all of it unraveling while America was wading through a serious economic depression set off by the financial panic of 1873. Although thousands were seriously hungry, America was celebrating its first 100 years—a celebration tainted by widespread want and suffering. Still, the Centennial in Philadelphia attracted large crowds of people all anxious to view the exhibits, almost as if standing among the examples of progress had some type of healing power. People were staring at the future and they liked it.

But there were so many head-spinning events happening outside of Philadelphia, and if a time frame had character traits, the year of the Centennial resembled a man experiencing wild mood swings. It was a year of one exciting event after another; among the standouts was the gold rush in Dakota's Deadwood Gulch, the massacre of Lieutenant Colonel George A. Custer's soldiers at Little Big Horn in Montana, the murder of the celebrated gunman, Wild Bill Hickok in Deadwood, Dakota Territory, a grasshopper invasion in the Northwest that caused widespread crop damage, and, finally, a scandalous, high-pitched, fraud-drenched presidential election that dumped the presidency on the former Civil War officer and mild-mannered Republican Rutherford B. Hayes.

One other unforgettable incident belongs in this distinguished group: the Northfield Bank robbery and subsequent remarkable and improbable escape by Frank and Jesse James from the clutches of the law.

The infamous brothers, whose names were on the lips of Americans throughout the land, had successfully eluded death or capture and made it back home to Missouri hungry, hurt and tired. It was once reported that the James brothers went directly to Waco, Texas, after Northfield, where their wounds were treated.[1] It was also speculated that Frank James would make Nebraska his destination, because the authorities suspected that he would meet his wife, Annie, in Omaha. A detective was assigned to Omaha "to keep a sharp outlook for her," but she stayed away.[2] In all likelihood the brothers stopped running once they got to Clay County, Missouri, more particularly to the family farm near Kearney.

On October 8, 1876, in a cheeky little piece under the heading "News and Gossip," a St. Paul newspaper declared that "two of that gang of Minnesota robbers have got [sic] back to Missouri, safe and sound." But they were both "so pale from fright that they can hereafter exhibit themselves in a side show as Albinos."[3] Another newspaper suggested that the brothers were in New Mexico, because two "masked men" had recently held up the stagecoach near Las Vegas. It was speculated that Frank and Jesse "fled to that section of the country after the lively little matinee" in Northfield.[4]

Then that same newspaper did a sudden about-face: the James brothers were back in Clay County, Missouri, having arrived at an unknown date. Nevertheless, there are other tidbits of information about their homecoming. A reporter for a St. Louis newspaper stated that he saw Jesse James, in October of 1876, in St. Louis. Moreover, he claimed to have talked to Jesse, who declared that he was in the city for the purpose of killing a Pinkerton, an obsession the outlaw could not ignore.[5]

The story about the arrest of John Goodwin thought to be Frank James caused people to speculate on the whereabouts Frank and his brother. But "no one could be found ... who was willing to state positively" that for the past three months he had seen "Jesse or Frank James in this section of the country." Then, on October 15, a man from Independence, "who is quite intimate with the James family," said that the brothers arrived in Jackson County, Missouri, "about ten days ago." The man was not identified in the newspaper article, but he said that Frank and Jesse rode on horseback through western Minnesota, eastern Dakota, Nebraska and Kansas, going as far south as the "Indian Territory," before traveling north to southwestern Missouri. Both men were wounded, "one in the leg and the other in the foot." This story ignores the fact that Iowa was on the brothers' travel itinerary, but it was deemed "reasonable enough" get the attention of the railroad and express companies, and, of course, the police.[6]

The sheriff of Clay County, John S. Groom, was at some point in time tipped off that the boys were at or near the old home place, for on the evening of November 22, 1876, he led a four-man posse to the Samuel farm near Kearney. It was raining gently when Frank spotted the lawmen and fired a shot to warn his brother. More shots were exchanged. Then the boys got on their horses and galloped away, shouting obscenities, and leaving yet another insulted posse with an empty bag.[7]

But the sheriff was in no mood to quit the chase. It had long been batted about that whoever held the office of Clay County sheriff was in cahoots with the bad brothers.[8] Sheriff Groom, serving his second term in that office, was determined to show that he was not "in" with the "brothers." So after having gained "positive proof" of their location in Platte County, the sheriff and his men moved in for an arrest. Some gunshots were exchanged, but no one was bagged. Next the James brothers were "traced into the neighborhood of Rushville" near St. Joseph in Buchanan County. "Here the trail was lost." Once again, however, the lawmen were not about to give up, and after it was ascertained that the fleeing brothers were about to cross the Missouri River into Kansas, the bridges at Atchison and St. Joseph were placed under guard for "several consecutive days and nights," but to no avail, for "no parties having the description of the brothers appeared." Once again, the trail was "entirely lost."[9]

How could they slip, ghost-like, out of every trap? In a "St. Louis special" to the *Chicago Tribune* that was copied by *The Faribault Democrat*, a sensational article claimed that Ed Miller, brother of the deceased Clell Miller, and "a man named Hoffman," were acting as spies for the James brothers.[10] That they had allies, both official and unofficial, who were looking out for them was undoubtedly true. Indeed their continued success was attributed to their ability to "retreat to regions where the community sympathized so strongly with them." The protection from among friends and neighbors provided a form of immunity, keeping them out of the coils of justice.[11] The well-traveled James boys were definitely back in Missouri, and despite pressure applied by the law, being home must have felt so good. Where else in America could they feel safe?

Their domineering mother had left Missouri and may not have been there to greet and care for them. *The Kansas City Times* reported that on November 1, Zerelda Samuel said tearful good-byes to a number of old friends and then boarded a train for Texas. The sad old lady, in the company of her black servants and "a little negro child adopted by me," confessed that she had no particular area in mind to live, but that people could write to her at Sherman, Texas. She told a reporter for the *Times* that her sons, Frank and Jesse, were "a thousand miles from Kansas City, ... hard at work, making an honest living." Clearly dejected and upset at being forced to leave the family home, she said, "I am very old now, not the woman I was thirteen years ago when trouble came upon me and mine with the [Civil] war."[12] But living out her life in Texas was not in the cards for Zerelda, for within a month she was back in Missouri.[13]

The Civil War radically shaped the lives of Zerelda Samuel and thousands others, including her outlaw sons, both of whom were about to lay low, and for good reasons. The mood in and around their old haunts had changed. When northwestern Missouri learned about the failed bank robbery in Northfield, and that the entire gang had been killed or locked up except Frank and Jesse, the feeling was that there would be no more bank and train robberies.[14]

Then, in September of 1877, a Kansas City, Missouri, reporter came out with a sensational article concerning the robbing of a Union Pacific Railroad train in Nebraska. The reporter did not name his sources, nor did he state that his information was from anonymous sources, but his story must have been read with great interest by the fans of the James and Younger brothers. The reporter said the robbery had all the hallmarks of previous similar crimes by the James brothers, "friends of the three Youngers," locked up in the Minnesota state prison. The robbery, he said, was something that had been planned well in advance, for the purpose of raising funds to assist in the escape of Cole, Jim and Bob from Stillwater. "The two men who alone escaped from the gang of eight which ventured into Minnesota" were known to have crossed the Union Pacific Railroad, "almost at the identical spot where the robbery occurred." The reporter didn't name "the two men," and, of course, there was no need to put the names of Frank and Jesse James in news print, for every American familiar with the daring exploits of brothers immediately read between the lines.[15]

The story, although artfully written, was in error in many ways, and although there was well-publicized robbery along the Union Pacific tracks, at Big Springs, 60 miles west of Omaha, it was done by another gang.[16] For the James brothers, with no gang to assist, were just then in no hurry to resume that particular line of crime. Frank and Jesse must have understood how lucky they were to have made such a miraculous escape from Northfield, a feat that was truly a life-changing event. It was time to engage in some serious, introspective thinking.

While the brothers had more star power because of the Northfield affair, much of the American press denounced them, and the authorities were pressured into making a genuine effort to find them. One noted writer suggested that Jesse secretly convalesced at the home of former Confederate general Joe Shelby in Lafayette County. Shelby openly admired his guest, an unrepentant rebel, who in 1872, all by himself, backed "down a mob bent on killing the general's teenage black servant."[17] But when Shelby was asked about harboring the Youngers and James, the old soldier angrily denied it, calling a lie and a slander.[18]

Be that as it may, Jesse and Frank could count on help from people, especially wartime comrades, in order to avoid detection and capture. Much of the pro–Rebel population sympathized with, and even supported, the ex–Rebel outlaws, giving them food and shelter while sharing information. Jesse and Frank seemed to be their favorites. Missourians more or less gave them a free pass, based on this pervasive sentiment: "They robbed the rich and gave to the poor." They were Rebels through and through and had fought hard for the South. And although the James brothers freely robbed banks, stagecoaches and trains, they never stole livestock from, nor did he rob the farmhouses of ordinary Missourians.[19]

While there were some people who would maintain that attitude, though the sky may fall, as time went on, the safety net protecting Frank and Jesse was beginning to fray along the edges. As crime piled upon crime the Robin Hood image took on some tarnish. And clearly, there had to be a change of attitude, a shift toward supporting law officers in their effort to clamp down on the violators. And change was coming, and while the number of people clinging desperately to the past was shrinking, the number of those rushing toward the future was surging. The James brothers' stubborn hold on the defeated Confederacy would ultimately prove to be a fatal liability.

One of the most courageous and persistent outlaw opponents was William H. Wallace, a lawyer, prosecutor and agent for change who decided that it was time to get tough. He was elected in 1880 to the office of prosecuting attorney in Jackson County, Missouri, and he threw himself into the business of convicting and locking up the bad men.[20] Wallace must have been inspired because of the capture of the Youngers and the widespread publicity over the event. Although the James brothers continued to get sympathetic coverage from some journalists, including the ever-faithful John Newman Edwards, the editorial opposition had established its own drumbeat.

Was the tide turning? Missouri was known in some quarters as the "meanest state in the Union," the state of "sin and misery."[21] Was she about to rid herself of these shameful labels?

Not according to the editor of the *Mankato Record* in Mankato, Minnesota. He tried his hand at combining outlaw behavior with politics in an editorial jab at South Carolina. The editor picked apart a speech by Wade Hampton, who both before and after the Civil War had been an iconic figure in the South. In 1876, when Hampton was running for governor of South Carolina, he gave a speech urging the need to protect the rights of white people that he believed were under siege from attacks by the northern Republicans. While denying that he was making threats, Hampton urged South Carolinians to vote Democratic to "protect ... your race ... for South Carolina belongs to her native sons."

To the Mankato man, this was rich with hypocrisy. He pointed out that if a black man in South Carolina wanted to vote Republican, he did so "at the risk of his life." He went on to write that at Northfield "the bank robbers ... said to Heywood open the safe or be shot, and they shot him," and now Hampton and "his cutthroat followers in South Carolina" were preparing to do the equivalent to black men who simply wanted to exercise their right to vote.[22] It was not the strongest analogy but it reflected the sharp policy division in America during the political firestorm of 1876, when the federal policy of Reconstruction was winding down and the campaign for enforcing civil rights was facing strong resistance.

The better editorials attacked crime directly, with thinly-veiled references to politics. Newspapers, especially those in Minnesota, a state directly impacted by crime from the James–Younger gang, attacked not only the outlaws, but the state of Missouri, calling it "the robbers' paradise." Officials from the governor on down were sharply challenged to show some backbone and go after the "robbers and cutthroats" that had enjoyed a free reign in the Missouri. The outlaws had been, for far too long, encouraged by the lack of punishment and by the "feebleness of pursuit." Add to this the "large numbers of the citizens to harbor and protect them" and "the many newspapers which admire, rather than condemn their dare-deviltry," and the result is that the law and society are diminished and disgraced. Missouri, by her own inaction, her lack of political will, was made to stand naked and ashamed in front of a nation where decency, law and order are the hallmarks of a civilized people.[23]

William H. Wallace found all this both troubling and embarrassing. So he spoke out with a powerful, courageous voice, knowing one man could make a difference. But he also understood that one man could not do it alone; leadership at all levels was needed. His beloved Missouri, whom he believed was as civilized and cultured as any other state, had suffered long enough from outlaw depredations. It was more than just a loss of reputation. The lawlessness had serious economic consequences, capital investment was withheld, jobs were lost, property values were lower than in neighboring states, and immigration into the state slowed to a trickle. People were avoiding the "Robber State," an insulting label—applied by an Iowa newspaper—that stayed with Missouri for about ten years. Because the "damage done to Missouri was incalculable," Wallace joined other law-abiding Southerners who "were tired of outlawry," lending his voice and legal expertise to arresting, trying, convicting and punishing the villains.[24]

No doubt sensing the pressure, the notorious James brothers kept a very low profile for about three years, following their escape from Northfield, Minnesota. There were no robberies, no letters to newspapers and no public appearances. There was even some suspicion that they might be dead.[25] In actuality, they had left Clay County and moved to Tennessee. There, under fake names, they lived in Nashville, with their families, living quietly among people who did not recognize them for what they were: America's most famous criminals. It was a life that kept them safe, but it was dull and boring compared to the guns a-blazing, hard-riding outlaw experience.

In February of 1878, Jesse and Zee became the parents of twin boys, born prematurely. The boys, named Gould and Montgomery, after the doctors that attended their birth, lived but a few days. Despite the doctors' best efforts, they died and the tragic loss was heartbreaking to Jesse and Zee.[26]

In August of 1878, it was reported that Jesse had been seen in Callaway County, Missouri, living under the protection of other ex–Confederates. According to an article in a Memphis newspaper, Jesse was still struggling to recover from "his wonderful and almost miraculous escape from his Minnesota expedition" when a "posse of Norwegians followed … him day and night," all of which took a heavy toll on his "once vigorous and wiry frame." The anxious reporter concluded that Jesse James was finished as an outlaw, and would, if allowed, transition to the role of an ordinary citizen.[27]

Jesse James, however, was probably laboring under the realization that he was careening toward a violent death. At any rate he could only take so much of the quiet, law-abiding life of a farmer, or in some other mundane line of work. Not even the birth of a daughter, Mary Susan, on June 17, 1879, could force Jesse to settle down for good. He needed an adrenaline rush, the kind that only came from danger, so he organized a new gang consisting of Tucker Basham, Bill Ryan, James A. "Dick" Liddil, Wood Hite, a cousin of the James boys, and Ed Miller, brother of the late Clell Miller, who had fallen dead in Northfield. On October 8, 1879, they pulled off what became known as the Glendale train robbery in Jackson County. The daring robbery of the Chicago and Alton Road netted the gang about $6,000. After dividing the loot, the gang members then went their separate ways.[28]

Soon after, in early November of 1879, Jesse James found himself back in the headlines. The man who subscribed to five daily newspapers to "keep himself posted,"[29] must have been stunned when newspapers all over America roared as one "Jesse James is dead!" It was reported that the celebrity outlaw had been shot and killed by a former gang member, the one-eyed ex–Confederate, ex-convict George Shepherd. Newspapers, including the *New York Sun*, declared that the ex-con was working as a teamster when he was recruited by Deputy Marshall James Liggett of Kansas City to act as a "detective" for the purpose of killing or capturing Jesse James. In the flurry of press coverage that excited all Americans, Liggett was proclaimed to be the mastermind behind the "dramatic death" of Jesse James.[30]

The alleged shooting took place about seven miles southwest of Joplin, Missouri. Jesse and Shepherd had been riding side by side with other gang members present, all heading in the direction of Texas, with a view of robbing a bank. Suddenly, without warning, Shepherd pulled his pistol and shot an unsuspecting Jesse in the head while yelling: "This is for killing my nephew, Ike Flannegan!" Shepherd put the spurs to his horse, and after he shot at the other gang members, namely Jim Cummins and Sam Kaufman, the alleged slayer of Jesse got away.[31]

Shepherd, who had lived in Kansas City, could now boast of having impressive outlaw credentials. In an interview with *The Kansas City Times*, Shepherd revealed bits and pieces of his outlaw past along with the details of the shooting death of America's best-known outlaw, Jesse James. He was well acquainted with Jesse, having served with him in the command of the raider William Clarke Quantrill during the late war. After the war he was involved in an attempted bank robbery in Kentucky, for which he was arrested, tried, convicted and spent "several years in the state prison in Kentucky."

After allegedly shooting Jesse, Shepherd told the reporter for the *Times* that during a shooting affair with another gang member, he lost both his pistol and his overcoat, but escaped to Kansas City, wounded in the leg. "I'm almost positive that I killed Jesse, but I don't think his companions will leave the body where it will be found," Shepherd explained, "with an air of authority." Jesse James "fell from his horse, and never uttered a word or even groaned." Shepherd closed the interview by saying, "they will … sink the body of Jesse in the creek."[32] He did not say who "they" were.

Shepherd's story did not, however, convince everyone that it was true. *The Kansas City Times* jumped on it with a fury, calling it a made-up tale, "a fraud, perpetrated for the purpose of securing the promised reward." But the *Times* warned Shepherd not count his money, for the truth will eventually be revealed. "It is hard to find a man now who believes that Jesse is dead or has been injured." According to the *Times*, the more accurate scenario was that when Jesse learned that Shepherd was about to betray him, he opened fire and shot George in the leg.[33]

About two and a half years following the alleged shooting, a Tennessee newspaper jumped on the strange report that had made George Shepherd "the hero of the day." In March of 1882, Shepherd came around to admitting the story was a fraud, an attempt by him and Jesse James to help themselves to "the large reward offered for Jesse dead or alive." Shepherd even confessed that his leg wound was more or less self-inflicted. In order for him to "square himself with the officers," Shepherd "deliberately held out his leg and allowed Jesse James to shoot a hole through it."[34]

Long before Shepherd came clean, other members of the press and public saw holes in the story and simply refused to believe that America's most beloved criminal was dead. Shocking rumors of Jesse's demise aroused a chattering gaggle of death deniers. "Jesse James is not dead!" shouted out *The Kansas City Times*, whose editor, John Newman Edwards, was an out-of-the-closet admirer and unabashed supporter of Jesse James.[35] Another newspaper, *The Ouachita Telegraph* from Monroe, Louisiana, called the death report a laughable "canard" that would have been entirely ignored had the accused murderer been someone other than George Shepherd, "one of his [Jesse's] old chums."[36]

A very much alive Jesse James got the last word on the issue. In a letter to a Hannibal, Missouri. newspaper editor, Jesse jumped into the minor mystery, saying, "your reporter and George Shepherd have the most brilliant imaginations in America." That was his opening salvo. He went on to write, "They can lie with more appearance of truth than any two men in Missouri," including none other than Mark Twain. Then Jesse waxed more seriously. "George Shepherd would never treat me that way. I shot his nephew because I had to, and he knows it. Besides George is no coward and would never have shot me in the back."

He wound down his rant with a couple of self-serving plugs. "I had no more to do with the Glendale robbery than you had." He inferred it was pulled off badly, hinting that had he been involved, the robbery would have been more stylish and the result more rewarding. Still he confessed a longing for "the old days and old deeds," and he would return to the kind of life he experienced in "the wild and reckless past" were it not for his wife and boy. If they were not in his life, he "would again take to the road."

One can almost hear a sigh coming from his letter when he advised the world that "I am playing a square game, and have settled down on a ranch [sic] about ten miles from this town [Brownwood, Texas] and am no longer known as Jesse James." If left alone, he would be a "good citizen and grow up in a new life with this great State of Texas." He praised his wife for standing by him, noting that she "has saved me from killing myself." In closing, he did not reveal his new name and instead signed the letter, "Believe me, yours in truth, Jesse James."[37]

In truth, Jesse did indeed have reason to praise his wife for she had stood by him in a manner that can best be described as heroic. That he loved her there can be no doubt, but he was not always faithful to her. He was reported to have had a woman in St. Louis whose name was Hattie Floyd. As the story goes, Jesse stole a "camel's hair shawl worth $1500.00 and gave it to her." Hattie wore it out in public and was stopped by the police. Since she couldn't convince them that it was really hers to wear, she was arrested, tried, convicted and served five years in jail—for a crime committed by her boyfriend! But when he was reminded of the girl, Jesse said that Hattie was now dead and the whole thing was something that made him laugh.[38]

A highwayman, it seems, meets many people under a variety of circumstances and many such relationships are of the throwaway kind. Jesse was a man who doubtlessly and casually discarded people left and right along the road of life. But he was not finished with banditry. It had provided too many thrills and rewards, and his rank and reputation as an outlaw leader remained at the top of the heap. A fellow outlaw once said of Jesse, "I think he was a brave man," and for that reason he never drank when on a raid. But he was hot-headed, petulant, suspicious and distrusting and would quickly turn against a gang member with savagery, betrayal was punished by death, and he "was known to kill his own men for their money."[39]

One gang member he was said to have killed was Ed Miller, a member of an outlaw family, whose brother Clell was shot dead in Northfield, Minnesota, in 1876. There are two reasons given for the impulsive shooting of Ed Miller in 1880.[40] One story is that Ed caught Jesse "fooling" around with his girlfriend, and to put an end to the angry issue, Jesse "drew a revolver and shot him dead." And in the other version, gang member Jim Cummins was messing with Ed's girl, a quarrel resulted, and Jesse, siding with Cummins, killed Ed. Either way, Ed Miller was shot dead and his body was left by the side of a road.

Whether his corpse was eventually laid in a grave is another matter. But the story about his alleged death found its way into a newspaper based on information provided by "ex-bushwackers [sic] and friends of all parties from Clay and Jackson counties" and was believed to be accurate.[41]

But was it accurate? Was Ed Miller really shot down like a dog? A note on the web site www.findagrave.com claims that "according to family history," Ed Miller's death was "faked" by himself and Jesse James as a way to get him out of the gang and secretly take him away safely to Kentucky "where he lived the rest of his life." Interestingly, the memorial lists his burial site as "unknown."[42]

And there is further confusion in the record. Jesse also claimed that Miller had become "seriously ill and had decided to go to Hot Springs, Arkansas for his health." But it was thought that this was a convenient lie told to cover up the fact that Ed was dead, and when he was pressed by Jim Cummins, Jesse said that "Ed was in East Tennessee" due to illness and, sadly, he would not recover.[43]

Shot dead or simply disappeared, outlaw Ed Miller was gone for good. But the mystery lingered on until at least 1896. In September of that year, when the ground behind a St. Joseph house where Jesse James had lived with his family was being excavated, a skeleton—believed to be that of a middle-aged man—was found. It had been buried without the benefit of a coffin "or any preparation whatever." Knowing men theorized that they had discovered the body of gang member, killed by Jesse, and the name of Ed Miller came up again, because "it is the belief of friends that he [Ed Miller] was made way with by Jesse James."[44] Maybe he was and maybe he wasn't.

Under the alias "J. T. Jackson," Jesse James brought his family out of Nashville to Kansas City where they rented a four-room house. He carried on as if he was simply a gambler but all the while he and his gang were plotting a major train robbery. On July 15, 1881, Jesse and Frank, along with gang members Wood and Clarence Hite and Dick Liddil, boarded a Rock Island and Pacific train at either Cameron or Winston, Missouri. With the train still moving, and after the command "Hands up!" Jesse shot and killed the conductor William Westfall who may have been reaching for a pistol or who may have been killed simply because he "was slow in complying" with the command to raise his hands. After the train had stopped, the robbers ordered the U.S. Express Company agent to open the safe. He did as commanded, and to the dismay of the robbers, their payday amounted to a paltry $130 per man.

Both the Rock Island officials and a Pinkerton detective insisted that "the work was undoubtedly done by Frank and Jesse James who are the only survivors of the famous James and Younger gang." But it was a dismal day for the "famous" James gang. They had robbed the wrong train and killed William Westfall, the conductor, and a passenger, Frank McMillan, who looked up when he should have ducked. Robbery along with murder meant each man had committed a capital crime for which the penalty was death.[45]

This latest brazen train robbery, known as the Winston robbery, that resulted in the death of two men aroused the public, press and law enforcement to a fever pitch. The governor, a former Union Civil War officer, Thomas T. Crittenden, was facing tremendous pressure to act in a manner that would once and for all rid Missouri of the scourge otherwise known as the James brothers. For too long the state had labored under the moniker "The Bandit State." That had to change. As time went on, Crittenden would step up and take action.

Still there were some men who liked the edgy excitement provided by the famous bandits. One of them, James W. Buel, a St. Louis writer and journalist, penned and published a book entitled *Border Outlaws* in 1881. Included in the book were, of course, the James brothers. Buel dutifully sent a copy to Frank James through an intermediary who was related to the eldest James brother. Frank sent a letter to Buel acknowledging receipt of the book.

Not long after that, the relative of Frank James went to St. Louis, met Buel and the two men discussed a proposition put forth by the relative. Later Buel spoke to his publisher "upon the advantages which we might reap by a sudden stimulation in the sale of *Border Outlaws*, for which he [the relative] was then acting as an agent." Buel went on to explain the details of the hot deal. It was known that Frank James and Jim Cummins were making plans to pull off another sensational robbery, one that would set off another wave of excitement. The relative would provide Buel with all the juicy details of the robbery and Buel could use the information as an appendix to a new edition of *Border Outlaws*. If he issued the new edition "contemporaneously with the newspaper reports," sales of the book would soar, making money for all concerned. The publisher wisely rejected the offer, but the naming of names satisfied Buel that Frank James and Jim Cummins were involved in the Winston robbery.[46]

Then, in August of 1881, a report from a faraway newspaper informed America that Jesse James was back in Dakota, this time at Grand Forks, in the far northern reaches of the territory. A man from Northfield, who had photograph of Jesse, was certain that he saw the famous, and seemingly ubiquitous, outlaw "accompanied by several suspicious companions." Large sums of money were just then filtering into Dakota "for investment and to handle the crops." Fittingly, all the leading banks were alerted. People got ready. But there were the usual problems with this latest Jesse James sighting. The man believed to be Jesse James was described as over six feet tall and more than 160 pound with a finger missing from his left hand. On the whole the man thought to be an outlaw was too big to be the real Jesse James even though he too was missing part of a finger on his left hand.[47]

There was some other criminal activity by the James brothers that summer of 1881, but not in northern Dakota. By November, it was reported that they and their families were "IN CLOVER" in Nelson County, Kentucky, where they had lived in the post-war years. Among friends in the town of Bardstown, they moved about openly and freely. A newspaper correspondent noted, having talked to an acquaintance of the James brothers, "that a goodly part of their earnings is annually paid to the police force of St. Louis, Kansas City and other places." Furthermore they had spies at all the "detective agencies and no movement for their capture is unknown to them."[48]

12. The Dark River

They roamed freely and without fear among the heavily wooded hills and rocky ravines, near the Salt River, within a mere 15 miles of Bardstown. Although there were only 50 miles from Louisville, "the outlaws were perfectly secure in the retreat," where they camped, divided their booty, and shot intruders. With a line of guards stretched all the way to Louisville, the James brothers could detect "any sign of a detective campaign" against them.[49]

They had protection in high places in Nelson County too. One protector was the sheriff, Don Pence, who, during the late war, had proudly ridden with Quantrill. During a skirmish with Union soldiers, Pence (also spelled Penz) was wounded. Frank James rescued the young man at the risk of his own life and took him to a place of safety in Nelson County where he recovered and over time became a "good citizen." Pence was "but one of hundreds of friends of the James boys in this [Nelson] county." The journalist declared: "it is safe to say that a thousand men could not capture the outlaws if they chose to remain in this vicinity." Besides, he added, "the people here all believe that the James boys will do no robbing in this vicinity."

And there was more to report. A "lady friend of the James boys" told a reporter for the *Courier Journal* that Jesse was about to make a very aggressive play. He had every intention of going to Chicago to kill "Pinkerton, chief of the Chicago detectives" to avenge the death of his brother Archie and the disabling injury to his mother. The lady was referring to the time when a Pinkerton agent threw "a shell into his mother's room," shattering her arm and killing his younger brother. The "lady friend" also informed the reporter that the James brothers and their families only associated with the upper-class people of Kentucky and Missouri, people who would not betray them for a reward. The "high-toned" folks included former Confederate army officers who, under no circumstances, would do or say anything detrimental to their former comrades in arms, the James brothers.[50]

In Missouri, Jesse James made headlines in *The Sedalia Weekly Bazoo* on October 18, 1881. And if the article speaks the truth, Jesse had strayed away from his Kentucky safe-haven. In Rich Hill, an old settler who claimed to have known Jesse for 30 years, including a stint as his school teacher, swore he saw the notorious outlaw and "was willing to make an affidavit" to that effect. The poor fellow was "trembling with fear when he conveyed the news to the bank officer" of the Rich Hill bank. Then the old settler saw Jesse a second time that day, riding on a "spirited bay horse," with a companion riding beside him. As if expecting a robbery, banks in the region were telegraphed and warned. A spasm of fear generated by the supposed sighting of the king of bandits caused a terrible "furor of excitement" to surge through the community that autumn afternoon.[51]

The Rich Hill incident speaks volumes about the outlaw reputation of Jesse James. He had been successful for so long and maybe he believed he was invincible. But he was a mere mortal and it would have been wise for him and his family to remain in Nelson County, Kentucky, where prospects were such that they could have all lived happily ever after. But Jesse took his family out of Kentucky, and in less than six months from the report in the *Weekly Bazoo*, Jesse James would be dead, really and truly dead. And George Shepherd would not be in the spotlight for he had nothing to do with it.

13

A Desperado Dies

> "It is graphic both in statement and illustration of this sensational tragedy that terminates the long and wonderful career of this noted outlaw."
> —*Weekly Graphic* (Kirksville, Adair County, MO), April 14, 1882

On Christmas Eve, 1881, Jesse James—using the alias T. D. Howard—and his family moved into a house in St. Joseph, Missouri, in what was known as the "Cracker Neck district."[1] An 1882 directory contained a listing for a "Thomas Howard," but "no avocation was given."[2] While this seems curiously funny in retrospect, at the time the directory was published, it did not draw suspicion. Outwardly, at least, the Howard family was happy and doing well in a friendly and peaceful neighborhood.

So unsuspecting were the people of St. Joseph that "Mr. Howard" rode on a "blooded horse" with his young son in a "municipal procession" led by a squad of city policemen.[3] It was also reported that the affable Mr. Howard, following a winter storm, engaged in a lively snowball fight with a group of young ladies at 1320 Lafayette Street one afternoon. As it turned out he outgunned the girls and "with loud screams of laughter" they turned and ran from "the domesticated guerrilla" who, in "close pursuit," was "showering snow on the heads of the fleeing bevy of beauties."[4]

The Howard house, at 1318 Lafayette Street, was rented for $14 per month. It was situated on a hill that offered a nice view in all directions, a convenient feature for a man who is always looking over his shoulder. It was a small, plain, one-story house that "was well situated for defense and retreat,"[5] and would prove to be the last residence of Jesse James. In their new dwelling place, the James family passed a pleasant Christmas together with the father playing Santa Claus. The yuletide celebration went convincingly well until young Jesse Edwards discovered that Santa had a brace of Smith and Wessons strapped around his waist.[6]

Good cheer, however, was rapidly eroding in the James household. For not long after the holiday season ended, men secretly gathered together to plan the capture or the death of Jesse James. The leader of the major undertaking was none other than Thomas T. Crittenden, the governor of Missouri. Crittenden was laboring under his very own painful and inconvenient truth: his adopted state, his Missouri, was nicknamed "The Bandit State." The rib and ridicule that attended the label was deemed wholly unacceptable by the governor, a man with political ambitions willing to take great risks in order to work his way up the ladder. In his inaugural address, Crittenden strongly condemned the outlaw element in Missouri, vowing to cleanse the state of "lawlessness of any character."[7] He wanted to make Missouri as "safe to dwell in as New York or Massachusetts."[8]

Crittenden—a member of a prestigious Kentucky family—served the Union in the Civil War after being appointed a colonel of the 7th Missouri State Militia Cavalry, so he had no Southern sympathies to toy with. He was the nephew of the powerful Senator John J. Crittenden of Kentucky, the man who had worked desperately on a grand compromise that he hoped would prevent war between the North and South. It failed and the war came and the ravenous grim reaper was turned loose upon the land. Two of the senator's son served in the war, one for the North and the other for the South.

Thomas T. Crittenden ran for governor of Missouri as a Democrat in 1880 and was elected. But he was beset with problems from the outset of his term, because the Democratic Party had been soft on, or sympathetic to, the Confederacy during the late war, and the party was widely blamed for allowing lawlessness to fester in Missouri in the post-war years. The Republicans and their friends in the press made it a political issue that dogged Crittenden night and day. The tipping point was the robbing of the Chicago, Rock Island and Pacific Railroad in July of 1881, known as the Winston robbery, where two innocent men were murdered. This heinous crime outraged the press and public, testing their patience as never before.[9]

And again, the names Frank and Jesse James came up when it was time to assign blame for the terrible crime. No one knew it at the time, but the 1880s would prove to be the most violent decade in Missouri history, with both "lynchings and legal executions" reaching historic heights.[10]

Pressure was placed directly on the governor, forcing him to act quickly and effectively. It has been charged that Crittenden chose to dip into the well of polluted waters for help. To deal with Jesse James, he needed an assassin and he brought into his plan a pair of young outlaws, Robert and Charlie Ford. The plan was simple: the Ford brothers would kill Jesse James and the governor would hold his nose and issue a pardon if and when they were convicted and sentenced for the crime of murder.

It has been written that the Ford brothers met privately with the governor and Clay County sheriff James H. Timberlake on January 13, 1882, at a Kansas City hotel where strategy was discussed. The Fords agreed to assist the sheriff and governor in rounding up outlaws, including and especially Frank and Jesse James. They were to receive "$10,000 apiece for Jesse and Frank, dead or alive," according to Bob Ford, but the governor later insisted that the reward money was for the capture, only, of the notorious and legendary brothers.[11]

Another story about their cloak and dagger meeting emerges from a Louisiana newspaper. It contends that on February 22, 1882, the secretive governor, under the stealth of night, spoke to "Mysterious Bob," who agreed to come to the St. James Hotel, room number 17, at 9 o'clock the next morning. Bob Ford was there at the appointed time and at that meeting, he pledged to "deliver Jesse James dead or alive."[12] A Michigan newspaper agreed with the foregoing, and added that Ford was to "receive one-fourth of the reward and immunity."[13] In an even more bizarre newspaper report, it was hinted that a "veiled woman in black," who the governor acknowledged had come to him on February 16, 1882, was really Bob Ford in disguise.[14]

The man who needed no disguise was Sheriff Timberlake. A large, broad-shouldered man with a domineering personality and a dark-eyed countenance to match, Timberlake was known by friend and foe to be strong, brave and fearless. He was a Civil War veteran devoted to his work as a lawman, and in his pursuit of lawbreakers, Timberlake was determined and relentless. He instilled "fear in the hearts of desperadoes." Even a clever man like Jesse James had to be concerned because the lawman with a "black, drooping mustache" was more than a match for any outlaw.[15]

Many years after the offer of the reward, Finis C. Farr, at one time the private secretary of Governor Crittenden, sat for an extensive interview for an article in a Kansas City newspaper in 1895. He wanted to cut through years of speculation, false reporting and dark intrigue, and set the record straight. "I probably know more about the circumstances leading up to the death of Jesse James than any other man except Gov. Crittenden," he said. Farr went on to say that Crittenden had been bedeviled by the public and press over lawlessness and especially the crimes of the James gang. He had to take action, and it was the Winston train robbery, where two men were killed, that prodded him into making a plan.

According to Farr, the governor's options were very limited, because the state law placed a $200 cap on a reward for the capture of an outlaw, a sum that most bounty hunters or outlaw turncoats would scoff at. The governor met with representatives from railroads and express companies and they were willing to put up serious cash. With money available, the governor then issued a proclamation offering a $10,000 reward for the apprehension of Jesse and Frank James, and other key members of the James gang including Dick Liddil, Wood Hite and Jim Cummins. An additional $10,000 would be paid for the conviction of Frank or Jesse James in connection with the Winston robbery. There was no "dead or alive" clause attached to the offer, because the governor had no authority to do so.

Dangling that kind of cash in public was certain to get the attention of all kinds of men, and it attracted Bob Ford to the table. Farr and Ford met with Sheriff Timberlake, who, along with Henry H. Craig, the police commissioner of Kansas City, was one of the governor's strongest allies. (Farr did not say that Crittenden was at the meeting.) Ford told Timberlake that Jesse James was hiding out somewhere in northwest Missouri and that his brother Charlie was with Jesse. Ford also informed the sheriff: "I believe Jesse will be after me before long to help him hold up something." According to Timberlake, Bob Ford "seemed anxious to earn the reward." The sheriff instructed Ford to "go with Jesse" and then report on the outlaw's location by mail or telegram. "Nothing was said about the killing of Jesse James nor was it thought of," according to Farr.[16] Crittenden himself also emphatically denied that there was a plan to kill Jesse James, saying, "I would be the last to think of such a thing."[17]

Crittenden put his foot down on at least one other occasion. It came when Mattie Collins, the girlfriend or wife of Dick Liddil, came before the governor and attempted to negotiate the terms of her man's surrender. Liddil's tenuous position was characterized as this: he "feared the law less than he did Jesse." Crittenden would make no deal. He told Mattie that "if Liddil surrenders, he must do so unconditionally."[18]

Through the medium of his lady, Liddil was handed an ultimatum: surrender to the law or get killed by Jesse James. He finally did give himself up on January 24, 1882, but the arrest was not publicized so that Jesse James would not learn of Liddil's surrender.[19] As it turned out surrendering was probably a wise decision. A correspondent claimed that Mattie Collins possessed a letter purportedly from Jesse James that contained a powerful threat: Jesse would stay "in this country until he had killed Dick Little [sic]" and after Dick was dead, Jesse and Frank and their families "would put the Atlantic Ocean between them and the United States."[20]

Farr repeated much of what he said in the 1895 interview in one given in 1902, once again saying "there is not a syllable of truth" to the report that

Governor Crittenden offered money for Jesse James "dead or alive." He added this stark statement: "Bob Ford killed Jesse James through terror of being killed himself." Ford told the governor about his intense fear of Jesse and "we never had cause to suspect the truth of his assertion."[21]

The statements of Farr and Crittenden were corroborated by M. H. Stevens who at the time of the so-called plot was the managing editor for *The Kansas City Journal*. Stevens said that he attended a meeting at Henry H. Craig's office "when Bob Ford started out on his mission of bringing Jesse James to justice." He recalled that Ford was instructed to "shoot in self-defense, but not to assassinate" Jesse James. Stevens always believed that the James boys were more "honorable than the Ford brothers."[22]

Concerning the reward money, a Jesse James biographer who had access to "official files at the state capital" stated that the sum of $5,000 was offered for the "apprehension of the outlaw" and another $5,000 "for his conviction in any court." The writer also concluded that Crittenden was not involved in a conspiracy or a plot to assassinate Jesse James.[23] Others back in the day believed that the governor had decided to fight fire with fire.

That Crittenden and the others wanted to put him out of business is certain, thus the undoing of Jesse James had begun. Charlie Ford, age 24, pretended to be one of his new outlaw allies. They hung out at the James residence in St. Joseph and he traveled with Jesse while they laid out plans for new bank robberies. In early March, Charlie suggested that his brother Bob, just 20 years old, be made a member of the new gang.[24]

It is curiously odd that a shrewd man like Jesse James would collude with the Ford brothers. They were shifty and sneaky, and all the while egotistical, overbearing and full of themselves. They were caught up and carried away by the romance of the outlaw experience and the high status they could claim by riding with a famous bandit chief. But to see them was enough to question their ability to handle that role. A reporter once described them as looking like "poor actors" or "underfed theological students."[25] In his own crazy way, Jesse was a man who valued courage, loyalty and trustworthiness, and he should have seen through them—as did his mother—and sent them packing. Maybe he was planning to use them and then kill them. Or maybe he "had a premonition of his fatal ending," as Kit Dalton, who claimed Jesse as a friend, once told reporter.[26]

Suddenly, one day, out of the clear blue, a small-town newspaper, demanding to be heard, tossed out an attention-getting headline: "Jesse James Mortally Wounded and Ed. Miller Killed." The sensational article—that had nothing to do with the Ford brothers—appeared on March 10, 1882, in the form of a special report. At a train depot in Kansas City, "a sheriff's officer worn out and splattered with mud, arrived from the west" with a report that was expected to "cause rejoicing in railroad circles." The officer claimed that a posse had trapped Jesse James and Ed Miller in a log cabin and a shootout ensued. In "a brief but bloody" fight, the "sheriff's officer claimed that Ed. Miller was instantly killed and that Jesse James received a large number of bullets" and was "mortally wounded."[27]

There was an immediate attempt to corroborate the report but the effort fell flat. Although Jesse James did indeed have but a short time to live, Ed Miller had been dead for more than a year, believed to have been murdered by Jesse himself, or if he was not killed he simply disappeared and remained well hidden. The outlandish claim made by the "sheriff's officer" had a very short life for there was no truth to it. A couple of outlaws could have been killed in a log cabin shootout but they were badly (or intentionally) misidentified.

Most likely, Crittenden did not assign any credibility to the story, nor did he let it get in the way of his grand plan to get Jesse James. But according to Finis C. Farr, Bob Ford failed to contact Sheriff Timberlake as to the whereabouts of Jesse James.[28] With the concerned sheriff and his allies in the dark, the Ford brothers went ahead with their own plan to find a way to kill Jesse; they wanted nothing to do with trying to take him alive. That would be far too risky. So they kept their cool and waited for the right time and place.

The only time to take on a tiger is when he is off-guard and unaware. The time was the warm spring morning of April 3, 1882, with peach blossoms in bloom and the prospect of warm weather in the air. The place was the James house on the high hill in St. Joseph, the scene of what many called a cowardly betrayal. But for others it was, at long last, a hallelujah moment. Either way a powerful excitement was created that has long endured.

Sometime later, Bob Ford, freely and in great detail, told the following story to Governor Crittenden and Finis C. Farr. He started out by saying: "Mrs. James poured out the coffee then sat down at one end of the table." The Ford brothers, Jesse and his kids were seated as well. Jesse picked up a newspaper and, after glancing at it, he turned toward Bob and, with eyes ablaze, he told all those present that Dick Liddil, a member of the gang since 1879, had surrendered.

Of course Jesse was worried about what Liddil might say to the lawmen that would tend to incriminate him and Frank. A blanket of silence fell upon the breakfast table. Bob denied knowing anything about the surrender. Jesse's focus on Bob intensified for he knew that he had caught the young outlaw in a lie, for the denial was weakened by an expression of obvious fear. Jesse said the whole thing looked "fishy."

Bob got up and went into the front room, believing that some shooting was about to start and that he was about to die. "I knew I had not fooled him. He was too sharp for that. He knew at that moment ... that I was there to betray him," said Bob Ford to his eager listeners. Jesse followed him into the room, but instead of shooting, he acted as if he had a sudden change of heart, saying, "well, Bob, it's all right any way."

Then, strangely, Jesse "seemed to want to busy himself with something," he took off his pistol belt, "with four revolvers in it, and threw it on the bed." Then he picked up a duster and said "that picture is awful dusty." Without another word, he stepped up on a chair "and began to dust the picture on the wall." Up to that point, Bob said "the thought of killing him never entered my mind," but suddenly he knew right then and there that now was his best, and probably only, opportunity to kill Jesse James. Charlie had just entered the room. The legendary outlaw's back was turned toward the two men. Both men drew their pistols, but it was a nervous Bob Ford who fired, the bullet striking the back of Jesse's head, killing him. In talking about the incident later, Bob recalled "that there wasn't a speck of dust" on the picture.[29]

With Zee holding her dying husband's head in her arms, the Ford brothers rushed out the door and went straight to the telegraph office. While they were on their way, C. E. Flanders, the telegraph operator, stepped out of his office and glanced up at the "house on the bluff." Just then "the hill looked like an anthill with men swarming up its sides from all directions." Soon Charley and Bob Ford entered the telegraph office, and with the former nervously twisting his mustache, the latter, with grim determination, wrote out two telegrams, one to the governor and the other to the Kansas City chief of police.[30]

Finis C. Farr was alone in the governor's office when the telegram arrived there; Crittenden was away in St. Louis. Farr immediately telegraphed St. Joseph for more details and met with the governor who arrived on the noon train. Crittenden expressed great disappointment that the legendary outlaw had not been taken alive.[31]

But many private citizens didn't care. Soon St. Joseph streets were filled with anxious, inquisitive people. Soon all of Missouri was erupting in celebration, happy that the famed outlaw was dead but displeased with the governor because of the perceived classless manner of bringing about Jesse's death.[32] On the lighter side, a Kentucky newspaper suggested rather whimsically that the "Jesse James hat will be the next love-a-thing on the market."[33]

Jesse James was dead, killed by a gun he had gifted to Bob Ford—Governor Crittenden's "mysterious man."[34] The body was taken to William Siedenfaden's undertaking firm in St. Joseph for embalming and photographing. The opportunity to cash in on the famous death was not lost on the thrifty undertaker who charged the on-rushing mass of people 50 cents each to have a look at the dead outlaw.³⁵

Of course relatives, friends and acquaintances were anxious to view the remains. The famous outlaw's body—with two visible "bullet scars" near the nipple of his right breast—was positively identified by several knowledgeable people.³⁶ The missing fingertip on his left hand was also a dead giveaway. Dingus was dead. Among those who viewed the remains was former gang member Dick Liddil and his wife Mattie Collins,³⁷ Sheriff James H. Timberlake, Jesse's distraught mother, his weeping widow, and, of course, reporters.

On April 4, a reporter for *The Sedalia Weekly Bazoo* swooped down for interviews of anyone who was willing to talk. He first spoke to the Ford brothers whom he described as "mere youths." Without hesitation or mental reservation, the boys made a full confession, saying they killed Jesse James for the reward money. They were damned cocky and seemed proud of themselves as if they had done something heroic, something that would have widespread and wholesome ramifications. "We are all grit," said Charlie, "you never expected to see Jesse James' dead body in St. Joseph, but we thought we would create a sensation and put him out of the way."³⁸

Jesse James was killed by a gun he had gifted to Bob Ford, shot dead in a cowardly manner that dogged Ford to an early grave. And while Ford was not mourned, the entire nation, it seemed, was fixated on the dead bandit king. Jesse's body was taken to a local undertaking firm where it was embalmed and prepared for burial. Although many skeptics were prepared to come out of the woodwork, and deny that he was dead, the body was positively identified by a number knowledgeable people, including Jesse's mother and his grieving widow. At an inquest, a coroner's jury ruled that the body before it was that of Jesse James and that he had been murdered by Bob Ford. After a splashy funeral, his body was buried at the James–Samuel farm near Kearney, Missouri. Thereafter, everything touching the life and death of Jesse—including pebbles from his grave—was valuable (Library of Congress).

13. A Desperado Dies

Both Bob and Charlie believed, for certain, that the body of the famous outlaw would be stolen by grave robbers.[39] But it didn't take long for the Fords to lose their bravado. For they were soon arrested, and while behind bars, a disconsolate Bob told a reporter that "had he known that he would be thrown into a dingy cell he would not have killed Jessie [sic]."[40]

The *Bazoo* reporter sought out Zee James and she was free with her thoughts, although heavy with sorrow. At first she said the dead man was Howard, but she quickly admitted that it was her husband, Jesse James, who had been killed. She said, "the deed is done, and why should I keep quiet any longer?" Then she pointedly said that the Ford brothers were responsible, but admitted that "little did I think they would ever kill him." Later, at the inquest, under oath, she said that not more than three minutes after her husband had left the kitchen, "I heard a pistol shot."[41]

The legal process was quickly set in motion for the purpose of announcing that Jesse James was "legally dead" and to determine the cause of death. The coroner's jury met on April 4 to take testimony. They deliberated and returned a verdict: the body before them was that of Jesse James, he was the victim of murder, and a charge of first degree murder was lodged against Robert Ford, a man whom many believed was in mortal danger "from members of the gang."[42] Among them was Dick Liddil, who identified the body because of the missing fingertip.[43] The sneaky Liddil, who was accused of being a part of the plot to bring down Jesse,[44] was quoted as saying, "I would know his [Jesse James] hide in a tan-yard."[45] Liddil may have been thinking about money too, for a Missouri newspaper declared that the body of Jesse James was "That $10,000 Corpse."[46]

Another key figure at the inquest was the one-armed mother of the dead outlaw, who had taken an early train to St. Joseph. When the train stopped at Camden, "some crank attempted to shoot Mrs. Samuel." This cowardly act, against "a defenseless woman," who had just lost her son, aroused the fury of the editor of a Ray County, Missouri, newspaper. The perpetrator was denounced as "a disgrace to the race they belong to."[47]

When she arrived in St. Joseph, Mrs. Samuel, "a large woman with a kindly face and eyes, and a rather prominent nose," caught and held the attention of all observers. All eyes were on the large woman, dressed in black and "partially veiled," and she "moved with a slow step and bowed head to the witness stand." When asked by the coroner during the inquest if the body she had just looked down upon was that of her son Jesse, she said, "It is. And then she added, "And would to God it were not." Then placing her hands on her two grandchildren, she said, "And these are his orphan children."[48]

As Zerelda was leaving the witness stand, she turned and noticed Liddil standing in the doorway. With her angry eyes fixed on the outlaw who once rode with Jesse, she let him have it "with the ferociousness of a tiger." Zerelda Samuel shouted, "Traitor! Traitor! Traitor! God will send vengeance on you for this. You are the cause of all this, oh you Villain!" Liddil (referred to as Little in the article) cringed and shrank like "a whipped dog," all the while denying any blame for the death of Jesse James.[49]

The inquest ended but there was still one important step to be taken. The governor had deputized William H. Wallace, the respected Kansas City attorney, to travel to St. Joseph and view the remains of the dead outlaw. Wallace, who was acquainted with Jesse James, took a close and careful look and knew he was looking at the body of Jesse James. The governor was telegraphed that the body of the famous outlaw had been officially identified. Satisfied and relieved, Crittenden sent word to the local authorities to turn the remains over to the widow and mother for burial.[50]

Speaking somewhat gravely from Jefferson City, the Missouri capital, Governor Crittenden said: "I am satisfied that Missouri will never be bothered with Jesse James again." He went on to say, rather weakly, that more than once he had thought of abandoning the plan, for he had experienced much difficulty in getting men to "work together and keep at it." Crittenden teasingly promised to reveal details of "my mysterious man Bob, as they call him, [who] did the work." But for now he simply said, "I am not at liberty to tell."[51] Of course the governor didn't have to say anything more, for the story poured out in the nation's presses with a Niagara-like fury.

It would take time for the fiery Zerelda Samuel—once referred to as "a general in petticoats"—to wind down from her high state of grief and anger.[52] Her beloved son had lived and died in the manner of a desperado and she was forced to grieve in the macabre circus atmosphere that swirled madly throughout the nation. Of the many bizarre incidents that weighed heavily on Zerelda, none could cause more torment than the telegram sent to her and Jesse's widow, with an offer to purchase the outlaw's body for the sum of $10,000. The offer came from a "meat preserving company" in Cincinnati. "They propose … to treat it by their process and then exhibit as an advertisement."[53] The company, also called an "embalming firm," promised to pay the two women a generous share of the $100,000 it expected to make from the morbid sideshow.[54]

The dead outlaw's coffined body never left Missouri. It traveled by train, in the baggage car, to Kearney, stopping in the town of Cameron where it remained for the night. "By a strange coincidence it [the body] was placed in exactly the same position as that occupied by the body of [William] Westfall the conductor," who had been killed by the James gang during the Winston train robbery.[55]

When the body arrived at the depot in Kearney, a large group of people were there, including Zerelda Samuel. Upon seeing the body of her beloved Jesse, she let her feelings show; holding back nothing she told a reporter, "I knew it had to come, but my boy Jesse is better off in heaven to-day than he would be here with us." Later, at the Kearney House, a hotel, the body was viewed by other family members and friends, amid "shrieks, moans and curses." The grieving mother seemingly lost all control, and a distraught Dr. Samuel struggled to get his wife away from the body of her son.[56]

Sam Kaufman, called a "noted desperado," a man who once rode with Jesse James, arrived at the hotel with a party of comrades to view the remains of his former outlaw mate. Kaufman responded to a telegram sent to him by Luther James, a cousin of the deceased.[57] Another curious visitor was the mother of Clell and Ed Miller, both of whom died violent deaths—Clell in Northfield, Minnesota, and Ed by none other than the man whose body she looked upon in silence, "her palsied lips refused to speak her thoughts."[58]

Jesse James was buried at the James–Samuel farm near Kearney, Missouri, the place of his birth, in the presence of family and friends. His favorite hymn, "What a Friend We Have in Jesus," was performed. Among the pallbearers was, oddly enough, Sheriff Timberlake.[59] Brother Frank did not attend the funeral, as he was out of town, but it was generally believed that he would "avenge Jesse's death."[60] In 1901, a newspaper reporter wrote that Frank attended the funeral "in disguise."[61]

It was a memorable funeral, one that the James family would not soon forget. In 1902, Luther James, who attended the funeral, was interviewed by *The St. Louis Globe-Democrat*, for the purpose of correcting "accepted history." But rather than illuminating that sad part of the past, he turned it into a horror story. Luther claimed that he was in charge of the body of his cousin Jesse, telling the reporter that "some of my relatives were too good ... to have anything to do with the family, but I was not." He went on to say that when he and Sheriff Timberlake opened the casket so that Jesse's half-brother, Johnny Samuel, could view the body, "to our horror we found there were no limbs on the body, the limbs having been taken off at St. Joseph." The sheriff replaced the cover on the casket, and when Zerelda Samuel demanded that it be reopened so she could see the mutilated remains, Timberlake said that reopening would be impossible because he "broke off one of the bolts" that fastened the cover to the casket. Luther closed his interview by saying that Mrs. Samuel "has worried" about the matter "all through her life since."[62]

Luther James was a minor player in the drama surrounding the tumultuous life and death of his larger-than-life cousin, Jesse James. He was just a tiny flicker, barely a flame at all, compared to the conflagration, the wild blaze that carried his cousin onto the pages of history. Why he would want to come up with a story that is patently false, and bizarre in the extreme, is either a question for the ages, or something better left alone for all time to come.

In the aftermath of the shooting death of Jesse James, excitement and consternation ruled the day for many days. The small death house on the big hill was visited by many "traveling men and theatrical people." The carpet where Jesse's body had laid dead was cut up "into little chunks by momento-hunters [sic]." The woman who owned the house opened it to the public and charged people 25 cents each to see the room "where the outlaw fell."[63]

But soon after the death of her infamous tenant, the widow landlady Henrietta Salzman launched a complaint against the state and its "agents" for

The grave of Jesse Woodson James became a tourist attraction with people coming to visit the site from all over America. There was some concern that the grave might be robbed, and for that reason, Jesse's mother Zerelda Samuel watched it like a hawk. She placed host to people who came to visit the grave, giving tours that included a look into the log house where the family had once lived. Sad over her loss but sensing a money-making opportunity, she charged tourists twenty-five cents to visit the grave and another twenty-five cents for a photograph of the grave. Young Jesse was involved too, selling pebbles from his father's grave to gullible visitors. In 1902, the bones of Jesse Woodson James were exhumed at what can best be described as a media event, and reburied at Mt. Olivet Cemetery in Kearney, Missouri (The State Historical Society of Missouri).

nearly wrecking the house and carrying away "the greater part of her house." She claimed that the damage done to her property amounted to $2,000 and she demanded that the state cover the loss.[64] Clearly, she was thinking short term, but there was no way she or any other person could have foreseen the intense public fascination with the death house of Jesse James. The plain, little house on Lafayette Street became a tangible, lasting representation of the wild times of the legendary outlaw.

When an ordinary man or woman was shot and killed, he or she was simply the victim of murder, an ordinary killing. But when a person highly placed, or when one who wore the crown of celebrity, was shot to death, that person was not simply murdered: that person was assassinated, apparently a more stylish—an elitist—way to die. And of course this particular assassination, the shocking demise of the outlaw celebrity Jesse James, set in motion the presses of the nation.

Reaction to the shooting varied wildly. The associated press picked up the story and newspapers were not slow in spreading the news, although one Arizona Territory newspaper, *The Arizona Weekly Enterprise*, called the report "improbable." It noted that "press agents have reported this man killed no less than a dozen times" over the past few years, and, as such, the story should be taken "with a large grain of allowance."[65]

But to other newspapermen, there was no allowance for skepticism. And to no one's surprise, the editorial thrust by John Newman Edwards easily surpassed all others in terms of its passion, pathos and verbal gymnastics. Calling Jesse James a "wonderful outlaw," acting in the role that fate created for him, Edwards condemned the conspirators and assassins in the strongest terms: it was murder, plain and simple, done by "cowards" for "blood money." The white-hot article admitted that Jesse James had been an outlaw, but it was not his fault, "fate made him so." His aggressive character had been molded in the fiery crucible of the late war. After the war ended, he was hunted mercilessly so he instinctively fought back, as was his nature. Praising the dead outlaw while condemning the man who killed him, Edwards declared that the heroic Jesse James would not have been taken had he not disarmed himself. "Would to God he were alive to make a righteous butchery of a few more" of those who had hunted him and had given him no peace. Then, exceeding the bounds of good journalism, and sounding a warning, the article angrily declared that "sooner or later there comes a day of vengeance."[66]

Another Kentucky newspaper took a more optimistic approach, saying that when news of the outlaw's death was made public, the value of Missouri land immediately shot upward. "It was worth to the state millions of dollars for the day after Jesse James died every foot of real estate in Western Missouri was worth ... at least forty percent more than the day before."[67]

The *National Tribune*, in Washington, D.C., came out with a thoughtful editorial that must have caused its readers to stop and think about the wisdom and justification of the act that brought down Jesse James. Although Jesse James was an outlaw and deserved to be punished, the editorial called killing of the famous outlaw an act that closely resembled "personal vengeance rather than the stern impersonal punishment of the law." The rash act "bodes no good for the future," and because it had aroused widespread sympathy for the dead outlaw and his family, would likely inspire some form of retaliation.[68]

The *Richmond Democrat*, from Ray County, Missouri, jumped on Governor Crittenden, calling him a coward for dashing off to Washington, D.C. Instead of staying in Missouri to deal with the aftermath of the shooting of Jesse James, he meekly slipped away, quitting "his post of duty" until such time as "matters become more quiet." Had he been a real man, he would have faced the music for having plotted "with the Ford boys to slay Jesse James." The article also took a colorful poke at Missouri's Democrats for having "clothed little Tom with the gubernatorial garment."[69]

The *Kansas City Journal*, no friend of the James boys, while ignoring the governor, solemnly declared: "The state of Missouri is at last rid of the most daring outlaw that has ever disgraced the Western country, Jesse James." Believing he deserved death "a thousand times over," the *Journal* scoffed at the "maudlin sympathy expressed for him by some people."[70]

In the north, *The Indiana State Sentinel* expressed great satisfaction that the well-known outlaw was, at long last, dead. Reaching deep into its journalistic arsenal, the *Sentinel* stated with ferocity: "And thus the bloodiest murderer the most incarnate fiend that ever cursed the land, was finally disposed of." The article then went on to lay dozens of murders at the now motionless feet of Jesse James. In closing, the writer coyly noted that, with Jesse James numbered among the dead, "it might be safe to run railroad trains through Missouri."[71]

The *New York Times* mocked and belittled those mourning Missourians who called Jesse James a hero, noting also that the "governor, who hired the Ford boys to shoot Mr. James, does not mourn to any great extent." The sarcastic editorial revealed that "three hundred and seven new male infant Missourians have been named" after the dead outlaw and that a Baptist church is to be built "in a leading Missouri town" as a memorial to his life.[72]

The editor of a Washington state newspaper wrote as if he were appalled at the "slobber and gush" from the teary-eyed masses that were unable to simply accept that "the scoundrel is finally brought to grief." Reminding his readers that the many victims of the guns of Jesse James should be the object of public concern and sympathy, not their treacherous killer, he snidely declared that a "wash basin" was needed to hold the tearful downpour from the sad eyes of the outlaw admirers. The editor even took a swipe at Jesse's widow, saying, "a world of sympathy is extended to the outlaw's wife," while a legion of sad weepers conveniently forgot that she had "aided and abetted" him for years.[73]

Although Jesse had once lived in Tennessee, it is clear from an article in a Memphis newspaper that he had enemies in that state. Commenting on his death, an article praised the "ending of a most cowardly and blood thirsty ruffian in a civilized State of the American Union. In all the records of brigandage and murder there is no instance more astounding than this of Jesse James."[74]

Perhaps the wry, pithy piece in *The Emporia Weekly News* best expressed the feelings of most thoughtful Americans: "The ends of poetic justice were never more fully served than when Jesse James died with his boots on."[75]

The reaction from the people who knew Jesse well varied from person to person. Many were greatly surprised to learn that "laid his revolvers down" just before he was shot. One man said that when Jesse slept, "he always had a revolver in his hand, and the slightest noise" would cause him to "jump up straight in bed and cock his weapon," for he was always "afraid of being betrayed." And if anyone was looking for an avenging angel, the explosive Mrs. Samuel was viewed as the candidate for the role. It was said in an interview: "Old Mrs. Samuel, Jesse's mother, will raise h-ll about this and will kill somebody before this thing is over. I tell you she is a holy terror," and she passed that form of willfulness on to "her boys, especially Jesse."[76]

A Dodge City, Kansas, newspaper had a different take on the significance of Jesse's death. It boldly declared that the demise of the famous outlaw would have profound political ramifications in Missouri, and all for the better. With Jesse gone, the state will abandon "Bourbonism," another word for the Democratic Party. "Democracy in Missouri has received a fatal blow," costing the party "thousands of votes." It was reasoned that the long-held sympathy for the dead outlaw had expired with his death and at long last people could expect political change.[77]

Suddenly, Governor Crittenden was the center of attention, and he did not seem to like it. The governor was hunted down at a hotel by a persistent reporter looking for an interview and an explanation. The weary governor was reluctant to talk, but succumbed. The reporter asked if "there was any arrangement between himself and Ford in the matter of the capture of Jesse James." His reply was weasel-wordy. "Put that in writing and let me answer in writing." The reporter pressed on and repeated the question in modified form, asking if there was any agreement between him and Ford "in regard to the killing of Jesse James." The governor mumbled something about being hungry and needing to eat, but at a later time and place, he would answer more questions. As he turned to walk away, the testy reporter asked when it was he met with Ford, to which Crittenden replied: "On the night of February 22nd." He added that it was at this time Ford presented a plan to capture Jesse James. In response to one final question, the governor said that it was his "friends" that put the reward money, meaning, of course, the railroads. Soon thereafter, the governor was safely alone in the dining room of the hotel where he could "refresh the inner man." It clearly had not been a pleasant exchange.[78]

About two weeks after the interview and the rather weak explanation, Crittenden made an official statement. "I have no excuse to make; no apologies to render to any living man for the part I played in this bloody drama." Rather than give in to his detractors, he said "the life of one honest, law-abiding man, however humble, is worth more to society and a state than a legion of Jesse Jameses." He concluded his carefully worded explanation by saying, "I am not regretful of his death, and have no words of censure for the boys who removed him. They deserve credit, is my candid, solemn opinion."[79]

The city of Sedalia came to the rescue of the beleaguered governor when, on May 15, 1882, it celebrated the death of Jesse James, while praising Governor Crittenden for his part in the matter. "A large and enthusiastic meeting was held at City Hall, for the purpose of endorsing Governor Crittenden's action ... in the removal of the notorious bandit, Jesse James." There was cheering, speech-making, back-slapping, glad-handing during the feel-good program attended by "democrats and republicans alike." The highlight of the evening was a speech by John I. Martin, one of the men in charge of the celebration. While confessing he was no orator, he lauded Crittenden "as the representative of law [and] order" and for having "wiped a stain from the escutcheon of this grand state" by bringing about the death of a "man who has so long been a blot and a curse on this commonwealth."

Another speaker, Colonel Richard Ritter, seemingly swept up in the moment, informed the world that "we are in favor of law and order." He noted that "there has been a lack of enforcement of the laws of Missouri," something that every honest man would have to admit. His "beloved Missouri has a bad name abroad. Why, even in Texas they throw it up to the Missourians that they hail from the robber state." For 15 years, Missouri citizens were forced to hear such slurs and insults. He went on, "even in Europe the people of Missouri are called outlaws" due to the criminal exploits of the James and Youngers. Ritter informed his audience that if Mrs. James "needed assistance, I might donate to her on behalf of humanity, not because she was the widow of Jesse James."

A wordy resolution was read to the crowd that wildly cheered its approval. It noted that for years desperadoes had freely committed crimes and had gone unpunished, despite efforts to put an end to the outrage. All efforts were without success until Governor Thomas T. Crittenden took matters in own hands: "by his prompt, brave and unflinching pursuit of these desperadoes has succeeded in landing some of them in the penitentiary" and by "removing" the "acknowledged leader of the bandits, Jesse James." In a splashy finish to the upbeat meeting, a final resolution was read and adopted "Resolved, That we, the citizens of Sedalia, in mass meeting assembled, do most emphatically endorse the action of Governor Crittenden in ridding the state of the curse and terror in the person of Jesse James."[80]

The Missouri legislature took a similar stance. A member of the House of Representatives introduced a rather poorly written resolution praising the method used to kill Jesse James. It read in part, "That in the death of Jesse James the State of Missouri has received a great benefit" and "We approve of the action of the Governor in breaking up and capturing and destroying this band of outlaws, and therefore, we are glad that Jesse James is dead."[81]

Many men believed that Crittenden had acted with courage and strength, but over time, his political career took a hard hit. For example, in 1886, President Grover Cleveland refused to appoint Crittenden to a political position because it "is believed in the East that Crittenden ... bargained with the Fords for the assassination of Jesse James." While allowing that Crittenden might be guiltless of such a conspiracy, "it is pretty generally believed in Missouri that the Fords were well paid for making away with Jesse James."[82]

Another Missouri newspaper responded to the Cleveland message by calling out the president and praising Crittenden, calling him an "honest, fearless executive" who "no more connived at the assassination of Jesse James than did the man in the moon."[83]

Crittenden left office in 1884. But before his term of office as governor ended, he all but admitted his political career was at an end. He was heard to say, rather mournfully, that he could not get elected to the office of coroner, anywhere in Missouri.[84] But he would never be arrested for his part in the death of Jesse James, even though a California newspaper pointed out that "neither under the United States Constitution nor those of any of the states is it permissible to procure the killing of even the worst ruffian by hired assassins." Still there was the fuzzy but prevailing belief that since Jesse James was a notorious outlaw, with a price on his head, anyone, even the governor, was free to kill him.[85]

14

A Gathering of Death Deniers and Myth Makers

"The Ford boys never killed Jesse James but they did kill somebody that looked like Jesse for the identification of the corpse as Jesse was complete."
—*The Caldwell Tribune* (Caldwell, ID),
May 16, 1891

Jesse James was deader than a proverbial doornail, as dead as he would ever be. His body was identified by many knowledgeable people, including those most qualified—his mother and wife—but it didn't take long for the death story take on a different aspect. On April 15, 1882, the *Blount County Democrat* from Marysville, Tennessee, came out with Jesse James assassination article simply entitled: "Killed Again." The cheeky, sarcastic piece alive with skepticism stated that "it is not at all improbable that the story will be contradicted in a day or two."[1]

Actually a contradiction occurred four days before the article in the *Democrat* was in print. Maybe Jesse James wasn't dead after all—maybe it was an elaborately staged hoax. Less than two weeks after he was reportedly assassinated, rumors were swirling in the press that took on the tune of a strange, discordant melody. The *Chicago Times* had a special correspondent in Missouri, investigating the circumstances of the shooting death of America's favorite outlaw celebrity. The reporter encountered many Missourians who "persist in the belief that it was not Jesse James who was killed."[2]

And so it began: the "Great Death Denial" and the making of an American myth. If a man is so well known and wildly popular, whether from the good or bad he does, and is therefore elevated in the public mind to celebrity status, there will emerge a segment of the population that deify this individual, blindly and feverishly believing that death is impossible. For any number of bizarre reasons, some people could not let go of Jesse James, for he had become larger than life—and death.

Two lines of thought emerged around the takedown of the legendary Missouri outlaw. Those who most happily accepted his death, and sought to profit from it, and those wishful thinking folks who denied his death and with their own motives and desires, pushed forward their "he faked his death" agenda, their bugles blasting a ridiculous rant that would be heard for decades. Because of this second group, there emerged from time to time, an old man who claimed he was the "real" Jesse James.

This convenient mythology picked up steam in the early 20th century, when, from time to time, an elderly man would claim to be Jesse James and would provide some lame story about how he faked his death. When a circus came to town, it was often accompanied by "an original Jesse James." Gullible people smiled, weakly but respectfully, nodding their approval while the claimant basked in the warm, phony celebrity. The tales of fake Jesses were often companioned with false claims about someone's father or grandfather who knew or rode with Jesse and played pool with him, or put horseshoes on his horses. The number of blacksmiths who came out of the woodwork was so large that a "wag," with tongue firmly in cheek, said that Jesse must have had dozens of horses and that their shoes were changed "twice a day."[3]

In 1930, an impostor claiming to be Jesse James showed up at a St. Joseph, Missouri, theater and asked if he go on stage and convince the audience that he was indeed the noted outlaw who had faked his death. The crowd was skeptical, causing the would-be star to say: "If I'm not Jesse James, then who am I?" When someone in the audience shouted, "Maybe Clara Bow," the place erupted in wild laughter, bringing an embarrassing end to the career of the impostor.[4]

In addition to the phonies and opportunists, there was a third group of people who were "on the fence," so to speak. Among them was a man who claimed that he went to the morgue to see for himself that the man he feared was actually dead. He asked the "morgue keeper" to permit him to view "all that is mortal of the honorable Jesse James." The morgue keeper led him to the slab where the dead outlaw's body was laid out and said: "Why did you call the dead man the honorable Jesse James?" The visitor promptly replied: "Because I wasn't quite certain he was dead."[5]

There were periods of time when calm seemed to have returned to Missouri, but everyone seemed to be on edge as if waiting for some new and startling revelation. Finally, in August of 1889, *The Sedalia Weekly Bazoo* jolted its readers with a bolt of journalistic lightning. "JESSE JAMES ALIVE" was the headline and wake up call.

News was received from a Philadelphia man, living quietly in that city, identified only as "R. Smith," to the effect that the "man killed by Bob Ford was not Jesse James, but rather "Sam Hill," a former gang member." R. Smith claimed to have been a boyhood friend of the James brothers and he knew them well enough to state with authority that had Bob Ford actually killed Jesse James, with the support of his brother Charlie, "Frank would have killed them." Smith, who claimed to have ridden with Quantrill, said that Sam Hill looked a lot like Jesse and that photographs of the two would bear this out. "I correspond regularly with Jesse and Frank James ... and less than ten days ago I received a letter from Jesse." Smith said that Ford killed Sam Hill "to get the reward and notoriety." As for Jesse James, Smith insisted with firmness: "I know he is alive."[6]

Two years after Smith made his bold statement, another man surfaced with his version of the "Sam Hill" theory. He too insisted that a substitute was killed, a gang member who looked like the twin of Jesse James, "whose resemblance to the outlaw chief was startling in every respect." The author of the claim created a few family members for Sam Hill, including a wife. They were all mystified because one day "Sam Hill left home for a short time ... and his family to this day has never seen or heard from him."[7]

The bizarre stories have many holes in them. First of all, "Sam Hill" sounds like a made-up name. Furthermore, the name does not come up in the literature about Jesse James, nor is it mentioned in countless other newspaper reports, so unless Hill was a very minor player in the outlaw saga, and therefore escaped all attention, he is pure fiction. The "Sam Hill" story only proves that if a man wanted to invent a Jesse James yarn, he could always find a reporter who would listen and write about it.

In 1900, many years after the "Sam Hill" story was forgotten, a man from Fort Worth, Texas, insisted that it was a detective—not a former gang member—that Bob Ford shot on April 3, 1882. The Texan said that Jesse James was very much alive, "running a grocery store near Trinidad, Colorado."[8]

For those who liked him dead, it could be argued that Jesse's death was a good career move that would provide income for his family. It would also be the golden opportunity for any number of enterprising men to make a quick buck. Within two weeks of his well-publicized funeral, the first book, *The Illustrated Lives and Adventures of Frank and Jesse James and the Younger Brothers, the Noted Western Outlaws*, was in print and available for purchase. It was promised that all those who loved the Wild West would not be disappointed, for the book included details of an outlaw's life of crime as well as "an exhaustive account of the recent successful pursuit of the robbers under the direction of Gov. Crittenden" that resulted in the killing of the star of the book, Jesse James.

14. The Gathering of Death Deniers and Myth Makers

"JESSE JAMES IS DEAD" shouted the advertisement in the *Weekly Graphic* out of Kirksville, Adair County, Missouri. "In an age of rapid book making," agents were wanted to market the book by Dr. J. A. Dacus, Ph.D. "Profusely illustrated," the book was hyped to be "the most salable and profitable book published."[9] News of the book spread like wildfire as several other newspapers picked up the ad. The widespread interest in the Dacus book was a strong indicator that more were in the offing.

Word was out that the widow, Zee James, was "preparing or dictating" a biographical account of the criminal exploits of her late husband and his brother Frank. But when she was interviewed, she emphatically denied any such thing, declaring, instead, that "under no circumstances would I lend my name to any [such] publication." She was aware, however, that a publisher, J. H. Chambers, was working with Frank Triplett, a St. Louis writer, on a book about the notorious James brothers. But when asked if it was true that she was assisting Triplett, she again denied the allegation, saying: "this statement is absolute false."[10]

Triplett's book, entitled *The Life and Treacherous Death of Jesse James*, published by J. H. Chambers and Company, was hurriedly put together and released in May of 1882. In it Triplett states that, while involved in writing the book, he was aided by both Zee James and Zerelda Samuel. In the publishers' preface, it is stated: "The public may rest assured that in this work they are receiving the facts as dictated by Mrs. James and Mrs. Samuels [sic]."[11] Someone wasn't telling the truth.

A strange woman might have been fudging a bit when she claimed to have contacted the ghost of Jesse James. That woman was "Madam Silva, a well-known spiritual medium" in St. Louis who boasted of her ability to contact the dead, a practice that went hand-in-hand with wildly popular 19th century religious movement called Spiritualism. A newspaper reporter came to her place of business for the purpose of contacting the spirit of Charles Guiteau. Guiteau had been executed on June 30, 1882, for the assassination of U.S. president James A. Garfield. In life, Guiteau was a bit of a gadfly, a busy, self-absorbed man who dabbled in a number ventures, all of which had failed. On July 2, 1881, he shot Garfield in the back at a Washington, D.C., train station because of the president's refusal to give him a job. The president suffered for weeks before dying on September 19, 1881. After his arrest, Guiteau exhibited textbook signs of insanity, and yet he was tried, found guilty of murder, and hung.

Madam Silva asked the reporter to sit down at a wooden table, and then she contacted "a sister spirit" who "told her that the spirit of Charles Jules Guiteau had just arrived and they were making a great fuss over him." It seems that his sudden appearance, after having dropped "through the trap" of the gallows, attracted a number of his "old friends and cranks who rushed forward to greet him." The giddy Guiteau was excited to be questioned by familiar faces and he proved to be just as much a blabber-mouth in death as he was in life. Speaking through the voice of the medium, he gushed over "the beautiful place he was in" and his hopes for advancing a better place yet, but for now his hands were "tied with penitence." He also insisted, as he did over and over again when he was alive, that he was "not crazy," but that he was still a "crank."

The reporter asked if "he had seen anything of Jesse James since his arrival." Guiteau replied, "Yes, Jesse was one of the first to welcome me." Not long after that remark, "the interview was interrupted by Jesse James who heard his name called." Jesse then went on a tirade against Governor Crittenden, slamming him for his recent pardoning of some gamblers. Guiteau abruptly pushed Jesse aside and took charge of the conversation, mentioning that he had seen John Wilkes Booth, and telling the reporter that there was "no such place as hell." It should have struck the reporter as odd that three the evil spirits, Charles Guiteau, John Wilkes Booth and Jesse James, were in a place other than hell. But the reporter departed the mysterious chamber, having been promised a future interview with Guiteau "in his presence."[12] His flowery article was written without even the slightest hint of skepticism.

Nor was this the only time that Jesse allegedly emerged from the spirit world, for one night in Philadelphia, he shared center stage at a séance with none other than William Penn, the famous colonialist for whom Pennsylvania was named. The séance was conducted by Clarence F. Henshaw, a 28-year-old prodigal son of wealthy parents. Henshaw was known for his prowess as a billiard player and for his popularity among the young ladies.

It all started when Henshaw came home following a night on the town. "The family was aroused by a terrible racket in the front hall." Rushing toward that area, his father found his son "lying under the hatrack, with a lot of canes, umbrellas and chairs piled upon him." Suddenly, Clarence blurted out that the noise was the work of spirits, which his father declared was true: it was spirits the young man had consumed from a flask that caused the ruckus. But no, Clarence then and there declared that he had been given clairvoyant abilities. He soon set out to prove his newfound skills as a medium to gullible audiences.

Chairs were said to be flying through the air along with other otherwise inanimate objects during a séance in the parlor of the Henshaw home. Suddenly, the competing spirits of Jesse James and William Penn dominated the proceedings, each one desiring to "run the show." The matter was settled when "Jesse James vanquished his older opponent," after which Clarence declared that he "was under the influence of the great Missourian." But there was more for the excited audience to experience. "A snare drum was produced" and the youthful Clarence told those present that Jesse James would play "Marching through Georgia" on it.

A pair of skeptical young ladies coated the drumsticks with a liberal dose of printer's ink and put them in the cabinet, knowing that Henshaw, whose hands were tied, would sneak into the cabinet. The lights went out and soon Jesse could be heard beating the drums "like a circus player." After the performance the lights were turned on and Henshaw's hands were exposed, both covered with black ink. Henshaw offered an explanation that was "too thin" for the spectators. He had been exposed as a fraud and the twittering audience departed, knowing that Jesse James would not likely make another appearance in Philadelphia.[13]

Of the many tales, both short and tall, about Jesse James, one of the most unusual stories is about the "phantom horseman." Jesse was said to be superstitious and a believer in ghosts, and the apparition that concerned him the most was the "phantom horseman." The outlaw believed it was his "own peculiar banishee [sic]." Jesse was often heard to say that "the appearance of the apparition was intended as a warning or foreboded evil." The "phantom horseman" appeared out of nowhere one night in Kentucky, when Jesse and his friends were out riding. Suddenly, at a fork in the trail, "in the bright moonlight, sat a man on a coal black horse." Jesse drew his gun, but believing he was looking at a ghost, did not fire and rider turned and rode away. But the persistent spirit had attached itself to Jesse James and "is said to have appeared to him shortly before his death."[14]

In the weeks and months that followed the death of Jesse James, the dead outlaw remained in sharp focus in the mind of the public, members of the press, and, especially, the James family. It was even reported that Frank had recruited a gang of desperadoes from the "Missouri bottoms" and the mountains of New Mexico for the express purpose of hunting down and killing anyone associated with the death of Jesse James. The Ford brothers would know no rest or safe haven. But the plan went even further, and "all informants and witnesses in Cracker Neck" were marked for death. The report declared that "the death avengers are backed by the entire constituency of Jesse James."[15]

But the weary Frank James pursued no such plans. He was tired of the outlaw life. He was wanted to come out of hiding but was worried about being ambushed and killed for the reward money. He wanted to turn himself in but he was worried that he might be lynched or shot by a mob. The surviving

James brother, feeling the weight of the years, began communicating with the governor through a third party, John Newman Edwards, who called Frank his friend. Frank was assured that he would be treated fairly, meaning a fair trial, so with a sense of relief tempered by fear of conviction of the many crimes he had committed, in the company of Edwards, he surrendered, shook the governor's hand, unbuckled his pistol belt and handed it to Thomas T. Crittenden. The prisoner was taken to Independence, where he received a hero's welcome, and then he was turned over to the custody of the sheriff and charged with first degree murder, arising from the Winston train robbery.[16]

But Minnesota wanted Frank James in the worst way. When it was known that he had surrendered, Rice County officials sent Frank Wilcox to Independence, Missouri. His task was to take a look at the prisoner and then decide if he recognized Frank as one of the men who had held up the bank in Northfield in 1876, and, more important, if he was the man who had killed Joseph L. Heywood, the acting cashier. After seeing the prisoner, and talking to him, Wilcox returned to Minnesota and swore out an affidavit naming Frank James as the robber who shot and killed Heywood. On the strength of this affidavit, Minnesota governor Lucius F. Hubbard formally requested that Missouri turn Frank over to Rice County to stand trial for murder. Frank, of course, denied he had ever set foot in Minnesota.

The request for extradition was denied and Minnesota was left disappointed. Frank James would not hang in Minnesota for killing Heywood, but he would face justice in Missouri. In Gallatin, in September of 1883, at his trial for his role in the Winston train robbery, and, more particularly, for the murder of Frank McMillan, James provided a somewhat rambling account of his whereabouts and activities since the winter of 1876. With the court audience breathlessly hanging on every word, he spoke about wanting a safe place for his family to live, but he was not able to do so because he always seemed to be targeted and bedeviled by detectives. His testimony about his connection with his brother and other suspected outlaws was vague, as he clearly sought to convince the jury that he wanted nothing to do with their outlaw activities. Frank stated under oath that when the Winston robbery occurred he was far away in the "Indian nation" and stayed there for "about fifteen days."[17]

His well-rehearsed testimony along with his good legal representation and public support served Frank James well. At the trial in Gallatin, and another at Huntsville, Alabama, for robbery, he was acquitted. Finally, in March of 1885, his legal troubles ended, all other cases against him were dismissed.[18]

A relieved Frank James, at long last out of the shadow of a gallows,

14. The Gathering of Death Deniers and Myth Makers

despite his many crimes, was allowed to live out the rest of his life without fear of arrest. Still, he was no doubt haunted and troubled by his wayward past, knowing in his heart of hearts that he had committed multiple crimes, including murder, for which he had escaped just punishment. Sometime after the charges were dismissed against him, Frank met face to face with William H. Wallace, the tough-minded prosecutor. Wallace admitted that he had tried his "levelest [sic] to hang him but could not." But Wallace held no ill-will against the outlaw, hoping he would become a good citizen.[19]

He did become a good citizen, and he made a friend of Governor Crittenden, the man who put so much effort into the killing of Frank's brother, Jesse. After one of his acquittals, Frank gave the governor one of his dead brother's favorite pistols, the same one that he "laid aside when Bob Ford shot him in the back." It was said that Crittenden treasured the gift and carried it on him when he traveled.[20]

It was a strange gesture. Frank was able to divest himself of the pistol, but he was forever attached to the memory of his dead brother, with whom he had shared great hardship and

FRANK JAMES.

This newspaper illustration of Frank James was inserted into an article about one of his trials. Frank, who grew weary of hiding and dodging, had toyed with the idea of turning himself in to the authorities and submitting himself for trial for his many alleged crimes. Instead of avenging the death of his brother Jesse, Frank turned his attention to saving his own hide. Finally, with the aid of the outlaw-friendly journalist, John Newman Edwards, Frank surrendered to the Missouri governor, Thomas T. Crittenden. Minnesota tried to extradite him so he could stand trial for murder, but Governor Crittenden refused to allow it. Instead he was tried in September of 1883, in Gallatin, Missouri, for his role in the Winston train robbery, and to no one's surprise, he was acquitted. Next he faced charge of robbery in court in Huntsville, Alabama, and again was acquitted. Finally, in March of 1885, all charges against him were dismissed and Frank James was allowed to live out his days without fear of prosecution. In short, he had gambled and won, thus escaping just punishment for his many crimes, including murder (*The Butler Weekly Times*, Butler, Missouri).

danger, while the two men, devoted to each other, pulled off their remarkable escape from Northfield, Minnesota. Frank was alone and left with the memories of that hard and painful experience. While he spoke little of the outlaw life, he once told a listener that "we have been hungry with our pockets full of money" and that he and his brother had been "hunted like the wolves of the prairie."[21] Was he thinking back to September of 1876 and their valiant struggle to survive and evade death or capture on the Dakota frontier? Had he taken the time to write about their dangerous journey, or had he dictated the story to a ghost writer, what a book it would have made!

The death of the famous Missouri outlaw Jesse James had cast a pall of sorrow over his family and friends, but it proved to be the catalyst for many budding enterprises managed by men quick to see a money-making opportunity. His sizzling outlaw reputation would prove to have lasting and widespread appeal and a certain selling power. J. L. Miller, of Cloverport, Kentucky, the proprietor of a hardware store, saw and seized the opportunity. During the Christmas season of 1882, he launched an advertisement in a Cloverport newspaper in bold strokes: "JESSE JAMES was the greatest outlaw, and so is J. L. Miller the largest dealer in Stoves, Tinware and Hardware."[22] It was an interesting angle on the use of crime to promote a legitimate business.

J. L. Miller's gimmick was a modest start of what became a massive media and entertainment campaign under the Jesse James banner. Understanding the public interest in the life and death of the famous outlaw, and sensing a money-making opportunity, various shows and programs popped up like mushrooms in a damp forest. One of the earliest shows, staged in Louisiana in November of 1883, was soundly trounced and rebuked by a newspaper from that state. Without naming the "play" the sarcastic article noted that the show "represented the different scenes in James' illustrious career." The article went to mention a few, including "the maudlin drunken scenes in the way side bar room, the charming and beautiful scene where Jesse robs the ticket office at the Kansas City Fair, and his pals set fire to the building," all of which were "highly moral and ennobling." And if these scenes failed to provide enough thrills, one could enjoy the "act where the gang tied an unfortunate wretch to the back of a horse and drag [sic] him through the forest."

It was suggested by the writer of the article that the low-brow program should have included Governor Crittenden. It was regretted that a scene showing the governor "bartering in secret with the sneaking coward Bob Ford for the assassination of James" was missing, for it is "an act which ought [sic] by all means have been presented." The reporter that was forced to sit through the miserable and bumbling presentation ripped it up from start to finish, lambasting the producers of the "play" for heaping praise on Jesse

James, "the wholesale maker of widows and orphans." All in all, "this was too rich."[23]

Unfortunately for the virtue of good taste, heaping ridicule where it was more than appropriate failed to dim the ardor of the producers of such trash, nor did it discourage the growth of the fan base of Jesse James. The production of the "Bandit King," in St. Joseph, was next in line. It featured two horses, one of them named "Roan Charger" found in the stable of Jesse James. It was duly confiscated by the St. Joseph police until its legal ownership could be determined. The magnificent animal that impressed the audience had belonged to a "prominent farmer" and was stolen by Charlie Ford, who presented the horse to Jesse James.

After Jesse's untimely death, the "prominent farmer," upon hearing of the murder, made his way to the death house in St. Joseph, and seeing his horse in the stable, laid claim to it. Eventually the horse was returned to its rightful owner and was sold to a local man for $300, an amount deemed twice its actual value. Next, the horse named "Roan Charger" was sold to a wealthy New Yorker for a "fabulous sum." The new owner was very happy to possess "the horse that Jesse rode."[24] The New Yorker, wittingly or unwittingly, had joined hands with a growing crowd of believers in the great myth.

Horses were not the only form of contraband found at the residence of the late Jesse James. A watch that once adorned the vest pocket of John A. Burbank of Indiana, formerly the governor of Dakota Territory, was discovered among Jesse's possessions, with its owner's name engraved on it, courtesy of certain "territorial officers of Dakota."[25] One may wonder who these officers were, for the conniving Burbank was so unpopular in Dakota that he had been, in some respects, run out of the territory.

The beleaguered ex-governor was a passenger in a six-horse stagecoach bound for Hot Springs, Arkansas, in the spring of 1874. Years later Burbank recalled the incident, noting that the passengers were warned that there were highwaymen about and they might be held up. The former governor said there were six men and one woman on board the stagecoach. Each man was armed. Burbank said that he had a firm grip on a revolver in his "right overcoat pocket." As the stagecoach went on its way, the men boasted freely about how they would "slay a whole gang of robbers." But when the stage was stopped by the James gang, consisting of eight men, and the passengers were ordered to raise their hands, all the bravado vanished and every one of the men did so instantly. As Burbank told his interviewer, "obeying a highwayman comes as natural as winking."[26]

All the terrified passengers were lined up outside of the coach, and each was relived of money and other valuables. Burbank lost his watch, some cash, a ring and a diamond pin. It was a humiliating experience. Burbank was left dead broke but he wasn't dead. He was able to reclaim his stolen watch that had been on exhibition in St. Louis in the summer of 1882.[27]

Another watch, this one also engraved with the name of its owner, Judge R. H. Rountree, was discovered at the James residence. It was taken during a stagecoach robbery that occurred on September 3, 1880, between Mammoth Cave and Cave City, Kentucky. A man named Dr. Thomas J. Hunt, who bore a strong resemblance to Jesse James, was arrested, tried, convicted and sentenced to three years in prison for the robbery.[28] In addition to the judge, two other witnesses identified him "as the spokesman of the gang." Hunt's refusal to explain his whereabouts on the day of the robbery mystified everyone and hurt his cause.[29]

His lawyer moved for a new trial, and while the legal machinery was in motion, with Hunt behind bars, Jesse James was killed by Bob Ford. Charlie Ford told the authorities that the watch and other jewelry were taken from the judge and his daughter, "when Jesse robbed the Mammoth Cave stage in Kentucky."[30] Another source states that one of the Younger brothers, from his cell in the state prison at Stillwater, Minnesota, "made a confession of the Mammoth cave stage robbery" and told the authorities where to find the stolen items, and that this led to the exoneration of Hunt.[31]

When he was shown a picture of Jesse James, a shocked Judge Rountree said: "that man who took my watch looked so much like Hunt." The Kentucky governor was petitioned and Hunt was freed, having been arrested, charged and convicted because he was the "unlucky double" of the actual thief, whose death had cleared him.[32] Hunt may have felt cursed by the strange quirk of fate, his remarkable resemblance to the famous outlaw, but the odd connection brought him out of lifeless obscurity and, for a brief period of time, into the lively flow of journalistic discourse.

About three years after the death of Jesse James, his mother and his son, Jesse Edwards, were walking together on a Kansas City street. Suddenly, none other than Bob Ford appeared in front of them. The old spitfire immediately let him have it, giving him hell for the cowardly murder of her son. Ford seemed humbled and confessed that since he committed the foul deed, he "had been stricken with remorse." He begged to be forgiven; he told Zerelda Samuel that he and his brother had received "only a few hundred dollars" of the reward money. The old woman was apparently impressed by Ford's humility and sincerity. She said to him: "If God can forgive you, I can."[33] One wonders.

Among the unforgiven during the post-death years of Jesse James were the Younger brothers, all model prisoners in Stillwater, Minnesota, but with

14. The Gathering of Death Deniers and Myth Makers

little or no hope of being paroled or pardoned. But they were not forgotten, and in 1889, while Bob Younger was dying of tuberculosis, Cole Younger granted a reporter an extended interview in which he reprised the details of the Northfield raid and hardships the brothers suffered as they limped their way through the woods, marshes and over the undulating prairie, as if driven by some homeward instinct. "All of us," said Cole, "endured untold agonies from exposure, for it was cold and raining most of the time." In addition to fighting the elements, they were plagued by desperate pangs of hunger that "drove us to the farm houses for food."

When pressed by the reporter to identity other members of the gang, Cole stubbornly refused to do so. Although Charlie Pitts, Bill Chadwell and Clell Miller had been positively identified long ago, Cole still refused to admit that they were the gang members who had been killed. When he was reminded that Jesse James was dead and therefore confirming his role in the robbery would not "disgrace his [Jesse's] relatives," Cole clammed up, saying: "although our friends are gone we still owe an obligation to their surviving relatives not to speak their names. It would hurt innocent people and do no good."

As for himself and his brothers, Cole lamented the lack of forgiveness in some form. The governor of Minnesota bent the rules and allowed Jim Younger to grow a bushy mustache that concealed the ugly scar from the bullet wound inflicted at the shootout near Madelia.[34] That was considerate but it pained Cole that they were not accorded some substantial form of mercy, especially for Bob, who wanted very much to die among kinfolk in Missouri. There must have been a touch of sadness in Cole's eyes when he said: "I don't think that the fact that sensational stories have been told of us that we should be treated different from other men."[35]

15

Outlaw Stardom

"Jesse James was a man, Who from danger never ran, He robbed the railway train."
—*The Salt Lake Herald*, March 8, 1889

In the months and years following the death of Jesse James, the state of Missouri struggled to rid itself of the outlaw curse even though its most famous outlaw resident was dead. All the while the reputation of Jesse James was moving in high-gear, soaring to heights seldom, if ever, achieved by a criminal. If America had to choose its favorite outlaw, Jesse James would be selected. He was not only a celebrity, he was a hot commodity. Everything touching Jesse James was suddenly worth money. In the summer of 1890, the young son of the late outlaw, "little Jesse James," was making money by selling "pebbles from his father's grave to tourists."[1]

Pictures of Jesse's gravestone were a popular item among the thousands of tourists who came each year to visit his grave. His mother, Zerelda Samuel, was quick to grasp the money-making opportunity, charging curious folks 25 cents to visit the grave. The fee included a look at the log cabin that was "the former home of the James boys." And if someone wanted to take home a photograph of the gravestone, he or she was charged 50 cents.[2]

In life, the daring and dashing Jesse James had been so successful at crime that other criminals came to admire and emulate him. One such crook pulled off a bank robbery in Columbus Grove, Ohio, in the summer of 1891. He shot two men, killing one of them, and as he dashed out of the bank, he yelled for all to hear, "I am a second Jesse James." Unfortunately, the egotistical bank robber should have chosen another line of work; he wasn't as lucky or skillful as the man he revered, because he was "overtaken in the woods and shot to death."[3] For certain, he was no Jesse James. Jesse always got away.

The fortunes of the men who were responsible for his death—the Ford brothers—were destined to sag rather ingloriously, because their outlaw careers would turn out to be insignificant when compared that of their victim.

Not long after killing Jesse, the Fords were taken into custody. They were tried and convicted of murder and sentenced to hang, but Governor Crittenden, as many people expected, pardoned them almost immediately.[4]

At first it seemed as if the Ford brothers had some traction and were enjoying their high status for having bagged a larger-than-life outlaw. A Kentucky newspaper observed, "the Ford boys were pampered and toasted and receive friends and admirers in the most genial manner." They also expressed the belief that grave robbers would steal the body of Jesse James.[5]

Bob and Charlie hit the road and tried their best to capitalize on their newfound celebrity status, giving interviews that were like theatrical performances. In September of 1882, the Ford brothers were in New York, "on exhibition," at a Brooklyn museum.[6] They were later interviewed in Chicago en route to Kansas City where they would be tried for the murder of outlaw Wood Hite, a cousin of the James boys. They were both upbeat and cheerful, as if they were enjoying the star treatment. When asked about the probable fate of Frank James (who had surrendered), Bob said, "He is in a pretty bad fix." And even if Crittenden pardoned him, Frank was still "under indictment in Minnesota."[7]

In Cincinnati they were set to appear "on the boards at the Vine Street Opera House" in a short dramatic piece written for the Fords entitled "The Outlaws of Missouri." A large crowd of the curious was expected to see the brothers described as "quiet, modestly behaved young men, neither rough nor rustic in their carriage." Both were well spoken but the reporter noticed that Charles "seems rather weak" and willing to let Bob take the lead in the interview.

When asked how they were received in Missouri, one of the boys said that the people "seem well disposed toward us, with the exception of a few roughs. Those who knew the most of Jesse James liked him the least." They insisted that his death had brought economic benefits to the state in the form of increased land values and immigration. On the downside, the boys told the reporter that death threats against both of them, some "signed by Frank," were very disturbing and concerning. But, all in all, the Fords felt that they had to kill Jesse because taking him alive was impossible.[8]

In an interview in another city, Bob expressed some concern over his safety should Frank be released, saying, "the country isn't large enough to hold us both," and if they ever faced off, one of them would "croak." As for shooting Jesse, Bob said he had no "pangs of conscience about it." When asked about what they would do after their trial, Bob said that he and Charley would "play our engagements" in the Eastern cities and then "about January first we will sail for England."[9] Amazing! What kind of talent would it have taken to a write a play any better than the real life drama that was attracting a large and diverse audience.

The Fords concocted a "show" called "How I Killed Jesse James." It attracted a smattering of curious people but was not a success. After touring a number of cities under that banner, they returned to Missouri in 1884. By then Charlie Ford was terminally ill with tuberculosis and was addicted to morphine. He shot himself to death on May 4, 1884.

Nothing seemed to work out for the Fords. Bob lived to regret killing Jesse James, an act that he came to realize was based on a "foolish notion" that shooting a famous bandit would bring him "fame and wealth." But the Fords were never able to fully capitalize on the crime. They got some attention early on, but it was merely curiosity, and after that faded away the public turned against them and saw them for what they were, merely egotistical, low-brow, cowardly killers. As the years passed, Bob cursed "Gov. Crittenden and his brother Charles for leading him to commit such a crime."[10]

Bob Ford drifted west with Dick Liddil and in Las Vegas, New Mexico, they bought and operated a saloon.[11] The venture failed and Ford, the back shooter and a hated non-entity, eventually landed in Creede, Colorado. On February 18, 1892, there came word from Creede that "the report that Bob Ford ... had been shot and killed here is false."[12] Not long after, however, "the dirty little coward who shot Mr. Howard" was, in fact, shot and killed. His death came on June 8, 1892, when a man with a sawed off shotgun in a bar in Creede terminated Bob's life.[13] Bob had to know, as he lay dying, that it was one thing to kill a man and escape punishment, but it was entirely another matter to kill a man, larger than life, that, from the grave, had the power to haunt and hound him to the gates of hell and beyond.

As the years passed, the 19th century gradually became a curious object in the rearview mirror of all forward-looking people, and yet interest in the life and times of America's favorite outlaw was undiminished. Son Jesse Edward James was no chip off the old block, and yet he managed to get arrested for having participated in train robbery. In a sensational, well-publicized trial, he was acquitted. Young Jesse received offers from theatrical companies on a regular basis. One such offer came by mail in June of 1899, asking him to "play a minor part in a melodrama" in the "coming theatrical season." The melodrama, of course, was one that would feature the wild life and bloody deeds of his unforgettable father. Like all other such offers, young Jesse disregarded it.[14]

It was said that Zerelda "Zee" James would not permit her son to perform on stage, nor would she talk in public about her husband's outlaw exploits. She was a quiet, stay-at-home woman, but whenever she appeared in public, she was "dressed in black" with a "widow's veil."[15] The perpetually blackened widow, forever in love with a dead outlaw, "lived in constant fear" that young Jesse Edward would succumb to "evil associations." She avoided being photographed because she feared that "her picture would get into the paper in connection with some sensational story about her husband."[16]

Though she lived a life of sadness, she raised her two children well and made certain they were both educated. All the while she held on to her memories of Jesse, whom she loved dearly, who "at all times was kind and attentive."[17] It is said that love is blind, and yet one may wonder how she was able to hold her husband in such high esteem and at the same time wear jewelry that was stolen from another woman. Did it ever trouble her that the presents Jesse brought her were sometimes paid for by money taken from a victim of robbery and murder?

As for Jesse's death, Zee continued blame Governor Crittenden, insisting that he paid the "assassin" Bob Ford to shoot her husband in the back.[18] Of course she just had to live with it. She was in no position—nor did she have it in her—to hunt down and kill the governor to avenge her husband's death.

When her death came, on November 14, 1900, the press was quick to respond with kind obituaries that told of her religious convictions and her devotion to her late husband and their family. People who knew Zee well "say that she tried to persuade her husband to abandon his roving and robbing" and take the family away to a "remote part of the country or to a foreign country" and thereafter live a normal life. Jesse liked the idea, but he always needed one more robbery in order to get the needed money. As a consequence, she lived "in constant dread and anxiety while her husband was away on marauding expeditions."[19]

In life she was reclusive so it is reasonable to assume that when she died, her wish was to remain a forgotten woman. But some years later, in 1907, a woman in New Jersey claimed she was the real Mrs. Jesse James. It was at a "camp meeting" of stridently religious people that the woman loudly "testified" that she was Mrs. Jesse James. She then "waved aloft a Bible and said that she was brought up with sinners," but now she was saved. Frank James, who had been "traveling through Indiana as a starter at fair races," was quick to react to the nonsense, reminding everyone that Zee James "has been dead for several years."[20] True, but a bit of the mysterious sparkle of fame surrounding her husband found its way to her as if struggling to keep her alive.

The small house where Zee had lived with Jesse and their family maintained its high status as a "must see" place for visitors coming to St. Joseph. In May of 1902, the house was in the news because it was about to be torn down to "make way for a new and more pretentious building." By that time it was estimated that about 100,000 people had visited the death house, with sightseers taking with them some small souvenir and many people writing their names on the walls of the room where Jesse was killed. An observer said that the room looked like "a directory of the world." Other than that, the room was unchanged since the day that the "dirty little coward" Bob Ford brought down Jesse James. The stable in the back of the house, however, had succumbed altogether to "relic hunters," most of it having been carted off.[21]

In 1922, it was announced in a Kansas newspaper that Jesse James house at 1318 Lafayette Street was "rapidly falling into ruins" and there would be no attempt to stop the deterioration, for, sadly, "no historical society has ... come forward to save the house." Strangely, it had become a place of "inexhaustible relics" where gullible people believed every tale that was told about the place. The curious folks would buy "a piece of plaster from around the bullet hole" in the wall, "or a piece of the picture" that Jesse was dusting when he was killed, "or some other bit of doubtful value." Case in point: the chair Jesse stood on when he was shot. It was said that there could no accounting of the number of rungs from that chair that were sold over the years and yet "the original chair is still there!"[22]

A St. Joseph newspaper took offence over the article, insisting that the old Jesse James house on "High School hill" is not falling apart and stories to that effect are

JESSE JAMES, JR.

Jesse Edwards James was usually referred to as "Jesse James, Jr." While he was saddled with his father's reputation as an outlaw, young Jesse grew up fairly normal, under the tender tutelage of his gentle mother. She saw to it that Jesse and his sister were both decently educated and therefore prepared for life as self-reliant and honest individuals. The only brush with notoriety came when Jesse was arrested for train robbery. In a highly publicized trial, he was acquitted. He went on to become a lawyer and established a successful law practice. But he fell flat on his face, when he tried acting in a motion picture about his famous father. The experience left him in a mental fog from which he never fully escaped (*The Argus*, Holbrook, Arizona).

"without foundation." In fact, just the opposite was true, "as the house is almost as good as in the days when it sheltered the great outlaw," his family and other outlaw friends. Then the reporter shifted gears slightly and reminded readers that Jesse James had been "the world famed outlaw," who, in the years following the end of the Civil War, made "Missouri not only famous but interesting as well." The reporter scolded the "the moralists and purists" among his peers, who think that the old house should, and will, one day disappear, along with all memories of Jesse James.[23]

As the 20th century dawned, the Jesse James Wild West shows dominated the budding big-time entertainment industry. Jesse was rapidly becoming a superstar and a very bankable one at that. One of the first of the new century was a performance put on by the "Youth's Dramatic Club" in, of all places, Hawaii. Entitled "Jesse James Oath," the four-act play with a simplistic theme featured an angry Jesse bent on killing the villain who had "murdered the husband of the heroine." Between the acts there was "jig dancing," a "cakewalk," some "wiring walking" and a "piano selection." The theater was "filled to overflowing."[24]

The widow Zerelda James is shown standing next to a collection of weapons, guns that no doubt were once the possessions of her husband, the bandit king of Missouri. Zee never fully recovered from the death of her husband, and whenever she appeared in public, she was veiled and dressed in black. She avoided being photographed because she felt that doing so would only further the opportunity of others to sensationalize the life of the man she loved, Jesse James. The reclusive widow was forced to live with the fact that her husband, who had made his living by robbing and killing, only to be assassinated by a turncoat outlaw. It was a bitter, lonely life that ended on November 14, 1900, when Zerelda "Zee" James died (The State Historical Society of Missouri).

The "dark and dreadful" play, further described as a "penny horrible and dime novel drama," moved to another theater, but by then attendance had fallen off. It was panned by a newspaper reviewer who ridiculed the blood-drenched, violence-packed scenes and was also highly critical of Jesse's "strong Punchbowl dialect." What brought down the house was the dancing of a "newsboy with distorted feet." The footloose little fellow was treated to a shower of "small change." For all its shortcomings, it was successful to the extent that it entertained people who had an interest in the antics of the 19th century outlaws. The fact that people flocked to these programs shows that their interest and curiosity was genuine and rather intense.[25]

In 1902, Jesse James shows continued to be very popular events, not to be missed if at all possible, by people who wanted to explore the dark side of their curiosity. On April 21, 1902, a played entitled "Jesse James, The Bandit Hero" was performed at the Kentucky Theater in Paducah to a packed house. The Blue-Coat train robbery was the feature for which happy customers paid 25 to 50 cents for a seat.[26]

The following night, at Hopkinsville, Kentucky, a large, unruly crowd of fans "fought and struggled" to get find seats at Holland's Opera House to see the same play. The manager boasted of having an audience "at his playhouse that has seldom been equaled in numbers before in Memphis." The crowd, once seated, enjoyed itself immensely. After certain thrilling scenes, the "applause was deafening" and the "house fairly shook with the excitement of the occupants." Finally, "after the holdup scene," the "house went wild" and the cheering lasted for "fully five minutes."[27] Truly, there was good money to be made from bad business.

And there occurred some bad experiences too. Two East Sedalia youngsters, who had seen a Jesse James play, decided to act out in the manner of the outlaws. Edgar Allen, who played the part of Jesse, with a real gun, bullets and all, shot and killed his friend, 13-year-old Will Martin, who was playing the role of a Pinkerton agent. The accidental killing took place in front of an audience of about 50 other boys.[28]

Loud and wildly successful Jesse James shows were not the only big story in the summer of 1902. While various actors were playing Jesse James on stages throughout America, his body was exhumed and reburied. That event, of course, was well covered by the news media. Family members were present at the sad and solemn occasion. When the grave was opened and the skeleton revealed, Jesse Edwards James curiously "picked up the skull" of his famous father and "pointed out the hole made by the bullet from Bob Ford's pistol." Pallbearers, former comrades of the dead outlaw, accompanied the remains as the small party of mourners went to the Mt. Olivet Cemetery in Kearney, Missouri, where a funeral service was held, after which there was a reburial, beside the grave of his wife.[29] Jesse's grave continued to attract attention, much of it morbid, and by the mid–1930s, his tombstone was gone, having been carried off, chip by chip, by relic hunters.[30]

Whether the doubters were finally convinced that Jesse James was truly dead was still a looming question. And it probably didn't matter for his popularity had not diminished; it was alive and thriving. A rumor was floating about to the effect that the place of his birth, the family house near Kearney, had been sold "to the St. Louis world's fair and will be moved there in the near future." It was expected to be one of the leading attractions at the fair, and as noted in a Missouri newspaper, the life and reputation of Jesse James still commanded interest and was still the object of some strange, magnetic curiosity. Although the outlaw on horseback era had ended, people looked back longingly on that part of the past because, just as the "Swiss have their martyrs" and the "Norsemen their pirates," the "Saxons have their outlaws."

Those who revered the outlaw Jesse James were "heirs to the blood of a race" and for them the reverence for the dead bandit was natural and inevitable. A robber, thief and a killer becomes a hero for all time to come, so long as there is a valid excuse, an overweening experience, a powerful turning point that forces him into a life of crime. Such was the perceived truth about Jesse James. How could anyone, seeking the truth, deny such a man his full measure of greatness? After all it was the mad misfortunes of war that caused him to turn a hard face to the world. How indeed can he be forgotten when, throughout his wild life, he carried on with daring, leadership, foresight and the spirit of adventure, all good qualities, only to be cowardly assassinated?[31]

The prospect of moving the family home to the fair in St. Louis only served to increase the value of his brand. Anything associated with Jesse James, be it tangible or intangible, became something to covet, and, if obtained, to keep. As might be expected, the famous outlaw's guns started popping up. In 1903, a man named Sam Houser claimed to have in his possession "the famous 44 Colts [sic] revolver that the world's greatest outlaw, Jesse James, carried." Houser said that it was given to him by a man who was part of Quantrill's gang of killers. He further alleged that it was the pistol that Jesse James used "to kill the cashier of the Russellville bank." The proud collector of outlaw memorabilia apparently liked showing the gun to others while pointing out that it had on it "the marks of the thirteen deaths it has caused," the "death count as scratched by Jesse himself."[32]

In 1912, a revolver "supposed to have been owned by the great bandit Jesse James" found its way to a "curiosity shop" owned by J. F. Jerezy, in Chanute, Kansas. Jerezy acquired the gun from a man who was pressed for funds and wanted to sell the old firing piece. The stranger who needed money insisted that it had once belonged to Jesse James, and that Jesse had given to one of his friends, Texas Jack, who in turn had to give it up when he was sent to prison. The revolver was reputed to have been an "old fashioned Colt" with "six notches cut on the handle," and perhaps more interesting, "Texas Jack from Jesse James 1867, was inscribed on the handle.[33]

As the years passed by, more guns that had allegedly found sanctuary in the hands of Jesse James were publicized by their new owners. In 1917, a saloon keeper in St. Louis named Jake Johnson claimed that Frank James once presented him with a revolver that Jesse had owned. As it turned out, the giving of the gift was an unfortunate turn of events. Johnson quarreled with his spouse and she "used the revolver in the approved Jesse James style." In the heat of passion she fired it at Jake but missed. Police who were called to the Johnson residence learned that Mrs. Johnson, having found that her aim was off, proceeded to beat Mr. Johnson with "the butt of the pistol." The pair was taken to the police station, and after a cooling off, they went home together. There was no further word about the disposition of the gun, supposedly owned by the late outlaw that almost terminated a marriage.[34]

One of the most unique claims, and undoubtedly one of the phoniest, was made by M. M. Townshend, a "coal operator" in southern West Virginia. He proudly claimed that he possessed "Jesse James' last cartridge." He said a .44 caliber cartridge was taken from Jesse's gun belt that "hung across the chair at the time of his death" and was given to him by the mayor of Kansas City. When displaying the cartridge, Townshend pointed to the inscription on the side of the cartridge that read "From Jesse James' Belt."[35] No doubt some people believed it.

In May of 1901, an article in an Illinois newspaper declared that the improbable had happened: the Younger brothers, Jim and Cole, were about to be paroled. Bob had died in prison in 1889 of tuberculosis; his request to die in his native Missouri was denied. His older brothers, however, had survived the boredom and ravages of life in an iron cage. They were both model prisoners with Jim serving as the prison librarian and Cole engaged in an 11-year study of theology. They never spoke about the killing of Joseph L. Heywood at Northfield, except to deny having killed him, and they never said a word about the James brothers, except one time when Jim told a reporter, "Jesse James did not kill Heywood because he was not with us. He was in California." No one believed Jim Younger, including the journalist who reported on their release, a man who "had the word of one of the friends of the James boys."[36] So Jim's denial was brushed aside. In 1901, no one believed that the James brothers were in California at the time of the Northfield robbery and no one believes it now.

When he entered Stillwater prison in November of 1876, Jim's wound was so severe that it was thought he would soon die. But he held on, all the while suffering intensely. Finally, in April of 1879, the prison surgeon "made an incision in the roof of his mouth to where the bullet lay." The bullet, of course, was the one that, on September 21, 1876, tore into his "upper lip," splitting "his upper jaw," taking off the "right half of the jaw." Two days after the examination, the surgeon "safely dislodged the bullet," much to the "joy of the sufferer."[37] As a result of the painful surgical procedure, Jim Younger recovered and was in reasonably good shape when he and Cole were informed of their release.

Not everyone expected it to happen, but on July 10, 1901, they were free men, of sorts. Cole was tickled to death when he learned of the parole. To the deputy warden, he declared rather giddily: "Why, I feel just like a Methodist ..., I feel like shaking hands with everybody. I haven't got a grudge against anybody in the world, dead or alive."[38]

There were a number of restrictions attached to their release on parole. Among the most burdensome was that they could not get married and they could not leave Minnesota. These restrictions were too onerous for Jim, who wanted to marry the woman he loved, a writer named Alice J. Miller whom Jim called "Lassie." He put an end to his misery by shooting himself to death in the Reardon Hotel in St. Paul on October 19, 1902. Written on a manila envelope that contained the correspondence between the two lovers were these words: "No crocodile tears wanted. Reporters be my friends. Burn me up. Jim Younger."[39]

He also left a rambling suicide letter to "Lassie" that expressed his love for her, along with an expression of his political and religious beliefs. He declared that William J. Bryan, just then a nationally-known political figure, was "the brightest man in these United States," but that he failed the public when he refused to come out in favor of socialism. Jim wrote that he was a socialist and was "decidedly in favor of women's rights." Stating that he "knew Him well," he penned the words there was "no such thing as a personal God," rather God is "universal." Having poured out the torment and sadness in his heart, the former outlaw concluded the letter by saying, "Good-bye sweet Lassie."[40] James Hardin Younger was dead but at least he was able to get back home to Missouri. He is buried in Lee's Summit Historical Cemetery, Jackson County, Missouri.

Cole was eventually allowed to return to Missouri and resume his friendship with Frank James. Like a man trying to wake up from a bad dream, Frank wanted desperately to forget about the outlaw days. He had kept a low profile over the years, working at menial jobs, including as a shoe salesman and a doorman. But seeing Cole must have lit once again the bright candle of life in Frank, for, after such a long time apart, they must have had a lot to talk about. In 1903, the two men started their own extravaganza, "The Great Cole Younger and Frank James Historical Wild West."[41]

The show proved to be very popular at first, but it lacked the staying power due to legal and personnel problems and it died an inglorious death within a year's time. The failure of the show stood in stark contrast to the success of the melodramas about the long-dead Jesse James, whose fame seemed limitless. Indeed, the halo of the hero would long adorn the head of Jesse James. In 1904 brother Frank tried his hand at acting in two melodramas entitled "Across the Desert" and "The Fatal Scar."[42]

But Frank's star faded rather quickly, while the Jesse James shows kept coming, getting bigger and brassier. A Jesse James drama featuring "solid comedy" and a "moral lesson" was advertised in a Louisiana newspaper as "one of the big shows of the season." It was scheduled for February 16, 1905, at St. Martinsville, Louisiana, under a "Big Water Proof tent." The company traveled in "magnificent private cars" and had performed "a long run" in New York. It was successful in New York and other cities, and "reports from this show are of a very flattering character."[43]

The W. I. Swain Jesse James show was another big production that entertained huge crowds in the year 1905. The show claimed to present "wild western life" that was "well recommended by the press." It featured roping, shooting, riding, and "music by the original cowboy band." People were advised to bring any "wild, unbroken horse or mule" to the show and it "will be rode free of charge." Showman Swain promised that his performance would not be the same old circus or a "dog and pony" show.[44]

Swain's action-packed three-hour Jesse James show traveled throughout the country, but mainly in southern and southwestern states. October 16, 1905, was the date it played in Amarillo, Texas. Swain thrilled large audiences by "portraying the James boys during their famous career," from the time of the Civil War until the death of Jesse. The show was called "moral," and instead of "shooting and dime novel play, it teaches a grand lesson, showing the hardships and deprivations of an outlaw."[45]

With 16 years' experience as a showman, Swain dominated the "Wild West" field of play. He laced all his productions with comedy and humor.

In the spring of 1906, the one and only Swain set up his big tent in Safford, Arizona, and then moved on to Albuquerque, New Mexico. An Arizona newspaper described the acting as "somewhat sensational" with surprising climaxes and western scenes that are "true to life," and, on the whole, "instructive and strictly moral." His company featured "Indians, cowboys, Mexicans, comedians, actors and a complete outfit of scenery, costumes, cowboy band, etc."

Press coverage was very good and complimentary.[46] In 1910, Swain expanded his outlaw reach, creating a new show: "The Younger Brothers."[47]

But Jesse James would always be the biggest draw, and W. I. Swain cleverly used the name and reputation of America's most famous outlaw in ways that exceeded the productions of his competitors. What Swain created was more than just a show about the life of Jesse James; it was a Wild West production, in the manner of Buffalo Bill Cody's shows, in that it featured people acting out in a manner of a cowboy or outlaw, living a life of excitement, danger and hardship. The frontier era was over and historians were busy doing research and writing. All this was fine for the academic or scholar who desired the truth. But entertainment is what the average person wanted and Swain knew how to dish it out. And dish it out he did, along with his son, who made certain the show went on well into the 1940s.

But Swain's production wasn't the only show traveling the roads of America. In Walla Walla, Washington, at the Keylor Grand, for one night only, October 21, 1906, the audience was treated to "The Sensational Life Drama." Incidents in the life of Jesse James were featured including "the Great Blue Cut Train Robbery" and "the realistic death of Jesse James." Tickets cost "25, 35 and 50 cents."[48]

The Opera House in Grant's Pass, Oregon, was thrilled to be the setting of

The bill for "Jesse James' Sweetheart" was one of many that made splashy attempts at attracting an audience. The western melodramas were a popular form of entertainment following the death of the famous outlaw. Large crowds would squeeze their way into tents, auditoriums and theaters, eager to watch some rendition of the outlaw exploits of America's favorite bandit. Shootouts were a popular feature and crowds cheered wildly as an actor in the role of Jesse James, defeated his enemies, leaving dead bodies on the stage. People applauded with enthusiasm when Jesse brought down a sheriff or his deputy, or single-handed robbed a bank or a train. There was some concern that the display of violence on stage had a negative effect on young men, but those voices were overcome by the much louder sounds of approval, as the show went on, town after town, night after night (*Missouri Valley Times*, Missouri Valley, Iowa).

the "sensational melodrama Jesse James" for one night only. Spectators were advised to expect the unexpected, including a "train dashing across the stage at full speed." The life of the "Missouri outlaw" will be on display, including the many "thrilling adventures and escapades."[49] The tiny article all but vindicates Jesse James, nullifying the destructive effect of his many crimes. He did not rob, steal and kill to benefit himself. Rather he did all those terrible things for unselfish reasons so that future generations could be informed and entertained.

In 1907, Sioux Falls, South Dakota—a town that the James brothers passed through in 1876, on their way back home from Northfield—was another stop for a Jesse James melodrama. It was announced in a local newspaper that the New Theater would be hosting the show entitled "The James Boys." The four-act play promised to provide thrills, chills and excitement: Act I: Clay County, Missouri, Act II: Quantrill's Camp, Act III: The Blue Cut Robbery, and Act IV: The Death of Jesse and Surrender of Frank James.[50]

There was something noticeably absent from the repertoire. There was no mention of their passing through Sioux Falls in the autumn of 1876 when it was a small, isolated frontier town, nor was there a word or two about Devil's Gulch, and the legendary Leap by Jesse James and his horse. That Devil's Gulch was not a part of the play probably means that the legend of the Leap had yet to be created. Nevertheless, the play, before a large audience, was a complete success. It so inspired the manager of the theater that he wanted the one-night stand to stay and perform another night. The automobile was rapidly replacing the horse as America's popular form of transportation, but it was the image of the outlaw on horseback that had captured the imagination of the masses, looking to the past for entertainment.

And producers were able to provide it. In June of 1906, in Albuquerque, New Mexico, Jesse James, "that penny-novel hero," came on stage, guns a-blazing. Having replaced on the boards "Rip Van Winkle" and his "flowing gray locks," Jesse cut quite a figure, a big man "loaded down with guns, knives and pistols." It was said he resembled "a walking arsenal." Of course he needed it because the show featured "plenty of killing," exactly what the crowd came to see. But the wildest and loudest cheers from the audience came when Jesse used his fists to get away from the police. "Biff! Bang! Bump!" and a passel of posse men were laid out on the ground "in picturesque attitudes, all stunned." The reporter covering the show asked pointedly and with no small amount of sarcasm: "Could anything be more stirring or sensational?"[51]

In St. Paul, Indiana, the actor playing Jesse James got a little taste of what the real Jesse felt when he was shot by Bob Ford. In this "blood-curdling, Wild West melodrama," the cast was short one revolver, but a citizen in the audience was kind enough to loan a gun to the actor so that the show could go on. The gun, a real .38 caliber pistol, contained a paper wad cartridge, and when the actor playing Bob Ford fired on his victim, the wad penetrated Jesse's back "an inch deep," causing him to fall down in actual pain. After which he sprang to his feet, cursing his fellow actor "Bob Ford." While the unintended back shooting was the highlight of the play, there was more: "buckets of blood flowed and men went down like tenpins."[52]

The writer of the preceding article was clearly not impressed with the show, but the reporter from the *Pullman Herald* heaped words of praise on the program that was scheduled to appear in Pullman, Washington, on August 28, 1907. Calling "Jesse James Coming" a "truthful reflection of wild western life," and a "beautiful heart story" with "exciting scenes," the enraptured reporter seemed to be swept off his feet by the grand spectacle. The play that had "been produced in every civilized country in the known world" was based on "the life of the most interesting character that American history has furnished—Jesse James." It was wholesome entertainment "intended for ladies and children" as well as men. "It will not corrupt the mind of the young but on the contrary teaches a great moral lesson."[53]

In a maudlin crescendo, the giddy reporter completely legitimized all of the outlaw's criminal activity, while reminding the world that America only exports its very best. He deftly contended that there were great moral lessons in life to be learned by everyone, and the best source available is the life experiences of a criminal: the bloody deeds of Jesse James. No need to study great philosophic treatises or religious works in search of virtue, truth and values. Ignore thinkers, theorists and scientists for they are all meddlers up to no good; better to sit at the feet of one who was a career criminal. All the great literature of the world pales in significance when compared to the wisdom one can attain by simply watching a play about a criminal and his crimes.

In 1902, a letter to the editor of a Butte, Montana, newspaper included a strongly-worded criticism of the Jesse James melodramas, citing the evil influence on the minds of young boys and girls that attend the shows. The writer, who had attended two shows, said, "Their influences upon the minds of the young are more pernicious than even the so-called 'burlesque' productions." He watched in horror as a boy, "perhaps 11 years," got worked up into state of excitement so bizarre and wild that he could "scarcely contain himself." The boy's eyes were "blazing with wrath; his hair stood on end," and he seemed to be transformed "into a fiend." Girls joined in the mad frenzy, "yelling to Jesse James to show no mercy." The writer concluded his letter with a gentle reminder that a truly civilized society would not permit children to be present at such classless and violent productions, and shame on parents who fail to keep their youngsters away from them.[54]

In the summer of 1908, another article in yet another Montana newspaper called for an end to the Jesse James shows. A number of Montana newspapers objected to the play and all of them wanted it suppressed "on the ground that it inculcates in the minds of the young criminal ideas." To bolster this position, the reporter noted that only recently, four boys, none older than 17, held up a train and killed a passenger. They were now facing a murder charge that can be traced to "bad literature and worse melodramas." The article called on all good people to condemn such literature and plays and insist that they be banned by state and local laws.[55]

In Minot, North Dakota, a 1908 Jesse James production did not go over very well. A snarky newspaper reporter was highly critical of what occurred on stage, saying that while Jesse James was indeed "a crooked criminal," in all likelihood he never "stooped to so low a trick as to get money from the public as did the mangers of an alleged production" that "appeared in Minot the other day."[56]

Elsewhere in 1908, the Jesse James melodrama was a welcome event. In Leon, Iowa, the town's newspaper stated, humorously, "Get your money ready Jesse James wants it. He will be at the opera house, Wednesday, September 30th." And as an extra added attraction, the "world's highest, diving dog, owned by Professor Auginson, will perform at 7:30 p.m., on the same bill as the Jesse James' performance."[57]

Although in some places where complaints were made, the shows were unwelcome, over the next several years Jesse James plays and other Wild West programs under his name were performed with regularity and seen by thousands of happy fans. In 1912, the "Blondin Show," under canvas, presented "that great sensational melodrama, Jesse James" in Meade, Kansas.[58] The following year, another company called "Brown & Roberts Famous Shows" presented "the Greatest of all Western Plays, Jesse James, The Missouri Outlaw," one night only, at Clay City, Kentucky. The trailer on their ad stated: "You have read the Book, now see the Play."[59] Now if we only knew: was the play better than the book?

On September 21, 1914, the Brinkman Theatre in Bemidji, Minnesota, was the place to be. The Margot Beaton Stock Company was presenting the play "Jesse James" starring Stewart Kemp in the role of Jesse. One of the other characters, the purely fictional Lige Snowball, Jesse's black servant, was played by a struggling young actor, originally from England, named Boris Karloff.[60] A complete unknown in 1914, he became one of America's best-known movies stars, following his appearance in the 1931 filming of *Frankenstein*. Karloff—

who blackened his face for the role of Lige—went on to appear in numerous other movies, especially thrillers and horror films.

The Bemidji show was not the first foray into the state of Minnesota by a Jesse James theatrical group. Back in 1903, "a melodrama entitled 'Jesse James the Bandit Hero'" was touring the state. The manager of the group had arranged a performance with the city of Northfield, of all places. When city officials changed their mind and cancelled the show, the manager of the company sued and recovered damages of $250 in a civil suit.[61] For old-timers who were around in 1876, the slap-in-the-face verdict must have felt like a second coming of the James and Youngers.

The last stages of the 19th century saw invention and innovation take the world to places and experiences long thought to be impossible, the stuff of dreamers only. The electric light, the telephone, the phonograph and the automobile were four of the most important magic-carpet marvels unveiled before the world, all of which were instantly and enormously popular. Then, on May 9, 1893, American inventor and promoter Thomas A. Edison made his first public demonstration of motion pictures in the form of a "peephole kinetoscope."[62] This was the humble beginning of motion pictures, a form of art and entertainment that all the world has since come to enjoy.

Edison's marvel was seized upon by the public, but its popularity was short-lived, and by 1896–97, the pleasure seeking public witnessed the birth of cinema, motion pictures projected on a screen.[63] Everyone forgot about the peep show. While people were fascinated with looking into wooden box and seeing film of people actually moving about, the peep show had its limitations because it could not be seen by mass audience.

Cinema was just the ticket, and those interested in the frontier experience were soon to be rewarded. In 1903, *The Great Train Robbery* was released and was shown in theaters called nickelodeons.[64] Then, in 1908, the first motion picture about Jesse James was released entitled *The James Boys in Missouri*. It featured numerous acts of violence including robbery, murder and the burning of buildings. It was, of course, a silent film, but it was, nevertheless, great fun because it was easy to imagine the dialogue and sounds. To ordinary fans it was pure enjoyment, but to others it was shocking and shameful, even without hearing voices or other sounds. So the movie was subjected to extensive criticism because it was thought to be "threatening" to "impressionable audiences."[65] *The James Boys in Missouri* and other movies like it gave rise to the regulation of content, in other words, censorship, a movement that has long been the bane of motion picture producers.

The threat to censor violent cowboy shows was apparently short lived, for in 1911, the second Jesse James movie, titled simply *Jesse James*, was released. In November of that year "the picture of three full reels" was shown at the Elite Theater in Pensacola, Florida. The review was favorable in the extreme; it was called a "truthful picture bare of all embellishments and strictly based on historic facts." But the reviewer was just getting started; he hailed the movie as "the greatest ever acted for a moving picture company and is playing to packed houses all over the country."[66]

Books and plays were the milestones on the long trail of the outlaw's odyssey. Their importance cannot be under stressed, but it was motion pictures, or "photoplays," that really set in stone, for all time to come, the story of Frank and Jesse James along with other frontier characters. As the unstoppable popularity of movies surged, the world got movie stars, and by way of the star system, the James brothers, and the actors that portrayed them, emerged as true American celebrities. The Western movie has been popular since the appearance of the first silent films about gunmen on horseback, and the movies about the James brothers, made with a colorful blend of myth and fact, are among the most entertaining in the Old West genre of film art.

Quite likely, had Jesse lived, he would like all the celebrity heaped upon him, but not his aging brother Frank. Old Frank was seriously burdened by regret and wanted to permanently put all memories of the outlaw days behind him. He could not wipe the slate clean so he tried to hide behind a façade of denial. He was deep in denial when pressed by a man for a response about the "effects of a life of crime." Frank faked indignation and said anyone who believes he "can violate the law and make a success of it" will end up on the "gallows or [in] the penitentiary."[67]

Frank's stepfather, Dr. Reuben Samuel, had been living with terrible memories too. Among them was the hanging by federal militiamen during the Civil War. The doctor had been hoisted up in order to torture information out of him, as to the whereabouts of Frank and Jesse. But not strung up long enough to kill him, and the tough old doctor survived that and other sensational events that eventually took him down. In 1901, "on the verge of [mental] collapse," he was admitted as "a private patient at Hospital for the Insane No. 2," in St. Joseph, Missouri.[68] He hung on to life until March 1, 1908.

His widow, the tough-minded Zerelda Samuel, aged rather gracefully and died on February 10, 1911, in a stateroom on a train as it approached Oklahoma City.[69] She was buried in Mount Olivet Cemetery, Kearney, Missouri. Her grave is in the company of her husband and her son, Jesse.

In 1914, Frank James was living near Kearney, Missouri, and was "dying at the age of seventy-two of complications of diseases incident to old age." To inquiring visitors, he would invariably say, "I don't care to talk about those days"; he wanted "to let bygones to be bygones." When he made personal appearances it was as "a starter of race horses" at fairs, where he modestly accepted the fact that, as an outlaw in his younger days, he was "a drawing card" as an old man.[70] He was also a "ticket taker at the Standard Theatre, a burlesque house in St. Louis."[71] He did what he could for as long as he could.

On February 18, 1915, the onetime desperado who in life was forced to look danger and death in the face, time and time again, died quietly, just the way he wanted to die. But death was not a safe haven; Frank James was fearful that his body would be stolen by grave robbers,[72] so he was cremated and the ashes stored in a bank vault. It was also reported that he had his ashes stored rather than buried because he "wished to avoid the constant procession of morbid persons" visiting his grave.[73]

There is a third reason for the cremation and storage of his ashes. Frank's beloved Annie lived much longer, and having over the years refused numerous high-paying offers to tell her story, she died July 6, 1944, at the age of 91. Frank's ashes were buried beside her at Hill Cemetery, Independence, Missouri.[74]

With the death of Frank, Cole Younger became the last living member of the James–Younger gang that had ventured into Minnesota in 1876. In 1914 he was interviewed by "a close relative" who swore not to talk about the conversation so long as Cole was alive. If there is any truth to the conversation, Cole—who always liked to talk—finally made some frank and startling revelations. He admitted that

The one-armed Zerelda Samuel is shown in this newspaper illustration when she appeared as a witness at the train robbery trial of her grandson. The grand old lady by any measure lived a tumultuous life from the outset of the Civil War until the day she died. All who knew her either like or disliked her domineering and fearless manner, but all would be forced to agree that she needed that fierce strength to struggle through the many crises that attended the outlaw activities of her boys, Frank and Jesse James. Their tough-minded and proud mother aged rather gracefully and died on February 10, 1911, in a stateroom on a train as it approached Oklahoma City. She was buried in Mount Olivet Cemetery, Kearney, Missouri. Her grave is in the company of her husband and her son, Jesse (*The Kansas City Journal*, Kansas City, Missouri).

Frank and Jesse James had participated in the Northfield raid, and that Frank, the rider of the dun horse, killed Joseph L. Heywood, the acting cashier. When asked if Jesse James had been killed in St. Joseph in 1882, Younger said: "he certainly was."[75] Cole Younger died at the home of his niece in Lee's Summit, Missouri, on March 21, 1916.

The interest in Frank and Jesse James did not end with their deaths, and in May of 1921, banditti fans at the Ramona Theater, in Phoenix, Arizona, were treated to a "real live, fast melodrama." None other than "Jesse James," along with a gaggle of other amateur actors, stepped on to the stage and soon the audience was cheering "knife fights, gunplay, red fire and trainrobberies [sic]" in three "thrilling acts of daring and adventure." It was written that the theater "fairly rung with cheers and peals of laughter."[76]

About the same time, on May 19, 1921, *Jesse James: Under the Black Flag*, an eight-reel silent motion picture starring Jesse Edwards James in the role of his infamous father, was shown at the Silver Moon Theatre in Fortescue, Missouri. It was billed as "startling in story and action—supreme in suspense—containing a wealth of adventure—tense in thrilling situations—a moral that is obvious." Jesse Edwards called the show "the only authentic photoplay every written of my father's life."[77]

Jesse Edwards James, often referred to as "Jesse James, Jr.," did not let his father's life of crime stand in the way of a successful career. The young man was ambitious and hard-working, and by 1906 he was an attorney, having attended law school at night, graduating with honors.[78] He was happily married to Stella Frances McGowan whom he had met in Kansas City.

He was convinced to try acting, but his own wife concluded that he was the worst actor in a cast of bumbling amateurs in *Jesse James: Under the Black Flag*.[79] He "starred" in another one entitled *Jesse James as the Outlaw* with a similar theme. Both were featured in various theaters, but they were not a financial success and young Jesse lost a lot of money, along with the money of other investors. The movie-making venture turned out to be both an emotional and financial disaster that weighed heavily on his mind.[80] Still, he may have liked the fact that smiling men wanted to shake his hand because he was the son of a great outlaw.

But to the budding movie industry, the late Jesse James was pure gold and the films kept coming in the 1930s, 40s and 50s. Some of them attempted to be an accurate portrayal of his life and that of his brother and their comrades, while others such as *Jesse James Meets Frankenstein's Daughter*, released in 1966, were simply ridiculous. The sheer volume of movies about the James brothers is rather telling about what we as a people think and feel but how little we know about the actual history of the American West and the frontier characters that lived and died in the storied past. It has been suggested that the "average horse opera has been mainly the adaptation, the exploitation of a formula rather than the careful reconstruction of the past."[81]

That passage contains more than a nugget of truth. We outwardly declare our love for peace, honor and justice for all. But all the while we listen to the dark side of our nature and fantasize about the old days and ways. We lap up with relish the details of the violent and sleazy lives of outlaws and other frontier characters. Law and order are the hallmarks of a life well lived, and yet we look beyond the platitudes and confess, ever so silently, a secret admiration for the gun-toting outlaws, those independent men and women who rejected good citizenship for the chance to follow a crooked trail.

There was also the stated opinion that the outlaw embodied the qualities of "genuine Americanism"—that is, the bad man who lived "without fear and whose life is made up of romantic, dramatic and tragic instances"[82] gave rise to the *real*, the ideal American character. We Americans have come to accept this as gospel, so is there any wonder that we have such a strong attachment to guns and gun-related entertainment?

This photograph, taken in 1898, shows an aging but determined-looking Frank James, a man who got a free pass from the legal system. Of all the members of the James–Younger gang, Frank was the lucky one, and so long as he stayed away from Minnesota, he could live out his life without fear of arrest. He disliked talking about the outlaw years, and when he questioned about those days on the run, he said very little, as if silence could change the past. He worked at menial jobs including that of a doorman and a shoe salesman. Although he was in denial, he nevertheless took advantage of his outlaw experience by making appearance at fairs or at horse races, where the old man was a drawing card. He even tried his hand at acting in a couple of obscure melodramas. Weakened by the complications of old-age, Frank James died peacefully on February 18, 1915 (Library of Congress).

The life of a desperado—that dashing, romantic figure on horseback—was not one of honesty and was often deadly, but it has left in its wake a revelation far more interesting than reading, for example, about the success story of an honest, hard-working sodbuster, a dedicated teacher or a persevering merchant. In accepting the truth of it, we elevate bad over good. But we have been able to live with our choices, and without serious qualms of conscience. The good often die in anonymity while the bad die amid song and celebration, and for a gunslinger like Jesse James, life never ends with death. It continues in the next book or movie.

Chapter Notes

Chapter 1

1. *The Adair County News* (Columbia, KY), March 1, 1911.
2. *St. Paul and Minneapolis Pioneer-Press and Tribune*, October 7, 1876
3. Yeatman, Ted P., *Frank and Jesse James: The Story Behind the Legend*, Nashville: Cumberland House, 2000, p. 26. The grave of Robert James has never been found.
4. *The Indiana State Sentinel* (Indianapolis), April 12, 1882; *The Columbian* (Bloomsburg, PA), April 14, 1882.
5. *The Adair County News*, March 1, 1911.
6. Yeatman, Ted P., p. 27.
7. *The Indiana State Sentinel* (Indianapolis), April 12, 1882.
8. *Cincinnati Inquirer* in the *Evening Star* (Washington, D.C.), May 27, 1882.
9. James, Stella Frances, *In the Shadow of Jesse James*, ed. Milton F. Perry, Thousand Oaks, CA: The Revolver Press, 1989, p. 59.
10. Yeatman, Ted P., p. 27.
11. *Lincoln County Leader* (Toledo, Lincoln County, OR), May 29, 1908.
12. Yeatman, Ted P., pp. 31–33.
13. *Ibid.*, pp. 35–54.
14. *Evening Star* (Washington, D.C.), April 18, 1882.
15. *The Central Record* (Lancaster, KY), August 8, 1901.
16. *Lincoln County Leader*, May 29, 1908.
17. Yeatman, Ted P., p. 49
18. *Ibid.*, 55–56.
19. Brant, Marley, *Jesse James: The Man and the Myth*, New York: Berkley Books, 1998, p. 37.
20. Love, Robertus, *The Rise and Fall of Jesse James*, New York: G. P. Putnam's Sons, 1926, p. 347
21. Yeatman, Ted P., p. 58.
22. *Ibid.*, p. 65.
23. *Ibid.*, p. 72.
24. *Ibid.*, p. 74.
25. *Ibid.*, pp. 76–77.
26. *The Hartford Herald* (Hartford, KY), January 20, 1904.
27. Yeatman, Ted P., pp. 76–77.
28. *Ibid.*, p. 80.
29. *St. Paul and Minneapolis Pioneer-Press and Tribune*, October 7, 1876
30. *The Herald* (Los Angeles), November 13, 1898.
31. *The Kansas City Times*, August 16, 1876.
32. Brant, Marley, p. 122.
33. *The Watchman and Southron* (Sumter, SC), September 20, 1881.
34. *The Kansas City Times*, August 16, 1876.
35. *Omaha Republican* in the *Las Vegas Daily Gazette*, August 10, 1881.
36. *The Manning Times* (Manning, SC), December 23, 1914.
37. *The Daily Morning Journal and Courier* (New Haven, CT), November 26, 1900.
38. Brant, Marley, p. 118.
39. Wallace, William H., *Speeches and Writings of Wm. H. Wallace with Autobiography*, Kansas City: The Western Baptist Publishers Co., 1914, pp. 264–265.
40. Love, Robertus, pp. 349–350
41. *Evening Bulletin* (Maysville, KY), April 17, 1882.
42. *The Watchman and Southron*, September 20, 1881.

Chapter 2

1. *New York Sun* in *The Fairbault Democrat* (Faribault, MN), July 7, 1876.
2. *Minneapolis Tribune*, September 8, 1876.
3. Dellinger, Herald, ed., *Jesse James: The Best Writings on the Notorious Outlaw and His Gang*, Guilford, CT: Globe Pequot Press, 2007, p. 92.

4. Lemann, Nicholas, *Redemption: The Last Battle of the Civil War*, New York: Farrar, Straus and Giroux, 2006, pp. 168–169.
5. *The Kansas City Daily Journal*, September 5, 1896.
6. *St. Paul Pioneer Press*, November 24, 1876.
7. *The Leon Reporter* (Leon, IA), April 6, 1916.
8. Settle, William A., Jr., *Jesse James Was His Name*, Lincoln: University of Nebraska Press, 1977, originally published in 1866, p. 23.
9. *The New York World* in *The Dakota Republican* (Vermillion, DT), October 26, 1876.
10. *The Daily Journal* (Sioux City, IA), October 21, 1876.
11. *The Butler Weekly Times* (Butler, MO), July 10, 1889.
12. *The Minneapolis Journal*, March 4, 1903.
13. Brant, Marley, *Jesse James: The Man and the Myth*, New York: Berkley Books, 1998, p. 94.
14. *The Faribault Democrat* in the *St. Paul Pioneer Weekly*, December 7, 1876; *Minneapolis Tribune*, November 15, 1876.
15. Brant, Marley, pp. 165 amd 172.
16. Settle, William A., Jr., p. 89.
17. *The Kansas City Times*, August 12 and 16, 1876.
18. Brant, Marley, p. 172.
19. *The Butler Weekly Times*, July 10, 1889.
20. *The Minneapolis Journal*, March 4, 1903.
21. *St. Paul and Minneapolis Pioneer-Press and Tribune*, September 9, 1876.
22. *The Kansas City Times*, October 1, 1876.
23. *The Daily Argus-Leader* (Sioux Falls, SD), March 29 1924.
24. *The Parkston Advance* (Parkston, SD), June 19, 1908.
25. Brant, Marley, pp. 161–162.
26. *The State Journal* (Jefferson City, MO), October 27, 1876; Settle, William A., Jr., p. 95.
27. *The Trial of Frank James for Murder, with Confessions of Dick Liddil and Clarence Hite and History of the "James Gang,"* New York: Jingle Bob/Crown, 1977, originally published in 1898, pp. 328–329; *The Topeka State Journal*, July 11, 1901.
28. *The Waco Daily Examiner*, May 3, 1882.
29. *Minneapolis Tribune*, September 23, 1876.
30. *Ibid.*, September 25, 1876.
31. *Rice County Journal* in the *St. Paul Weekly Dispatch*, September 22, 1876.
32. *The Daily Journal*, October 25, 1876.
33. *The Story of Cole Younger, by Himself*, St. Paul: Minnesota Historical Society Press, 2000 (originally published by Hennberry of Chicago, 1903), p. 74.
34. Stiles, T. J., *Jesse James: The Last Rebel of the Civil War*, New York: Vintage, 2003, p. 307.
35. *St. Paul and Minneapolis Pioneer-Press and Tribune*, September 26, 1876.
36. *The Fulton County News* (McConnellsburg, PA), June 27, 1901.
37. *The Topeka State Journal*, July 11, 1901.
38. *St .Paul and Minneapolis Pioneer-Press and Tribune*, September 9, 1876.
39. *The Kansas City Times*, August 18, 1876.
40. *Ibid.*, August 23, 1876.
41. Stiles, T. J., p. 323.
42. *The Daily Argus-Leader*, September 27, 1924.
43. *Minneapolis Tribune*, September 9, 1876.
44. *St. Paul and Minneapolis Pioneer-Press and Tribune*, September 9, 1876.
45. *The Butler Weekly Times*, July 10, 1889.
46. Stiles, T. J., p. 323; *Minneapolis Tribune*, September 19, 1876; *St. Paul and Minneapolis Pioneer-Press and Tribune*, September 20, 1876.
47. *The Kansas City Times*, September 24, 1876.
48. *The Butler Weekly Times*, September 1, 1886.
49. *St. Paul Press* in *The State Journal* (Jefferson City, MO), September 1, 1876.
50. *The Story of Cole Younger, by Himself*, pp. 77–78.
51. *The Daily Argus-Leader*, March 29, 1924.
52. Stiles, T. J., p. 326.
53. *The Story of Cole Younger, by Himself*, pp. 77–78.
54. *Minneapolis Tribune*, September 8, 1876.
55. *The Story of Cole Younger, by Himself*, pp. 77–78.
56. Dellinger, Harold, ed., p. 94.
57. *Minneapolis Tribune*, September 8, 1876.

Chapter 3

1. *The Faribault Democrat* (Faribault, MN) in the *St. Paul Pioneer Weekly*, December 7, 1876.
2. Dellinger, Harold, ed., *Jesse James: The Best Writings on the Notorious Outlaw and His Gang*, Guilford, CT: Globe Pequot Press, 2007, p. 78.
3. Brant, Marley, *Jesse James: The Man and the Myth*, New York: Berkley Books, 1998, p. 177.
4. *Minneapolis Tribune*, September 23, 1876.
5. Dellinger, Harold, ed., p. 113.
6. *New York Sun* in *The Fulton County News* (McConnellsburg, PA), June 27, 1901.
7. *The Faribault Democrat*, August 18, 1876.

8. *The Daily Argus-Leader* (Sioux Falls, SD), March 29, 1924.
9. *Minneapolis Tribune*, September 8, 1876.
10. *St. Paul and Minneapolis Pioneer-Press and Tribune*, September 8, 1876.
11. *Minneapolis Tribune*, September 8, 1876.
12. Stiles, T. J., *Jesse James: The Last Rebel of the Civil War*, New York: Vintage, 2003, pp. 328–330; *Minneapolis Tribune*, September 8, 1876.
13. Brant, Marley, p. 180.
14. *The Daily Argus-Leader*, April 5, 1924.
15. Gardner, Mark Lee, *Shot All to Hell: Jesse James, The Northfield Raid, and the Wild West's Greatest Escape*, New York: William Morrow, 2013, p. 68.
16. *The Faribault Democrat*, September 15, 1876.
17. *The Kansas City Times*, September 15, 1876.
18. *The Faribault Democrat*, September 15, 1876.
19. Gardner, Mark Lee, p. 83.
20. *Rice County Journal* (Northfield, MN), September 14, 1876.
21. *Minneapolis Tribune*, September 8, 1876.
22. *The Faribault Republican*, September 13, 1876.
23. *St. Paul Weekly Dispatch*, September 22, 1876.
24. *St. Paul and Minneapolis Pioneer-Press and Tribune*, September 27, 1876.
25. *Minneapolis Tribune*, September 11, 1876.
26. *Rice County Journal*, September 14, 1876.
27. *The Faribault Democrat* in the *St. Paul Pioneer Weekly*, December 7, 1876.
28. *Barbour County Index* (Medicine Lodge, KS), August 4, 1881.
29. *The Salt Lake Herald*, August 6, 1897.
30. *The Minneapolis Journal*, March 4, 1903.
31. *The Story of Cole Younger, by Himself*, St. Paul: Minnesota Historical Society Press, 2000 (originally published by Hennberry of Chicago, 1903), p. 81.
32. Dellinger, Harold, ed., p. 104.
33. Gardner, Mark Lee, p. 95.
34. Brant, Marley, p. 182.
35. *The Kansas City Times*, October 1, 1876.
36. *The Daily Argus-Leader*, April 5, 1924; *Minneapolis Tribune*, September 8, 1876.
37. *Mantorville* (MN) *Express* in the *Sioux Valley News* (Canton, DT), September 23, 1876.
38. *The Webster Journal* (Webster, SD), July 17, 1930.
39. *St. Paul and Minneapolis Pioneer-Press and Tribune*, September 27, 1876.
40. *Minneapolis Tribune*, October 17, 1876.
41. Kolbas, John, *The Jesse James Northfield Raid, Confessions of the Ninth Man*, North Star Press of St. Cloud, 1999, p. 9.
42. *Ibid.*, p. 13.
43. *Ibid.*, p. 9.
44. *Ibid.*, p. 14.
45. *Minneapolis Tribune*, October 3, 1876.

Chapter 4

1. *Rice County Journal* (Northfield, MN), September 14, 1876.
2. Yeatman, Ted P., *Frank and Jesse James, The Story Behind the Legend*, Nashville: Cumberland House, 2000, p. 175.
3. *St. Paul Weekly Dispatch*, September 22, 1876.
4. Christianson, Theodore, *Minnesota: A History of the State and its People*, Vol. I, Chicago: The American Historical Society, 1935, p. 478.
5. *Minneapolis Tribune*, September 8, 1876.
6. *The Faribault Democrat* (Faribault, MN), September 8, 1876.
7. *Ibid.*
8. *St. Paul and Minneapolis Pioneer-Press and Tribune*, September 10, 1876.
9. Yeatman, Ted P., p. 177.
10. Huntington, George, *Robber and Hero: The Story of the Northfield Bank Raid*, St. Paul: Minnesota Society Press, 1986, first published in 1895, p. 40.
11. *Ibid.*, p. xvii.
12. *The Kansas City Times*, September 13, 1876.
13. *St. Paul and Minneapolis Pioneer-Press and Tribune*, September 8, 1876.
14. *Ibid.*, September 9, 1876.
15. *The Faribault Democrat*, September 15, 1876.
16. *St. Paul and Minneapolis Pioneer-Press and Tribune*, September 9, 1876.
17. *Minneapolis Tribune*, September 26, 1876.
18. Gardner, Mark Lee, *Shot All to Hell: Jesse James, The Northfield Raid, and the Wild West's Greatest Escape*, New York: William Morrow, pp. 39, 115–116.
19. *Pioneer-Press* (Cato, KS) in *The Faribault Republican* (Faribault, MN), October 25, 1876.
20. *The Faribault Republican*, November 1, 1876.
21. *Ibid.*, October 24, 1877.
22. *Ibid.*, p. 46.
23. *Ann Arbor Register* in the *St. Paul and Minneapolis Pioneer-Press and Tribune*, October 5, 1876.
24. Brant, Marley, *Jesse James: The Man and the Myth*, New York: Berkley Books, 1998, p. 192.

25. *The Webster Journal* (Webster, SD), July 17, 1930.
26. *The Daily Argus-Leader* (Sioux Falls, SD), April 5, 1924.
27. www.findagrave.com, Find a Grave Memorial, Clelland D. Miller, consulted 9/13/16.
28. Huntington, George, p. xxxviii.
29. *The Webster Journal*, July 17, 1930.
30. *Minneapolis Tribune*, September 8, 1876.
31. *The Worthington Advance* (Worthington, MN), September 14, 1876.
32. *Minneapolis Tribune*, September 11, 1876.
33. *The Worthington Advance*, September 14, 1876.
34. *The Daily Argus-Leader*, April 12, 1924.
35. Yeatman, Ted P., p. 177.
36. *The Worthington Advance*, September 14, 1876.
37. Koblas, John, *The Jesse James Northfield Raid: Confessions of the Ninth Man*, North Star Press of St. Cloud, 1999, p. 83.
38. *Minneapolis Tribune*, September 9, 1876.
39. Gardner, Mark Lee, pp. 95 and 104.
40. Huntington, George, p. 50.
41. *The Daily Argus-Leader*, April 12, 1924; *Rice County Journal*, September 14, 1876.
42. *The Kansas City Times*, October 1, 1876.
43. *The Faribault Republican*, September 13, 1876.
44. *The Faribault Democrat*, September 15, 1876.
45. Yeatman, Ted P., pp. 177–178.
46. *The Faribault Democrat*, September 15, 1876.
47. *St. Paul and Minneapolis Pioneer-Press and Tribune*, September 9, 1876.
48. *Minneapolis Tribune*, September 9, 1876.
49. *The Story of Cole Younger, by Himself*, St. Paul: Minnesota Historical Society Press, 2000, originally published in 1903, p. 82.
50. *The Faribault Democrat*, September 15, 1876.
51. Yeatman, Ted P., p. 178.
52. *St. Paul and Minneapolis Pioneer-Press and Tribune*, September 9 and 10, 1876.
53. *The Faribault Democrat*, September 15, 1876; *The Faribault Republican*, September 13, 1876.
54. *St. Paul and Minneapolis Pioneer-Press and Tribune*, September 10, 1876.
55. *Minneapolis Tribune*, September 12, 1876.
56. *St. Paul and Minneapolis Pioneer-Press and Tribune*, September 10, 1876.
57. *Ibid.*, September 12, 1876.
58. *Ibid.*, September 10, 1876.
59. *The Daily Journal* (Sioux City, IA), September 9, 1876.
60. *Minneapolis Tribune*, September 11, 1876.
61. *St. Paul and Minneapolis Pioneer-Press and Tribune*, September 12, 1876.
62. *The Kansas City Times*, September 13, 1876.
63. *Daily Press and Dakotaian* (Yankton, DT), September 13. 1876.
64. *Minneapolis Tribune*, September 11, 1876.
65. *St. Paul and Minneapolis Pioneer-Press and Tribune*, September 12, 1876.
66. *The Kansas City Times*, September 13, 1876.
67. *Minneapolis Tribune*, September 11, 1876.
68. *St. Paul and Minneapolis Pioneer-Press and Tribune*, September 12, 1876.
69. *Daily Press and Dakotaian*, September 13. 1876.
70. *Minneapolis Tribune*, September 12, 1876.
71. *Ibid.*
72. *St. Paul and Minneapolis Pioneer-Press and Tribune*, September 13, 1876; *The Faribault Republican*, September 20, 1876.
73. *Mankato Record* (Mankato, MN), September 30, 1876.
74. *Minneapolis Tribune*, September 12, 1876.
75. *Ibid.*, September 13, 1876.
76. *The Faribault Republican*, September 20, 1876.
77. *Minneapolis Tribune*, September 13, 1876.
78. *St. Paul and Minneapolis Pioneer-Press and Tribune*, September 14, 1876.
79. *The Daily Journal*, October 27, 1876.
80. *The Daily Argus-Leader*, June 5, 1924.
81. *Mankato Record*, September 16, 1876.
82. *The Daily Journal*, August 27, 1924; *Faribault Democrat* in the *St. Paul Pioneer Weekly*, December 7, 1876.
83. *The Daily Journal*, October 27, 1876.
84. *St. Paul and Minneapolis Weekly Pioneer Press*, November 2, 1876.
85. *St. Paul and Minneapolis Pioneer-Press and Tribune*, September 14, 1876.

Chapter 5

1. *Omaha Daily Bee*, July 23, 1881.
2. *The Daily Argus-Leader* (Sioux Falls, SD), April 19, 1924.
3. *The Interior Journal* (Stanford, KY), May 5, 1916.
4. Triplet, Frank, *The Life, Times and Treacherous Death of Jesse James*, New York City: Promontory Press, 1970, originally published in 1882, pp. 153–160.
5. *The Life and Tragic Death of Jesse James, by "One Who Dare Not Disclose His Identity,"* Philadelphia: Barclay, 1883, pp. 46–47.
6. *The Waco Daily Examiner*, May 3, 1882.

7. *The Farmer and Mechanic* (Raleigh, NC), January 8, 1880.
8. Breihan, Carl W., *The Day Jesse James Was Killed: The Spine-Chilling True Story of the Most Hunted Outlaw in the Old West*, New York: Signet, 1979, pp. 81–82.
9. *The Faribault Republican*, September 20, 1876.
10. *Ibid.*, October 11, 1876.
11. *Daily Press and Dakotaian* (Yankton, DT), September 15, 1876.
12. *The Faribault Republican*, September 20, 1876.
13. *Minneapolis Tribune*, September 14, 1876.
14. *The Sedalia Weekly Bazoo* (Sedalia, MO) in *The St. Louis Globe-Democrat*, December 5, 1876.
15. *St. Paul and Minneapolis Pioneer-Press and Tribune*, September 15, 1876.
16. *Minneapolis Tribune*, September 15, 1876.
17. *St. Paul and Minneapolis Pioneer-Press and Tribune*, September 15, 1876.
18. *Ibid.*
19. *Daily Press and Dakotaian*, September 15, 1876; *Minneapolis Tribune*, September 15, 1876.
20. *The Faribault Democrat* (Faribault, MN), October 6, 1876.
21. Yeatman, Ted P., *Frank and Jesse James: The Story Behind the Legend*, Nashville: Cumberland House, 2000, p. 179.
22. *The Faribault Democrat* in the *St. Paul Pioneer Weekly*, December 7, 1876.
23. Brant, Marley, *Jesse James: The Man and the Myth*, New York: Berkley Books, 1998, p. 189.
24. *St. Paul and Minneapolis Pioneer-Press and Tribune*, September 24, 1876.
25. *Minneapolis Tribune*, November 15, 1876.
26. *St. Paul and Minneapolis Pioneer-Press and Tribune*, September 16, 1876.
27. *Mankato Record* (Mankato, MN), September 16, 1876.
28. Yeatman, Ted P., September 16, 1876.
29. *The Weekly Sedalia Bazoo* in *The St. Louis Globe-Democrat*, December 5, 1876.
30. *Mankato Record*, September 30, 1876.
31. *St. Paul and Minneapolis Pioneer-Press and Tribune*, September 16, 1876.
32. Nolf, Richard A., ed., "St. Joe Museum Graphic—Jesse James Special Edition," Published by St. Joseph Museum, St. Joseph, MO, 1972, p. 8.
33. Brant, Marley, p. 73.
34. Settle, William A., Jr., *Jesse James Was His Name*, Lincoln: University of Nebraska Press, 1977, originally published in 1966, p. 55.
35. *The Manning Times* (Manning, SC), December 23, 1914.
36. *Minneapolis Tribune*, September 16, 1876.
37. *The Weekly Sedalia Bazoo* in *The St. Louis Globe-Democrat*, December 5, 1876.
38. *St. Paul and Minneapolis Pioneer-Press and Tribune*, September 16, 1876; *The Faribault Democrat*, September 22, 1876.
39. *The Emporia Weekly News* (Emporia, KS), April 13, 1882.
40. Horan, James D., *Desperate Men, Revelations from the Sealed Pinkerton Files*, New York: Bonanza Books, 1949, p. 118.
41. *The Faribault Republican*, September 20, 1876.
42. Yeatman, Ted P., p. 180.
43. *St. Paul and Minneapolis Pioneer-Press and Tribune*, September 19, 1876.
44. *The Faribault Republican*, September 20, 1876.
45. *The Emporia Weekly News*, April 13, 1882.
46. *The Daily Journal* (Sioux City, IA), September 16, 1876; *The Worthington Advance* (Worthington, MN) September 14, 1876.
47. *Minneapolis Tribune*, September 16, 1876.
48. *The Weekly Sedalia Bazoo* in *The St. Louis Globe-Democrat*, December 5, 1876.
49. *St. Paul Weekly Dispatch*, September 15, 1876.
50. *The Worthington Advance* (Worthington, MN), September 21, 1876.
51. *Minneapolis Tribune*, September 16, 1876. Bresette is also spelled "Brissette."
52. *Ibid.*, September 20, 1876.
53. *The Worthington Advance*, September 28, 1876.
54. *The Faribault Republican*, September 20, 1876.
55. *The Daily Argus-Leader*, April 26, 1924.

Chapter 6

1. *St. Paul and Minneapolis Pioneer-Press and Tribune*, September 19, 1876.
2. Rose, Arthur P., *An Illustrated History of the Counties of Rock and Pipestone Minnesota*, Luverne: Northern History, 1911, pp. 135 and 142.
3. Rose, Arthur P., pp. 236 and 453; *The Daily Argus-Leader* (Sioux Falls), April 19 1924.
4. *Ibid.* The rock formations and mounds were real and are now are part of the beautiful scenery of Blue Mound State Park.
5. Croy Homer, *Jesse James Was My Neighbor*, New York: Dell, 1960, p. 107.
6. *The Daily Argus-Leader*, April 5, 1924.
7. *Ibid.*
8. *Ibid.*
9. *Ibid.*, April 26, 1924.
10. *Minneapolis Tribune*, September 19, 1876.

11. *St. Paul and Minneapolis Pioneer-Press and Tribune,* September 19, 1876.
12. *Minneapolis Tribune,* September 19, 1876
13. *St. Paul and Minneapolis Pioneer-Press and Tribune,* September 20, 1876
14. *Minneapolis Tribune,* September 19, 1876.
15. Rose, Arthur P., p. 236.
16. *The Daily Argus-Leader,* April 26, 1924. Split Rock River was renamed Split Rock Creek.
17. *Ibid.*
18. *Minneapolis Tribune,* September 19, 1876
19. *St. Paul and Minneapolis Pioneer-Press and Tribune,* September 19, 1876.
20. *The Worthington Advance,* September 21, 1876.
21. *Minneapolis Tribune,* September 16, 1876
22. *Ibid.*, September 15, 1876.
23. *Daily Press and Dakotaian* (Yankton, DT), September 20, 1876.
24. *Minneapolis Tribune,* September 16, 1876.
25. *Ibid.*, September 19, 1876.
26. *St. Paul and Minneapolis Pioneer-Press and Tribune,* September 29, 1876.
27. *Omaha Daily Bee,* July 23, 1881.
28. *The Sedalia Weekly Bazoo* (MO) in *The Pioneer Press, St. Paul and Minneapolis Weekly,* November 30, 1876.
29. *The Sedalia Weekly Bazoo* in *The St. Louis Globe-Democrat,* December 5, 1876.
30. *The Pioneer Press, St. Paul and Minneapolis Weekly,* December 6, 1876.
31. *St. Paul and Minneapolis Pioneer-Press and Tribune,* September 16, 1876.
32. *Ibid.*, September 19, 1876.

Chapter 7

1. *The Daily Argus-Leader* (Sioux Falls, SD), April 26, 1924.
2. *St. Paul and Minneapolis Pioneer-Press and Tribune,* September 19, 1876.
3. *The Dakota Pantagraph* (Sioux Falls, DT), April 18, 1878.
4. *History of Southeastern Dakota,* Sioux City: Western, 1881, pp. 113–114.
5. Smith, Charles A., *A Comprehensive History of Minnehaha County,* Mitchell, SD: Educator Supply, 1949, p. 429.
6. *The Daily Argus-Leader,* April 26, 1924.
7. *Ibid.*
8. *St. Paul and Minneapolis Pioneer-Press and Tribune,* September 19, 1876.
9. *The Daily Argus-Leader,* April 26, 1924.
10. *Mankato Record* (Mankato, MN), September 30, 1876.
11. *Pioneer History, Minnehaha County's Norwegian Pioneers, History from the Year 1866 to 1896,* published by Minnehaha County's Norwegian Pioneers, 1928; translated into English and reprinted in 1976, p. 381.
12. *Sioux Falls Independent* (Sioux Falls, DT), September 11, 1873.
13. *Ibid.*, October 2, 1873.
14. *Ibid.*, July 9, 1874.
15. *The Dakota Pantagraph* (Sioux Falls, DT), May 23, 1878.
16. *Sioux Falls Independent,* February 3, 1876.
17. *Celebrating a Century, Garretson, SD, 1889–1989,* compiled and published by the Garretson Book Committee, 1989, p. 445.
18. *Sioux Falls Independent,* March 30, 1876.
19. *Celebrating a Century, Garretson, SD, 1889–1989,* compiled and published by the Garretson Book Committee, 1989, p. 2.
20. *The Daily Argus-Leader,* April 4, 1924.
21. *The Dakota Pantagraph,* May 23, 1878.
22. *Saturday Blade* (Chicago) in the *Evening Argus-Leader,* August 1, 1894.
23. *Sioux Falls Daily Press* (Sioux Falls, DT), March 31, 1886.
24. *The Garretson News* (Garretson, SD), June 7, 1923.
25. STJ–Biographies, Jesse James #1, St. Joseph, MO, Public Library, unidentified newspaper article, July 3, 1938.
26. *The Garretson News,* July 27, 1922.
27. Breihan, Carl W., *The Escapades of Frank and Jesse James,* New York: Frederick Fell, 1974, pp 187–188.
28. *The Daily Argus-Leader,* May 3, 1924.
29. *Ibid.*
30. *The Garretson News,* June 7, 1923.
31. *Ibid.*, June 21, 1923.
32. *Ibid.*, January 3, 1924.
33. Bailey, Dana R., *History of Minnehaha County, South Dakota,* Sioux Falls: Brown & Saenger, 1899, pp. 888–889.
34. *The Daily Argus-Leader,* April 19, 1924.
35. *Ibid.*, May 25, 1948.
36. Letter from Charles E. Mason, St. Joseph, MO, to the Garretson Chamber of Commerce, July 12, 1966, posted at the Visitor's Center at Devil's Gulch, Garretson, SD.
37. *St. Paul and Minneapolis Weekly Pioneer Press,* December 7, 1876.

Chapter 8

1. *Daily Press and Dakotaian* (Yankton, DT), September 19, 1876.
2. *Sioux Falls Independent,* June 4, 1874.

Notes—Chapter 9

3. *The Dakota Republican* (Vermillion, DT), November 30, 1876.
4. *New York Sun* in *The Fulton County News* (McConnelsburg, PA), June 27, 1901.
5. This information is from a plaque at the Samuelson log house at the Beaver Creek Nature Area.
6. *Daily Press and Dakotaian*, September 19, 1876.
7. Interview with Bill Webster, Rowena, SD, May 27, 1976.
8. *The Daily Argus-Leader* (Sioux Falls, SD), July 21, 1949.
9. *The Weekly Sedalia Bazoo* (Bazoo, MO) in *The St. Louis Globe-Democrat*, December 5, 1876.
10. Yeatman, Ted P., *Frank and Jesse James: The Story Behind the Legend*, Nashville: Cumberland House, 2000, p. 183.
11. *The Weekly Sedalia Bazoo* in *The St. Louis Globe-Democrat*, December 5, 1876.
12. *The Faribault Democrat* (Faribault, MN), September 22, 1876.
13. *Daily Press and Dakotaian*, September 19, 1876.
14. Ibid.
15. Ibid., September 20, 1876.
16. Ibid.
17. *Dakota Herald* (Yankton, DT), September 24, 1876.
18. *Daily Press and Dakotaian*, September 20, 1876.
19. Ibid.
20. *The Dakota Republican*, September 21, 1876.
21. *The Daily Argus-Leader*, April 26, 1924.
22. *Pioneer History, Minnehaha County's Norwegian Pioneers, History from the Year 1866 to 1896*, published by Minnehaha County's Norwegian Pioneers, 1928; translated into English and reprinted in 1876, p. 311.
23. South Dakota Heritage Center, Pierre, SD, Jesse James Biographical File, article from an unidentified Sioux Falls, SD, newspaper.
24. *The Daily Argus-Leader*, May 3, 1924.
25. *Sioux Valley News* (Canton, DT), September 23, 1876.
26. *The History of Lincoln County South Dakota*, published by the Lincoln County History Committee, Canton, SD, 1985, p. 214.
27. *The Daily Argus-Leader*, May 3, 1924.
28. *The History of Lincoln County South Dakota*, p. 214.
29. *Minneapolis Tribune*, September 21, 1876.
30. *The History of Lincoln County South Dakota*, p. 214; *The Daily Argus-Leader*, May 3, 1924.
31. *The Daily Argus-Leader*, May 3, 1924.
32. *Dakota Farmer's Leader*, March 1, 1901.
33. *Sioux Valley News*, September 23, 1876.
34. *The Daily Argus-Leader*, May 3, 1924.
35. *Dakota Farmer's Leader*, March 1, 1901.
36. *The Worthington Advance* (Worthington, MN), October 5, 1876.
37. *Sioux Valley News*, September 23, 1876.
38. *The Daily Argus-Leader*, April 26, 1924.
39. Ibid., May 10, 1924.
40. *Daily Press and Dakotaian*, September 23, 1876.
41. *The Daily Journal* (Sioux City, IA), September 22, 1876.
42. *Minneapolis Tribune*, September 22, 1876.
43. *St. Paul and Minneapolis Pioneer-Press and Tribune*, September 22, 1876
44. *Swan Lake Era* (Swan Lake, DT), September 28, 1876.
45. Sutley, Zack T., *The Last Frontier*, New York: Macmillan, 1930, pp. 105–110
46. South Dakota Heritage Center, Pierre, SD, Jesse James Biographical File, article from an unidentified Sioux Falls, SD, newspaper.
47. *The Daily Argus-Leader*, May 10, 1924.

Chapter 9

1. *Mankato Record* (Mankato, MN), September 23, 1876.
2. *St. Paul and Minneapolis Pioneer-Press and Tribune*, September 22, 1876.
3. *The Daily Argus-Leader* (Sioux Falls, SD), June 6, 1924.
4. *St. Paul Evening Dispatch* in *The Dakota Republican* (Vermillion, DT), October 5, 1876.
5. *The Daily Argus-Leader*, June 5, 1924.
6. Huntington, George, P., *Robber and Hero, The Story of the Northfield Bank Raid*, St. Paul: Minnesota Historical Society Press, 1986, first published in 1895, xxxviii; Sorbel's phony last name is also listed as "Suborn."
7. *The Daily Argus-Leader*, June 5, 1924.
8. Huntington, George P., xxxviii.
9. *Minneapolis Tribune*, September 22, 1876.
10. *The Daily Argus-Leader*, September 20, 1924.
11. *Minneapolis Tribune*, September 23, 1876.
12. Ibid., September 22, 1876.
13. *The Daily Argus-Leader*, September 20, 1924.
14. *Mankato Record*, September 23, 1876.
15. *Sioux Valley News* (Canton, DT), October 28, 1876, from an unidentified Mankato, MN, newspaper.
16. *Mankato Record*, September 30, 1876.

17. *St. Paul and Minneapolis Pioneer-Press and Tribune*, September 22, 1876.
18. *The Philipsburg Mail* (Philipsburg, MT), July 27, 1893.
19. *The Daily Argus-Leader*, September 20, 1924.
20. *The Daily Journal* (Sioux City, IA), October 25, 1876.
21. *Minneapolis Tribune*, September 22, 1876.
22. *St. Paul and Minneapolis Pioneer-Press and Tribune*, September 23, 1876.
23. *Minneapolis Tribune*, September 22, 1876.
24. *Ibid.*, September 23, 1876. Also called George Wells.
25. *St. Paul and Minneapolis Pioneer-Press and Tribune*, September 22, 1876.
26. Gardner, Mark Lee, *Shot All to Hell: The Northfield Raid, and the Wild West's Greatest Escape*, New York: William Morrow, 2013, p. 236.
27. *St. Paul and Minneapolis Pioneer-Press and Tribune*, September 26, 1876.
28. *The Dakota Pantagraph* (Sioux Falls, DT), December 18, 1878.
29. *The Daily Argus-Leader*, September 20, 1924.
30. *Ibid.*
31. *The Faribault Democrat* (Faribault, MN), September 29, 1876.
32. *The Daily Argus-Leader*, September 20, 1924.
33. *Mankato Record*, October 7, 1876.
34. *St. Paul and Minneapolis Pioneer-Press and Tribune*, September 23, 1876.
35. Brant, Marley, *Jesse James, The Man and the Myth*, New York: Berkley Books, 1998, p. 191.
36. *St. Paul Weekly Dispatch* in *The Worthington Advance* (Worthington, MN), September 28, 1876.
37. *Mankato Record*, September 16 and 30, 1876.
38. *St. Paul Weekly Dispatch* in *The Dakota Republican* (Vermillion, DT), October 12, 1876.
39. *Minneapolis Tribune*, September 23, 1876.
40. *The Daily Journal*, September 23, 1876.
41. *Minneapolis Tribune*, September 23, 1876.
42. *St. Paul and Minneapolis Pioneer-Press and Tribune*, September 23, 1876.
43. *Minneapolis Tribune*, September 23, 1876.
44. *Ibid.*, September 25, 1876.
45. *St. Paul and Minneapolis Pioneer-Press and Tribune*, September 26, 1876.
46. *St. Paul Weekly Dispatch* in *The Dakota Republican* (Vermillion, DT), October 12, 1876.
47. *Minneapolis Tribune*, September 25, 1876.
48. *The Faribault Republican*, September 27, 1876.
49. *St. Paul and Minneapolis Pioneer-Press and Tribune*, September 26, 1876.
50. *Minneapolis Tribune*, September 23, 1876.
51. *The Faribault Republican*, September 27, 1876.
52. *Minneapolis Tribune*, September 23, 1876.
53. *The Faribault Democrat*, September 29, 1876.
54. *The Daily Argus-Leader*, April 12, 1924.
55. *Minneapolis Tribune*, September 25 and 26, 1876.
56. *St. Paul and Minneapolis Pioneer-Press and Tribune*, September 24, 1876.
57. *Ibid.*, September 26, 1876.
58. *Ibid.*, September 30, 1876.
59. *Minneapolis Tribune*, September 28, 1876.
60. *The Kansas City Times*, September 26, 1876.
61. *The St. Louis Globe-Democrat* in *The Worthington Advance* (Worthington, MN), October 5, 1876.

Chapter 10

1. *The Faribault Democrat* (Faribault, MN), September 29, 1876.
2. *The Faribault Republican* (Faribault MN), October 11, 1876.
3. *Minneapolis Tribune*, September 25 and 27, 1876.
4. *Ibid.*, November 15, 1876.
5. *The Faribault Democrat* in the *Mankato Record*, November 4, 1876.
6. *Minneapolis Tribune*, September 28, 1876.
7. *The Worthington Advance*, September 28, 1876.
8. *Minneapolis Tribune*, November 21, 1876.
9. Brant, Marley, *Jesse James, The Man and the Myth*, New York: Berkley Books, 1998, p. 192.
10. *The Faribault Republican*, October 4, 1876.
11. *The Journal*, Official Publication of the Western Outlaw-Lawman History Association, "How the James Boys Fled the Disaster at Northfield," by Nancy B. Samuelson, Vol. III, No. 1, Spring/Summer 1993, p. 5.
12. *The Faribault Democrat* in the *St. Paul Pioneer Weekly*, December 7, 1876.
13. *Minneapolis Tribune*, November 16, 1876.
14. *St. Paul and Minneapolis Weekly Pioneer Press*, November 16, 1876.
15. Samuelson, Nancy B., p. 7.
16. *Minneapolis Tribune*, September 28, 1876.
17. *St. Paul and Minneapolis Pioneer-Press and Tribune*, September 28, 1876.
18. *Ibid.*, September 27, 1876.

19. *Ibid.*, September 26, 1876.
20. *Ibid.*, September 22, 1876.
21. *Ibid.*, September 24, 1876.
22. *The Faribault Republican*, September 27, 1876.
23. *Mankato Record*, September 30, 1876.
24. *The Worthington Advance*, September 28, 1876.
25. *The Faribault Democrat*, October 6, 1876. The victim's last name is also spelled Cavernick and Kapanick and the shooter's name was also given as James Glyser.
26. *The Faribault Republican*, October 4, 1876.
27. *The Faribault Democrat*, October 6, 1876.
28. *The Worthington Advance*, October 19, 1876.
29. *The Webster Journal* (Webster, SD), July 17, 1930.
30. *Minneapolis Tribune*, November 14, 1876.
31. *Ibid.*, November 15, 1876.
32. *Ibid.*, November 16, 1876.
33. *Ibid.*, November 14, 1876.
34. *The St. Louis Globe-Democrat*, November 18, 1876.
35. *Minneapolis Tribune*, November 16, 1876.
36. *Ibid.*
37. *St. Paul and Minneapolis Weekly Pioneer Press*, December 14, 1876.
38. *Ibid.*, November 23, 1876.
39. *The Worthington Advance*, November 23, 1876.
40. *St. Paul and Minneapolis Weekly Pioneer Press*, November 30, 1876.
41. *Minneapolis Tribune*, November 23, 1876.
42. *New York World* in *The Dakota Republican* (Vermillion, DT), October 26, 1876.
43. *Ibid.*

Chapter 11

1. *Daily Press and Dakotaian* (Yankton, DT), September 24, 1876.
2. *The St. Louis Republican* in the *Minneapolis Tribune*, September 22, 1876.
3. *The Daily Argus-Leader* (Sioux Falls, SD), May 10, 1924.
4. *The Sioux Falls Journal*, November 21, 1913.
5. *Sioux Valley News* (Canton, DT), September 23, 1876.
6. *Minneapolis Tribune*, September 22, 1876.
7. *The Kansas City Times*, September 22, 1876.
8. *Minneapolis Tribune*, September 22, 1876.
9. *The Daily Journal* (Sioux City, IA), September 22, 1876.
10. *Ibid.*, January 22, 1876. An accoucheur was a doctor who assisted with births.
11. *Minneapolis Tribune*, September 26, 1876.
12. *The Daily Journal*, September 22, 1876.
13. *Ibid.*
14. *Ibid.*, September 23, 1876.
15. *Daily Press and Dakotaian*, September 22, 1876.
16. *St. Paul and Minneapolis Pioneer-Press and Tribune*, September 26, 1876.
17. *The Daily Journal*, September 23, 1876.
18. *The Kansas City Times*, September 26, 1876.
19. *The Journal*, official publication of the Western Outlaw-Lawman History Association, "How the James Boys Fled the Disaster at Northfield," by Nancy B. Samuelson, Vol. III, No. 1, Spring/Summer 1993, p. 7.
20. *Daily Press and Dakotaian*, September 24 and 26, 1876.
21. *The Daily Journal*, September 24 and 26, 1876.
22. *Ibid.*, October 22, 1876.
23. Samuelson, Nancy B., p. 4; Breihan, Carl W., *The Escapades of Frank and Jesse James*, New York: Frederick Fell, 1974, pp. 187–188.
24. *Bismarck Tribune*, February 28, 1877.
25. *St. Paul and Minneapolis Pioneer-Press and Tribune*, September 29, 1876.
26. *The Daily Argus-Leader*, May 10, 1924.
27. *The St. Louis Globe-Democrat* in the *Minneapolis Tribune*, October 9, 1876.
28. Samuelson, Nancy B., p. 7.
29. *Ibid.*
30. *The Sedalia Weekly Bazoo* (Sedalia, MO), April 11, 1882.
31. *The St. Louis Globe-Democrat*, October 19, 1876.
32. *The Kansas City Times* in the *Minneapolis Tribune*, October 17, 1876.
33. Samuelson, Nancy B., p. 7.
34. *The Daily Journal*, October 19, 1876.
35. *Minneapolis Tribune*, October 17, 1876.
36. *The Daily Journal*, October 19, 1876.
37. *The Monroe Journal* (Monroe, SC), September 25, 1914.
38. *Minneapolis Tribune*, October 17, 1876.
39. *The Daily Journal*, October 20, 1876.
40. *Ibid.*, October 19, 1876.
41. *The St. Louis Globe-Democrat*, October 19, 1876.
42. *The Daily Journal*, October 22, 1876.
43. *The Sedalia Weekly Bazoo*, April 11, 1882.
44. *The St. Louis Globe-Democrat*, October 19, 1876.
45. *The Daily Journal*, October 20, 1876.

46. *The Kansas City Times* in the *The Dakota Republican* (Vermillion, DT).

Chapter 12

1. *The Waco Daily Examiner*, May 3, 1882.
2. *Omaha Republican* in the *Las Vegas Daily Gazette*, August 10, 1881.
3. *St. Paul and Minneapolis Pioneer-Press and Tribune*, October 8, 1876.
4. *The St. Louis Globe-Democrat*, November 25, 1876.
5. *The Faribault Republican* (Faribault, MN), September 26, 1877.
6. *The Kansas City Times*, October 15, 1876.
7. Yeatman, Ted P., *Frank and Jesse James: The Story Behind the Legend*, Nashville: Cumberland House, 2000, pp. 190–191; Settle, William A., Jr., *Jesse James Was His Name*, Lincoln: University of Nebraska Press, 1977, originally published in 1966, p. 100; Gardner, Mark Lee, *Shot All to Hell: Jesse James, the Northfield Raid, and the Wild West's Greatest Escape*, New York: William Morrow, 2013, p. 214; *The St. Louis Globe-Democrat*, November 26, 1876.
8. *The St. Louis Globe-Democrat*, December 16, 1876.
9. *The Kansas City Times*, December 15, 1876.
10. *The Faribault Democrat*, December 15, 1876.
11. *Sacramento Daily Record-Union*, April 5, 1882.
12. *The Kansas City Times* in the *St. Paul and Minneapolis Weekly Pioneer Press*, November 2, 1876. The "little negro child" was most likely a reference to the illegitimate child of Dr. Reuben Samuel and one of the enslaved women owned by the James–Samuel family.
13. Brant, Marley, *Jesse James, The Man and the Myth*, New York: Berkley Books, 1998, p. 195.
14. *Omaha Daily Bee*, August 12, 1901.
15. *The Faribault Democrat*, September 28, 1877.
16. *The Faribault Republican*, September 26, 1877.
17. Gardner, Mark Lee, p. 202.
18. *The Butler Weekly Times* (Butler, MO), April 19, 1882.
19. McKiernan, F. Mark, and Launius, Roger D., eds., *Missouri Folk Heroes of the 19th Century*, Independence, MO: Independence Press Herald Publishing House, 1989, p. 151.
20. Brant, Marley, p. 206.
21. *Mankato Record* (Mankato, MN), October 14, 1876.
22. Ibid.
23. *St. Paul and Minneapolis Pioneer-Press and Tribune*, October 1, 1876.
24. Wallace, William H., *Speeches and Writings of Wm. H. Wallace with Autobiography*, Kansas City: The Western Baptist Publishing Co., 1914, p. 265.
25. *Alexandria Gazette* (Alexandria, VA), April 6, 1882.
26. Brant, Marley, pp. 196–197.
27. *Memphis Daily Appeal*, August 8, 1878.
28. Yeatman, Ted P., p. 215; Settle, William A., Jr., p. 102.
29. *The Sedalia Weekly Bazoo* (Sedalia, MO), September 19, 1882.
30. *New York Sun*, November 10, 1879; *Daily Press and Dakotaian* (Yankton, DT), November 6, 1879.
31. *The Ouachita Telegraph* (Monroe, LA), November 14, 1879. Cummins is also spelled "Cummings."
32. *Chicago Times* in the *Daily Press and Dakotaian*, November 6, 1879.
33. *The Kansas City Times* in the *Dodge City Times* (Dodge City, KS), November 15, 1879.
34. *The Milan Exchange* (Milan, TN), March 11, 1882.
35. *The Kansas City Times* in the *Memphis Daily Appeal*, July 28, 1880.
36. *The Ouachita Telegraph* (Monroe, LA), December 12, 1879.
37. Ibid.
38. *St. Paul and Minneapolis Pioneer-Press and Tribune*, September 20, 1876.
39. *The Sedalia Weekly Bazoo* (Sedalia, MO), September 19, 1882.
40. Yeatman, Ted P., p. 265.
41. *Lake Charles Commercial* (Lake Charles, LA), November 12, 1881.
42. www.findagrave.com, Find a Grave Memorial, Edward T. Miller, consulted 5/21/16.
43. Yeatman, Ted P., p. 227.
44. *Iron County Register* (Ironton, MO), September 10, 1896.
45. Yeatman, Ted P., pp. 249–250; Gardner, Mark Lee, p. 217; *The River Press* (Fort Benton, MT), August 3, 1881.
46. *The St. Louis Republican* in the *Sioux Valley News* (Canton, DT), August 12, 1881.
47. *Fargo Argus* (Fargo, DT) in *The Black Hills Daily Times* (Deadwood, DT), August 30, 1881.
48. *Courier Journal* (Bardstown, KY) in the *San Marcos Free Press* (San Marcos, TX), November 17, 1881.
49. *San Marco Free Press*, November 17, 1881.
50. *Courier Journal* (Bardstown, KY) in the

San Marcos Free Press (San Marcos, TX), November 17, 1881. This is probably a reference to Allan Pinkerton, founder of the famous Chicago detective agency.
51. *The Sedalia Weekly Bazoo*, October 18, 1881.

Chapter 13

1. *Weekly Graphic* (Kirksville, Adair County, MO), April 7, 1882.
2. *The County Paper* (Oregon, MO), April 14, 1882.
3. *Lincoln County Leader* (Toledo, Lincoln County, OR), May 29, 1908.
4. *The County Paper*, April 14, 1882.
5. *Helena Weekly Herald* (Helena, MT), April 13, 1882.
6. Yeatman, Ted P., *Frank and Jesse James: The Story Behind the Legend*, Nashville: Cumberland House, 2000, p. 265.
7. Settle, William A., Jr., *Jesse James Was His Name*, Lincoln: University of Nebraska Press, 1977, originally published in 1966, p. 107.
8. *The Breckenridge News* (Cloverport, KY), June 27, 1894.
9. Settle, William A., Jr., pp. 107–198.
10. Frazier, Harriet C., *Death Sentences in Missouri, 1803–2005, A History and Comprehensive Registry of Legal Executions, Pardons and Commutations*, Jefferson, NC: McFarland, 2006, p. 64.
11. Yeatman, Ted P., p. 266.
12. *St. Landry Democrat* (Opelousas, LA), April 15, 1882.
13. *Lake County Star* (Chase, MI), April 13, 1882.
14. *Weekly Graphic*, April 7, 1882.
15. *The Helena Independent* (Helena, MT), March 7, 1891.
16. *Kansas City Star* in *The Butler Weekly Times* (Butler, MO), October 31, 1895.
17. *The Breckenridge News*, June 24, 1894.
18. *Sierra County Advocate* (Kingston, NM), August 21, 1891.
19. Yeatman, Ted P., p. 266.
20. *Knoxville Daily Chronicle*, April 6, 1882.
21. *Mount Vernon Signal* (Mt. Vernon, KY), July 4, 1902.
22. *The Butler Weekly Times* (Butler, MO), September 1, 1886.
23. Love, Robertus, *The Rise and Fall of Jesse James*, New York: G. P. Putnam's Sons, 1926, p. 351.
24. Yeatman, Ted P., p. 267.
25. *The Indianapolis Journal*, June 12, 1892.

26. *The Daily Missoulian* (Missoula, MT), January 31, 1913.
27. *Weekly Graphic*, March 10, 1882.
28. *Kansas City Star* in *The Butler Weekly Times*, October 31, 1895.
29. Ibid.
30. *The Hickman Courier* (Hickman, KY), December 1, 1910.
31. *Kansas City Star* in *The Butler Weekly Times*, October 31, 1895.
32. Gardner, Mark Lee, *Shot All to Hell: Jesse James, the Northfield Raid and the Wild West's Greatest Escape*, New York: William Morrow, 2013, pp. 218–220.
33. *The Bourbon News* (Millersburg, KY), April 14, 1882.
34. *Lincoln County Leader*, May 29, 1908.
35. Nolf, Richard A., ed., "St. Joe Museum Graphic—Jesse James Special Edition," published by St. Joseph Museum, St. Joseph, MO, 1972, pp. 14 and 25; *The Rock Island Argus* (Rock Island, IL), April 4, 1882.
36. *Cheyenne Transporter* (Darlington, Indian Territory) Supplement, April 10, 1882.
37. *The Sedalia Weekly Bazoo* (Sedalia, MO), April 11, 1882. Mattie Collins may not have been Liddil's "real" wife. It was said that she once was an inmate in a Dallas house of ill-repute and had been the lover of the outlaw Joel Collins, a member of the Sam Bass gang.
38. Ibid.
39. *Daily Globe* (St. Paul, MN), April 7, 1882.
40. Ibid., April 6, 1882.
41. *The Sedalia Weekly Bazoo*, April 11, 1882.
42. *The Bourbon News*, April 11, 1882.
43. *The Rock Island Argus* (Rock Island, IL), April 5, 1882.
44. *El Paso Daily Herald* (El Paso, TX), February 6, 1901.
45. *The Butler Weekly Times*, April 19, 1882.
46. *Weekly Graphic*, April 7, 1882.
47. *Richmond Democrat* (Richmond, MO), April 13, 1882.
48. *The Rock Island Argus*, April 5, 1882.
49. *Daily Press and Dakotaian* (Yankton, DT), April 7, 1882.
50. *Iron County Register* (Ironton, MO), April 20, 1882.
51. *The Sacramento Daily Record-Union*, April 5, 1882.
52. *The News-Herald* (Hillsboro, OH), February 25, 1892.
53. *Butler Citizen* (Butler, PA), April 12, 1882.
54. *Northern Tribune* (Cheboygan, MI), April 15, 1882.
55. *New York Sun* in the *Bisbee Daily Review* (Bisbee, AZ), September 1, 1907.

56. *Daily Globe*, April 7, 1882.
57. *Ibid.*
58. *Omaha Daily Bee*, April 7, 1882.
59. *The Emporia Weekly News* (Emporia, KS), April 13, 1882.
60. *The Benton Weekly Record* (Benton, MT), April 20, 1882.
61. *El Paso Daily Herald*, February 6, 1901.
62. *The St. Louis Globe-Democrat* in *The Indianapolis Journal*, July 11, 1902.
63. *Omaha Daily Bee*, August 21, 1887.
64. *The Waco Daily Examiner* (Waco, TX), April 29, 1882.
65. *Arizona Weekly Enterprise* (Florence, AZ), April 8, 1882.
66. *Evening Bulletin* (Maysville, KY), May 4, 1882.
67. *The Breckenridge News*, June 27, 1894.
68. *The National Tribune* (Washington, D.C.), April 15, 1882.
69. *Richmond Democrat*, April 13, 1882.
70. *The Kansas City Daily Journal* in the *Cheyenne Transporter*, April 10, 1882.
71. *The Indiana State Sentinel*, April 12, 1882.
72. *New York Times* in *The Sedalia Weekly Bazoo*, May 30, 1882.
73. *The Vancouver Independent*, June 8, 1882.
74. *Public Ledger* (Memphis, TN), April 14, 1882.
75. *The Emporia Weekly News* (Emporia, KS), April 13, 1882.
76. *Daily Press and Dakotaian*, April 7, 1882.
77. *Dodge City Times* (Dodge City, KS), April 20, 1882.
78. *The Semi-Weekly Miner* (Butte, MT), April 26, 1882.
79. *Idaho Semi-Weekly World* (Idaho City, IT), May 9, 1882.
80. *The Sedalia Weekly Bazoo*, May 16, 1882.
81. *Iron County Register*, May 11, 1882.
82. *The Daily Telegraph* (Monroe, LA), February 1, 1886.
83. *The Butler Weekly Times*, February 10, 1886.
84. *The Scranton Tribune* (Scranton, PA), August 28, 1896.
85. *The Sacramento Daily Record-Union*, April 19, 1882.

Chapter 14

1. *Blount County Democrat* (Marysville, TN), April 15, 1882.
2. *Chicago Times* in the *Las Vegas Daily Gazette* (Las Vegas, NV), April 11, 1882.
3. *Sioux City Journal Tribune*, June 17, 1948.

4. STJ—Biographies, James, Jesse #1, Newspaper File, St. Joseph Library, St. Joseph, MO, unnamed and undated newspaper article.
5. *New York Globe* in *The Commoner* (Lincoln, NE), October 1, 1913.
6. *The Sedalia Weekly Bazoo* (Sedalia, MO), August 13, 1889.
7. *The Caldwell Tribune* (Caldwell, Idaho Territory), May 16, 1891.
8. *Daily Public Ledger* (Maysville, KY), August 28, 1900.
9. *Weekly Graphic* (Kirksville, Adair County, MO), April 14, 1882.
10. *The Daily Cairo Bulletin* (Cairo, IL), May 5, 1882.
11. Triplett, Frank, *The Life, Times and Treacherous Death of Jesse James*, New York: Promontory Press, 1970, originally published in 1882 by J. H. Chambers, St. Louis, MO, p. xxiii.
12. *The Sedlia Weekly Bazoo* (Sedalia, MO), July 11, 1882.
13. *Madison Times* (Tallulah, LA), May 23, 1885.
14. *The Butler Weekly Times* (Butler, MO), August 29, 1888.
15. *The True Northerner* (Paw Paw, MI), April 21, 1882.
16. Yeatman, Ted P., *Frank and Jesse James: The Story Behind the Legend*, Nashville: Cumberland House, 2000, pp. 279–283.
17. *The Butler Weekly Times*, September 5, 1883.
18. Gardner, Mark Lee, *Shot All To Hell: Jesse James, the Northfield Raid and the Wild West's Greatest Escape*, New York: William Morrow, 2013, pp. 224–225.
19. Wallace, William H., *Speeches and Writings of Wm. H. Wallace with Autobiography*, Kansas City: The Western Baptist Publishing Co., 1914, p. 266.
20. *Orleans County Monitor* (Barton, VT), August 19, 1895.
21. *The Richmond Climax* (Richmond, KY), September 23, 1914.
22. *The Breckenridge News* (Cloverport, KY), December 20, 1882.
23. *Louisiana Journal* in the *Mexico Weekly Ledger* (Mexico, MO), November 15, 1883.
24. *St. Joseph Gazette* in *The Sedalia Weekly Bazoo*, November 20, 1883.
25. *The Butler Weekly Times*, June 8, 1893.
26. *Ibid.*
27. Fanebust, Wayne, *Outlaw Dakota, The Murderous Times and Criminal Trials of Frontier Judge Peter C. Shannon*, Sioux Falls, SD: The Center for Western Studies, 2016, p. 102; *The Elk County Advocate* (Ridgway, PA), June 8, 1882;

Sioux Falls Independent (Sioux Falls, DT), January 29, 1874.
28. *Daily Globe* (St. Paul, MN), April 6, 1882.
29. *The Western News* (Stevensville, MT), July 9, 1902.
30. *Daily Globe*, April 6, 1882.
31. *The Western News*, July 9, 1902.
32. *Nashville Banner* in the *The Brownsville Daily Herald* (Brownsville, TX), March 26, 1904; *The Washington Herald* (Washington, D.C.), April 18, 1914. In other sources the judge's name is spelled "Rowntree" and Hunt's first name is also listed as "William."
33. Love, Roberrtus, *The Rise and Fall of Jesse James*, New York: G. P. Putnam's Sons, 1926, p. 361.
34. *The Philipsburg Mail* (Philipsburg, MT), July 27, 1893.
35. *The Butler Weekly Times*, July 10, 1889.

Chapter 15

1. *New York World*, June 1, 1890.
2. *The Topeka State Journal*, May 29, 1895.
3. *The Dalles Daily Chronicle* (The Dalles, OR), August 8, 1891.
4. Yeatman, Ted P., *Frank and Jesse James: The Story Behind the Legend*, Nashville: Cumberland House, 2000, p. 275.
5. *Evening Bulletin* (Maysville, KY), April 20, 1882.
6. *Daily Press and Dakotaian* (Yankton, DT), September 28, 1882.
7. *The Louisiana Democrat* (Alexandria, LA), November 1, 1882.
8. *The Sedalia Weekly Bazoo*, September 19, 1882.
9. *The Louisiana Democrat*, November 1, 1882.
10. *Hopkinsville Kentuckian* (Hopkinsville, KY), June 2, 1896.
11. Yeatman, Ted P., p. 291.
12. *The Durham Daily Globe* (Durham, NC), February 19, 1892.
13. Yeatman, Ted P., p. 291.
14. *The Kansas City Journal*, June 28, 1899.
15. *The St. Louis Republic*, November 14, 1900.
16. *The Daily Morning Journal and Courier* (New Haven, CT), November 26, 1900.
17. *Ibid.*
18. *Denver Republican* in the *Lewiston Teller* (Lewiston, ID), September 11, 1890.
19. *The St. Louis Republic*, November 14, 1900.
20. *The Butler Weekly Times* (Butler, MO), September 19, 1907.
21. *The St. Louis Republic*, May 4, 1902.

22. *The Topeka State Journal*, August 23, 1922.
23. *The St. Joseph Observer* (St. Joseph, MO), September 16, 1922.
24. *The Honolulu Republican*, July 16, 1901.
25. *The Pacific Commercial Advertiser* (Honolulu, HI), August 19, 1901.
26. *The Paducah Sun* (Paducah, KY), April 21, 1902.
27. *Hopkinsville Kentuckian*, April 22, 1902.
28. *The Hawaiian Star* (Honolulu, HI), April 10, 1902.
29. *Bismarck Daily Tribune* (Bismarck, ND), July 1, 1902.
30. Settle, William A., Jr., *Jesse James Was His Name*, Lincoln: University of Nebraska Press, 1977, originally published in 1966, p. 166.
31. *The Lexington Intelligencer* (Lexington, MO) August 2, 1902.
32. *It* (Lawrenceburg, KY), January 8, 1903.
33. *The Chanute Times* (Chanute, KS), March 1, 1912.
34. *The Washington Times* (Washington, D.C.), June 14, 1917.
35. *The Butte Daily Post* (Butte, MT), February 16, 1917.
36. *Rock Island Argus* (Rock Island, IL), May 25, 1901
37. *Rochelle Register* (Rochelle, IL), April 12, 1879.
38. *The Butler Weekly Times*, July 18, 1901.
39. Settle, William A., Jr., pp. 162–163; *Wood County Reporter* (Grand Rapids, WI), October 23, 1902.
40. *The Daily Morning Journal and Courier* (New Haven, CT), October 20, 1902.
41. Yeatman, Ted P., pp. 301–302.
42. *The Leon Reporter* (Leon, IA), February 25, 1915.
43. *The Weekly Messenger* (St. Martinsville, LA), February 11, 1905.
44. *The Falls Tribune* (Falls City, NE), July 7, 1905; *The Worthington Advance* (Worthington, MN), July 14, 1905.
45. *The Twice-a-Week Herald* (Amarillo, TX), October 10, 1905; *The Coconino Sun* (Flagstaff, AZ), June 9, 1906.
46. *Graham Guardian* (Safford, AZ), May 4, 1906; *Albuquerque Evening Citizen* (Albuquerque, NM), June 25, 1906.
47. *Hopkinsville Kentuckian*, August 4, 1910.
48. *The Evening Statesman* (Walla Walla, WA), October 17, 1906.
49. *Rogue River Courier* (Grant's Pass, OR), November 30, 1906.
50. *The Daily Argus-Leader* (Sioux Falls, SD), March 30 and April 1, 1907.

51. *Albuquerque Evening Citizen*, June 19, 1906.
52. *The Evening Statesman*, March 11, 1907.
53. *Pullman Herald* (Pullman, WA), August 28, 1907.
54. *The Butte Inter Mountain* (Butte, MT), July 7, 1902.
55. *The Billings Gazette* (Billings, MT), June 26, 1908.
56. *The Minot Optic* (Minot, ND) in the *Bismarck Daily Tribune*, August 9, 1908.
57. *The Leon Reporter*, October 1, 1908.
58. *Meade County News* (Meade, KS), September 12, 1912.
59. *The Clay City Times* (Clay City, KY), May 15, 1913.
60. *The Bemidji Daily Pioneer* (Bemidji, MN), September 21, 1914. His real name was William Henry Pratt.
61. *Warren Sheaf* (Warren, MN), January 29, 1903.
62. Gaudrecault, Andre, ed., *American Cinema 1890–1909*, New Brunswick: Rutgers University Press, 2009, p. xiv.
63. *Ibid.*, p. 45.
64. *Ibid.*, p. 15.
65. *Ibid.*, p. 207.
66. *The Pensacola Journal* (Pensacola, FL), November 15, 1911.
67. *Forest City Press* (Forest City, SD), August 1, 1903.
68. *The St. Louis Republic*, October 20, 1901.
69. *The Washington Times*, February 11, 1911.
70. *The Manning Times* (Manning, SC), December 23, 1914.
71. *The Leon Reporter*, February 25, 1915.
72. Settle, William A., Jr., p. 165.
73. *The Blackfoot Optimist* (Blackfoot, ID), February 25, 1915.
74. Yeatman, Ted P., p. 326.
75. Breihan, Carl W., *The Day Jesse James Was Killed: The Spine-thrilling Story of the Most Hunted Outlaw in the Old West*, New York: Signet, 1979, originally published in 1861, pp. 84–85.
76. *Arizona Republican* (Phoenix, AZ), May 27, 1921.
77. *The Hold County Sentinel* (Oregon, MO), May 13, 1921.
78. *The Spokane Press*, July 18, 1906.
79. James, Stella Frances, *In the Shadow of Jesse James*, ed. Milton F. Perry, Thousand Oaks, CA: The Revolver Press1989, p. 96.
80. www.findagrave.com, Jesse Edwards "Tim" James, consulted 11/30/16.
81. Everson, William K., and Fenin, George N., *The Western: From Silents to Cinerama*, New York: Bonanza Books, 1962, p. 36.
82. *The Marion Daily Mirror* (Marion, OH), December 18, 1907

Bibliography

Books

Bailey, Dana R., *History of Minnehaha County, South Dakota*, Sioux Falls: Brown & Saenger, 1899.

Brant, Marley, *Jesse James: The Man and the Myth*. New York: Berkley Books, 1998.

Breihan, Carl W., *The Day Jesse James Was Killed: The Spine-Chilling True Story of the Most Hunted Outlaw in the Old West*, New York: Signet Book, 1979.

_____, *The Escapades of Frank and Jesse James*, New York: Frederick Fell, 1974.

Celebrating a Century, Garretson, SD, 1889–1989, compiled and published by the Garretson Book Committee, 1989.

Christianson, Theodore, *Minnesota: A History of the State and its People*, Vol. I, Chicago: The American Historical Society, 1935.

Croy, Homer, *Jesse James Was My Neighbor*, New York: Dell, 1960.

Dellinger, Harold, ed., *Jesse James: The Best Writings on the Notorious Outlaw and His Gang*, Guilford, CT: Globe Pequot Press, 2007.

Everson, William K., and Fenin, George N., *The Western: From Silents to Cinerama*, New York: Bonanza Books, 1962.

Fanebust, Wayne, *Outlaw Dakota: The Murderous Times and Criminal Trials of Frontier Judge Peter C. Shannon*, Sioux Falls, SD: The Center for Western Studies, 2016.

Frazier, Harriet C., *Death Sentences in Missouri, 1803–2005: A History and Comprehensive Registry of Legal Executions, Pardons and Commutations*, Jefferson, NC: McFarland, 2006.

Gardner, Mark Lee, *Shot All to Hell: Jesse James, the Northfield Raid, and the Wild West's Greatest Escape*, New York: William Morrow, 2013.

Gaudrecault, Andre, Ed., *American Cinema 1890–1909*, New Brunswick: Rutgers University Press, 2009.

The History of Lincoln County South Dakota, published by the Lincoln County History Committee, Canton, SD, 1985.

History of Southeastern Dakota, Sioux City: Western Publishing Co., 1881.

Horan, James D., *Desperate Men, Revelations from the Sealed Pinkerton Files*, New York: Bonanza Books, 1949.

Huntington, George, *Robber and Hero: The Story of the Northfield Bank Raid*, St. Paul: Minnesota Historical Society Press, 1986, first published in 1895.

James, Stella Frances, *In the Shadow of Jesse James*, ed. Milton F. Perry, Thousand Oaks, CA: Revolver Press, 1990.

Johnson, Michael L., *Hunger for the Wild: American Obsession with the Untamed West*, Lawrence: University Press of Kansas, 2007.

Kolbas, John, *The Jesse James Northfield Raid, Confessions of the Ninth Man*, North Star Press of St. Cloud, 1999.

Lemann, Nicholas, *Redemption: The Last Battle of the Civil War*, New York: Farrar, Straus and Giroux, 2006.

The Life and Tragic Death of Jesse James, by "One Who Dare Not Disclose His Identity," Philadelphia: Barclay & Co., 1883.

Love, Robertus, *The Rise and Fall of Jesse James*, New York: G. P. Putnam's Sons, 1926.

Mackay, James, *Allan Pinkerton: The First Private Eye*, New York: John Wiley & Sons, 1996.

McKiernan, F. Mark, and Launius, Roger D., eds., *Missouri Folk Heroes of the 19th Cen-*

tury, Independence, MO: Independence Press Herald Publishing House, 1989.
Pioneer History, Minnehaha County's Norwegian Pioneers, History From the Year 1866 to 1896, published by Minnehaha County's Norwegian Pioneers, 1928; translated into English and reprinted in 1976.
Rosa, Joseph G., *The Gunfighter, Man or Myth?* Norman: University of Oklahoma Press, 1969.
Rose, Arthur P., *An Illustrated History of the Counties of Rock & Pipestone Minnesota*, Luverne: Northern History Publishing Co., 1911.
Settle, William H., Jr., *Jesse James Was His Name*, Lincoln: University of Nebraska Press, 1977.
Smith, Charles A., *A Comprehensive History of Minnehaha County*, Mitchell, SD: Educator Supply, 1949
Stiles, T. J., *Jesse James: The Last Rebel of the Civil War*, New York: Vintage, 2003.
The Story of Cole Younger, by Himself, St. Paul: Minnesota Historical Society Press, 2000, originally published by Hennberry of Chicago, 1903.
Sutley, Zack T., *The Last Frontier*, New York: Macmillan, 1930.
The Trial of Frank James for Murder, with Confessions of Dick Liddil and Clarence Hite and History Of the "James Gang," New York: Jingle Bob/Crown, 1977, originally published in 1898.
Triplett, Frank, *The Life, Times and Treacherous Death of Jesse James*, New York: Promontory Press, 1970, originally published in 1882.
Wallace, William H., *Speeches and Writings of Wm. H. Wallace with Autobiography*, Kansas City: The Western Baptist Publishers Co., 1914
Yeatman, Ted P., *Frank and Jesse James: The Story Behind the Legend*, Nashville: Cumberland House, 2000.

Articles, Journals, Websites, Archives and Interviews

Bill Webster Interview, Rowena, SD, May 27, 1976.
Garretson Museum and the Visitors' Center at Devil's Gulch, Garretson, SD.
Nolf, Richard A., ed., "St. Joe Museum Graphic, Jesse James Special Edition," p.ublished by St. Joseph Museum, St. Joseph, MO, 1972
The Journal, official publication of the Western Outlaw-Lawman History Association, "How the James Boys Fled the Disaster at Northfield," by Nancy B. Samuelson, Vol. III, No. 1, Spring/Summer 1993.
STJ—Biographies, James, Jesse #1, Newspaper File, St. Joseph Public Library, St. Joseph, MO.
South Dakota Heritage Center, Pierre, SD, Jesse James Biographical File.
www.findagrave.com, Find a Grave Memorial, Jesse Edwards "Tim" James, consulted 11/30/16.
www.findagrave.com, Find a Grave Memorial, Clelland D. Miller, consulted 9/13/16.
www.findagrave.com, Find a Grave Memorial, Edward T. Miller, consulted 5/21/16.

Newspapers

Albuquerque Evening Citizen (Albuquerque, NM)
Alexandria Gazette (Alexandria, VA)
Ann Arbor Register (Ann Arbor, MI)
Arizona Republican (Phoenix, AZ)
Arizona Weekly Enterprise (Florence, AZ)
Barbour County Index (Medicine Lodge, KS)
The Bemidji Daily Pioneer (Bemidji, MN)
The Benton Weekly Record (Benton, MT)
The Billings Gazette (Billings, MT)
Bisbee Daily Review (Bisbee, AZ)
Bismarck Daily Tribune (Bismarck, ND)
Bismarck Times (Bismarck, ND)
The Black Hills Daily Times (Deadwood, DT)
The Blackfoot Optimist (Blackfoot, ID)
Blount County Democrat (Marysville, TN)
The Bourbon News (Millersburg, KY)
The Breckenridge News (Cloverport, KY)
The Brownsville Daily Herald (Brownsville, TX)
Butler Citizen (Butler, PA)
The Butler Weekly Times (Butler, MO)
The Butte Daily Post (Butte, MT)
The Butte Inter Mountain, Butte, MT)
The Caldwell Tribune (Caldwell, ID)
The Central Record (Lancaster, KY)
The Chanute Times (Chanute, KS)
Cheyenne Transporter (Darlington, Indian Territory)
Chicago Times
Cincinnati Inquirer
The Clay City Times (Clay City, KY)

Bibliography

The Coconino Sun (Flagstaff, AZ)
The Columbian (Bloomsburg, PA)
The Commoner (Lincoln, NE)
The County Paper (Oregon, MO)
Courier Journal (Bardstown, KY)
Daily Globe (St. Paul, MN)
Daily Press and Dakotaian (Yankton, DT)
Dakota Farmer's Leader (Canton, SD)
Dakota Herald (Yankton, DT)
Denver Republican
Dodge City Times (Dodge City, KS)
El Paso Daily Herald (El Paso, TX)
The Elk County Advocate (Ridgway, PA)
The Emporia Weekly News (Emporia, KS)
Evening Bulletin (Maysville, KY)
Evening Star (Washington, D.C.)
The Evening Statesman (Walla Walla, WA)
The Falls Tribune (Falls City, NE)
Fargo Argus (Fargo, ND)
The Faribault Democrat (Faribault, MN)
The Faribault Republican (Faribault, MN)
The Farmer and Mechanic (Raleigh, NC)
Forest City Press (Forest City, SD)
The Fulton County News (McConnellsburg, PA)
The Garretson News (Garretson, SD)
Graham Guardian (Safford, AZ)
The Hartford Herald (Hartford, KY)
The Hawaiian Star (Honolulu, HI)
The Helena Independent (Helena, MT)
Helena Weekly Herald (Helena, MT)
The Herald (Los Angeles, CA)
The Hickman Courier (Hickman, KY)
The Hold County Sentinel (Oregon, MO)
The Honolulu Republican
Hopkinsville Kentuckian (Hopkinsville, KY)
Idaho Semi-Weekly World (Idaho City, IT)
The Indiana State Sentinel (Indianapolis, IN)
The Indianapolis Journal
The Interior Journal (Stanford, KY)
Iron County Register (Ironton, MO)
It (Lawrenceburg, KY)
The Kansas City Daily Journal
Kansas City Star
The Kansas City Times
Knoxville Daily Chronicle
Lake Charles Commercial (Lake Charles, LA)
Lake County Star (Chase, MI)
Las Vegas Daily Gazette (Las Vegas, NV)
The Leon Reporter (Leon, IA)
Lewiston Teller (Lewiston, ID)
The Lexington Intelligencer (Lexington, MO)
Lincoln County Leader (Toledo, Lincoln County, OR)

Louisiana Journal
Madison Times (Tallulah, LA)
Mankato Record (Mankato, MN)
The Manning Times (Manning, SC)
The Mantorville Express (Mantorville, MN)
The Marion Daily Mirror (Marion, OH)
Meade County News (Meade, KS)
Memphis Daily Appeal
Mexico Weekly Ledger (Mexico, MO)
The Milan Exchange (Milan, TN)
Minneapolis Tribune
The Minot Optic (Minot, ND)
The Monroe Journal (Monroe, SC)
Mount Vernon Signal (Mt. Vernon, KY)
Nashville Banner
The National Tribune (Washington, D.C.)
New York Globe
New York Sun
New York Times
The New York World
The News-Herald (Hillsboro, OH)
Northern Tribune (Cheboygan, MI)
Omaha Daily Bee
Omaha Republican
Orleans County Monitor (Barton, VT)
The Ouachita Telegraph (Monroe, LA)
The Pacific Commercial Advertiser (Honolulu, HI)
The Paducah Sun (Paducah, KY)
The Parkston Advance (Parkston, SD)
The Pensacola Journal (Pensacola, FL)
The Philipsburg Mail (Philipsburg, MT)
Pioneer-Press (Cato, KS)
Public Ledger (Memphis, TN)
Pullman Herald (Pullman WA)
Rice County Journal (Northfield, MN)
The Richmond Climax (Richmond, KY)
Richmond Democrat (Richmond, MO)
The River Press (Fort Benton, MT)
Rochelle Register (Rochelle, IL)
The Rock Island Argus (Rock Island, IL)
Rogue River Courier (Grant's Pass, OR)
The Sacramento Daily Record-Union
St. Joseph Gazette (St. Joseph, MO)
The St. Joseph Observer (St. Joseph, MO)
St. Landry Democrat (Opelousas, LA)
The St. Louis Globe-Democrat
The St. Louis Republic
The St. Louis Republican
St. Paul and Minneapolis Pioneer-Press and Tribune
St. Paul Pioneer Press
St. Paul Pioneer Weekly
St. Paul Weekly Dispatch

The Salt Lake Herald
San Marcos Free Press (San Marcos, TX)
Saturday Blade (Chicago)
The Scranton Tribune (Scranton, PA)
The Sedalia Weekly Bazoo (Sedalia, MO)
The Semi-Weekly Miner (Butte, MT)
Sierra County Advocate (Kingston, NMT)
Sioux Falls Daily Press (Sioux Falls, DT)
Sioux Falls Independent (Sioux Falls, DT)
The Sioux Falls Journal
Sioux Valley News (Canton, DT)
The Spokane Press
The State Journal (Jefferson City, MO)
Swan Lake Era (Swan Lake, DT)
The Adair County News (Columbia, KY)
The Topeka State Journal

The True Northerner (Paw Paw, MI)
The Twice-a-Week Herald (Amarillo, TX)
The Vancouver Independent
The Waco Daily Examiner (Waco, TX)
Warren Sheaf (Warren, MN)
The Washington Herald (Washington, D.C.)
The Washington Times (Washington, D.C.)
The Watchman and Southron (Sumter, SC)
The Webster Journal (Webster, SD)
Weekly Graphic (Kirksville, Adair County MO)
The Weekly Messenger (St. Martinsville, LA)
The Western News (Stevensville, MI)
Wood County Reporter (Grand Rapids, MI)
The Worthington Advance (Worthington, MN)

Index

Numbers in **_bold italics_** indicate pages with illustrations

Allen, Edgar 200
Allen, J.S. 38, 41
American Revolutionary War 8
Ames, Adelbert 21, 27–28, 46
Ames, Blanche 46
Ames, Jesse 21, 50
Ames, John 21, 50
Anderson, Andrew 114–115
Anderson, William "Bloody Bill" 14–17
The Arizona Weekly Enterprise 177
Armes, George B. 63
Avery, Dr. H.N. 81
Axlund, Martin 108

Bailey, Dana R. 94
Baker, Millard 101, 107
Banning, Abraham 100
Banning's Crossing 100
Bardstown, KY 162–163
Barnum, P.T. 130
Barr, Henry Lafayette 63
Basham, Tucker 157
Barton, Ara 53, 69, 123, 127, 130
Batchelder, George W. 131
Bates, C.E. 38
Baxter, George N. 64, 132
Beloit, IA 105, 136–137
Big Sioux River 77, 90, 98, 100–102, 104–107, 136
"Big Woods" 52, 55, 63
Black Hills 25, 28, 45, 75, 78, 101, 147
Blount County Democrat 182
Blue Earth River 64–65, 121
Boland, Morgan 146–147, 149
Booth, John Wilkes 186
Border Outlaws 162
Bottalfson, B.M. 25
Bow, Clara 183
Bradford, George ***116***, 117
Braley, Win 137–138
Brant, Marley 33, 40
Breihan, Carl W. 92
Bresette, John B. 53, 71
Bridgewater, Capt. James H. 15
Broadbent, R.A. 139, 141

Broken Kettle Creek 142–143
Brown, C.W. 51
Bryan, William J. 203
Buckham, T.S. 13`
Budd, John 136
Buel, James W. 162–163
Buffalo Bill Cody 205
buffalo in Dakota 84
Bunker, Alonzo E. 34–37, 39, 42, 49, 124–125, 132
Burbank, John A. 191–192
Burgess, B.L. 109
Butler, Benjamin 27

California gold rush 9, 11
Calliope, IA 137
Callender, John W. 101
Cameron, John D. 106
Cameron, MO 161, 174
Cannon Falls, MN 47
Cannon River 20, 31, 52–53
Canton, SD 75
Canton, Dakota Territory 104–107, 136–137
Carleton College (Northfield, MN) 21, 35
Carter, Cal (Al) 126–128, 148–149
Centennial Exposition 30, 35, 50, 71, 151
Center, MN 73
Chadwell, Bill 22, 26–27, 29, 34, 36, 41–44, 47–49, ***119***, 124, 126, 136, 143, 193
Chadwell, M.E. 48
Chadwick, Bill 42
Chambers, J.H. 185
Chicago Times 182
Chicago Tribune 153
Church, Miles 127
Civil War 6, 7, 9, 10, 11, 17, 19, 21, 22, 24, 27, 46, 67, 75, 78, 83, 97, 107, 144, 151, 154–155, 166–167, 204, 210
Clements, Archie "Little Archie" 16
Cleveland, Grover 181
Collins, Charley 145
Collins, Mattie 168, 172
Colt, Samuel 6
Como Lake 119
Converse, Walter 72

233

Cooper, H.N. 25
Cordova, MN 31, 52
Corey, William A. 43
Correctionville, IA 144
Corson, Harry 101
Council Bluffs, IA 107
Courier Journal 163
Cox, Maj. Samuel P. 15
"Cracker Neck District" 165, 187
Craig, Henry H. 168-169
Crittenden, John J. 166
Crittenden, Thomas T. 161, 166-171, 174, 178-181, 184, 188-190, 195-197
Crystal Lake, MN 63, 66, 82
Cummins, Jim 61, 158, 160-161, 162
Custer, Lt. Col. George A. 151

Dacus, Dr. J.A. 185
The Daily Argus-Leader 75, 77, 92, 112, 117, 145
The Daily Journal 147
Daily Press and Dakotaian 102
Dakota Territory 8, 25, 47, 60, 62-63, 72, 74, 77-79, 81-84, 89, 96, 98-99, 107-109, 136, 138-139, 144, 152, 162, 191
Dalton, Frank 94-96
Dalton, Kit 169
Dampier Hotel (Northfield MN) 21, 41
Davis, Jefferson 14
Dell Rapids, DT 72
Dement, Jack 77
Dennison, IA 141
Derome, J.A. 5, 61, 75, 77, 93, 145
Des Moines River 63, 70, 73
Devil's Gulch (aka Spirit Canyon) *86*-88; legends 89-96, 206
Devil's Stairway 92
Dill, William H. 69, 73, 76-77
dime novels 6, 7
Donaldson, Robert 51
Doon, IA 138
Duncan, Leroy 16
Dundas, MN 50-51, 130
Dunham, Sam 53
Dunning, Thomas Jefferson 57-58, 64-65, 112

East Orange, IA 107, 138
Edwards, John Newman 155, 159, 177, 188-189
Elk Point, DT 89, 102, 136
Ellsworth, Mollie 29-30
Elysian, MN 56
Elysian Road 53
Empey, Philip 50, 52

Fairview, Dakota Territory 105
Fargo, DT 43
Faribault, MN 27, 50, 53, 101, 123, 126, 129-131
The Faribault Democrat 40, 45, 127, 153
The Faribault Republican 48, 130
Farr, Finis C. 167-171
Finlay, Dakota Territory 103

First National Bank of Northfield 21, 34, *36*, 132
Flanders, C.E. 171
Flandreau, Dakota Territory 82
Flannegan, Ike 158
Floyd, Hattie 160
Floyd River 141-142
Ford, Charles 166, 168-169, 171-173, 178, 181, 191-192, 195-196
Ford, Robert 166-173, 178-181, 184, 189, 192, 195-198, 200, 206-207
Fort Dodge, IA 62-63, 71
Fort Sully, Dakota Territory 79
Fort Sumter 11

Gallatin, MO 188-189
Garden City, MN 67-69, 80-81, 86
Gardner, Mark Lee 47
Garfield, James A. 185
Garretson, SD 87-88, 92-93, 95
Gayville, Dakota Territory 101, 109
Georgetown University 8
German Lake, MN 56
Gigge, Theodore 109
Glazier, Frank 130
Glendale Train Robbery 157
Glispin, James 111-113, *116*, 118, 123
Goodwin, John (Goodin) 147-149, 152
Grand Forks, DT 43, 47, 49, 162
Granite, IA 104
Grant, Gen. U.S. 16, 121
"The Great Cole Younger and Frank James Historical Wild West" 204
The Great Train Robbery 209
Grigsby, Melvin 106
Groom, John S. 152-153
Guiteau, Charles 185-186
Gustavson, Nicolas 41, 123, 132

Ha-Schootch-Ga 89
Hall, Richard S. 150
Hampton, Wade 155-156
Hannibal, MO 159
Hanska Slough 79, 112, 115-116
Hardin, C.H. 143, 146
Harding, James 90
Harding, Nellie 90-91
Hardwicke, Samuel 26
Hawn, Dan 106
Hayes, Rutherford B. 37, 151
Hazen, Larry M. 40, 128
Henshaw, Clarence F. 186-187
Heywood, Joseph Lee *34*-37, 39-40, 57, 121, 124-125, 129, 132, 141, 156, 188, 202, 212
Hickok, James Butler "Wild Bill" 75, 151
Hill, Sam 184
Hill Cemetery, Independence MO 211
Hite, Clarence 161
Hite, Wood 157, 161, 168, 195
Hobbs, Elias 38
Hoffman, Harry 40, 65, 153

Holt, Billy 106
Hot Springs, AR 160, 191
Houser, Sam 201
Hoy, Mike 56, 64-65, 69, 121
Howard, T.D. 165, 173, 196
Howe, Perry E. 77, 83
Howk, Orvus L. 94-95
Hubbard, Lucius F. 188
Hunn, C.B. 126
Hunt, G.W. 144-145
Hunt, Thomas J. 192
Huntsville, AL 188-189
Hurd, Dr. 101, 142

The Illustrated Lives and Adventures of Frank and Jesse James and the Younger Brothers, the Noted Western Outlaws 184
The Indiana State Sentinel 178

Jackson, T.J. (alias for Jesse) 161
Jackson farm 68
James, Alexander Franklin 5; birth 8, 11; Dakota and Devil's Gulch 91-96, 97, 128; death 211-212, *213*; in Iowa 136-137, 140-142, 144, 146-150, 151; joins confederate forces 12, *13*, 14-16; marriage 17-18, 21, 22, 24, 28, 30; in Missouri 152-155, 161-164, 167-168, 170, 175, 184-185, 187; Northfield bank robbery 33-34, 36-37, 39-40, 50, 61-63, 65, 67, 70, 73-74; surrendered 188, *189-*190, 195, 202-204, 206, 210
James, Annie Ralston 17, 18, 152, 210
James, the Rev. Billy 18
James, Drury 9, 67
James, George 52
James, Gould 157
James, Jesse Edwards 22, *63*, 165, 176, 192, 194, 196, *198*, 200, 212
James, Jesse Woodson 5, 7; birth 8; Dakota and Devil's Gulch 86, 89, 92-96, 97, 124, 128; death 171, *172*, 173-175, *176*, 177-181; fatherhood 22, 23, 24, 26, 27, 28, 29-30; as guerrilla *9*, 11, 12; immortalized 182-187, 189-202, 204-212, 214; in Iowa 136-138, 144, 146-147, 150, 151; joins Quantrill *13*, 14-17; marriage 18, 21; in Missouri 152-155, 157-161, 162-164; moves to St. Joseph 165-170; Northfield bank robbery 33-34, 36-37, 39-40, 46, 50, 55, 62-63, 65, 67, 70, 73-*74*
James, Luther 175
James, Mary Susan *63*, 157
James, Montgomery 157
James, Robert 8-9, 11
James, Susan Lavenia 9, *10*
James, Zerelda Cole *see* Samuel, Zerelda
James, Zerelda "Zee" 17-18, 22, 157, 159, 170-173, 180, 185, 196; death 197, *199*
The James Boys in Missouri (first movie about Jesse James) 209
James brothers 6, 8, 19, 22, 27, 45, 60-61, 64-66, 68-69, 72, 75, 78, 80-85, 89, 98-100,
102-110, 111, 118, 122-123, 133, 136-137, 139, 140-146, 148, 150, 152, 155, 157, 162-163, 166, 184, 202, 206, 209
James River 103, 138
James-Younger gang 5, 7, 17, 21, 22, 24-26, 30, 41, 50, 52, 54, 126, 128, 149, 156, 161, 180, 208, 211, 213
Janesville, MN 54, 56
Jefferson City, MO 174
Jeft, J.G. 21
Jennison, Charles R. 23
Jerezy, J.F. 201
Jesse James (second movie about Jesse James) 209
Jesse James as the Outlaw 212
Jesse James Cave 91, 95
Jesse James Meets Frankenstein's Daughter 212
Jesse James: Under the Black Flag 212
Jesse James Wild West shows 199-200, 204, *205*, 206-210, 212
Johnson, Maj. A.V.E. 15
Johnson, Jake 202
Jones, John J. 16
Joplin, MO 25, 158

Kansas City, MO 8, 24, 99, 138, 143, 147, 153, 158, 161, 162, 167-168, 171, 190, 192, 195, 212
The Kansas City Journal 169, 178
The Kansas City Times 28, 30, 125, 153, 158-159
Kapernick, Henry 130-131
Karloff, Boris 208-209
Kaufman, Sam 158, 175
Kearney, MO 8, 18, 152, 172, 174-176, 200-201, 210
Kellar, George 106
Kellar, Jim 106
Kemp, Stewart 208
Kenny, Patrick 45
Kerry, Hobbs 24, 28-29
King, James 79
Kingsbury, George W. 109-110
Krogness, A.D. 136-137
Krogness, the Rev. S.N. 136-137
Krunz, George 58-59

Lake Crystal, MN 66-67, 72, 141
Lake Shetek, MN 69-70, 82
Lamberton, MN 69
Larson, Albert 104-105
Larson, F.M. 145
Larson, John 145
The Last Frontier 108-109
Leavenworth, MN 69
Leavenworth Times 55
Lee, Gen. Robert E. 16
Lee and Hitchcock's store (Northfield, MN) 33
Lee's Summit, MO 23, 150, 212
Lee's Summit Historical Cemetery 203
Le Mars, IA 139, 142

Index

Le Sueur Center, MN 31
Liddil, James A. "Dick" 60, 157, 168, 170, 172, 196
The Life and Treacherous Death of Jesse James 185
Ligget, James 158
Lincoln, Abraham 11
Little Sioux River 140–141, 145, 161
Lommen, Peter 103
Loon Lake, MN 66
Lord, Judge Samuel 129, 131–132
Los Angeles, CA 42, 67
"Lost Timber" of Dakota 82
"Lost Timber" of Minnesota 73
Louisville, KY 163
Luna Lake, MN 82
Luverne, MN 70, 73–74, 76–77, 83, 86, 90, 93–94, 105

Madam Silva 185
Madelia, MN 31, 68, 79, 86, 111–115, 120–121, 123, 131, 139, 193
"Madelia Seven" 116, 120, 131
Mankato, MN 25, 27, 31, 46, 55, 57–58, 64, 69–70, 81, 113, 132, 155–156
Mankato Record 67, 130, 155
Manning, Anselm R. 41, 124
Marks, C.R. 142
Martin, John I. 180
Martin, Will 200
Mason, Charles E. 95
McCarthy, Mike 77
McDermott, Tom 101
McDonald, Dan 138
McDonald, John 102–103, 107, 111, 138, 141–143, 145
McDonough, James 120, 126, 143, 146
McFarland, William C. 144
McGarvin, J.C. 25
McGowan, Stella Frances 212
McMillan, Frank 161, 188
Memphis, TN 157, 179, 200
Miller, Alice J. "Lassie" 203
Miller, Clelland "Clell" 22, 34, 36–38, 41, 48–49, 56, *119*, 124, 126, 143, 153, 157, 160, 175, 193
Miller, Ed 153, 157, 160–161, 169–170, 175
Miller, H.S. "Doc" 22
Miller, J.L. 190
Miller, Theodore 38
Millersburg, MN 31
Millersville, MN 51
Mimms, Benjamin 10, 11
Mimms, John 13, 16
Mimms, Zerelda "Zee" 9, 13
Minneapolis, MN 25, 29, 31, 39, 56, 124
Minneapolis Tribune 31, 40, 42, 47, 49, 54, 57, 71, 76–77, 107, 127, 147
Minneopa Falls, MN 65, 121
Minnesota River 52
Missouri River 25, 78, 101–102, 109, 138, 145, 154

Monticello, MN 47
Morey, Dan 109
Mosher, Dr. Sidney 139–144, 148–150
Motion Pictures 209–210, 212
Mount Olivet Cemetery, Kearney, MO 176, 200, 210–211
Mountain Lake, MN 69
Muddy Fork Cemetery, Clay County, MO 49
Murphy, Dr. John H. 118–119
Murphy, W.W. *116*, 117

Nashville, TN 157, 161
The National Review 178
Nelson, Andrew 84–86, 94, 99–100, 107
Nelson, Nels 84–85
New Ulm, MN 113
New York Sun 34, 99, 157
New York Times 178
Nicollet Hotel (Minneapolis, MN) 29
"Ninth man theory" 32, 42–44
Noland, Dr. William W. 146–147, 149
North, John W. 20
Northfield, MN 8, 20–22, 24, 25, 27, 31–32, 33, 35–36, 38–43, 46, 49, 50–51, 53, 54, 56, 60, 62, 68, 72, 74–75, 91, 93, 96, 98–99, 101–102, 105–106, 108–110, 111–112, 119–122, 124–125, 127, 130–131, 137, 141, 143–144, 146–148, 151–152, 154, 156, 160, 162, 175, 188, 193, 202, 206, 209, 212

O'dell, Nellie E. 50–51
Olivet, Dakota Territory 103
Omaha, NE 152, 154
Otterville, MO 24, 29
The Ouachita Telegraph 159
Outdoor Life 75
Owen, Anton 113
Owen, Mads 113

Palisades 77–78, 83–84, 87–*88*, 89, 91, 93–94
Parke, Clay 107
Parmer, Allen H. 10
Patterson, Billy 77
Patton, Charles W. 89
Pence, Don 163
Penn, William 186–187
Phillips, George M. 35
Pillsbury, John S. 54, 71
Pinkerton, William 10
Pinkerton Detective Agency 10, 26, 152, 161, 163, 200
Pitts, Charlie (alias for Samuel Wells) 22, 29, 33–34, 40, 50, 57, 61, 111–116; death 117–118, *119*, 121–126, 139, 193
Pomeroy, Charles *116*
Ponca, NE 102
Portlandville, IA 138
Pruist, August 142

Quantrill, William C. 9, 10, 12, 13, 14, 15–17, 23, 83, 158, 163, 184, 201, 206

Index 237

Ralston, Annie 17, 18
Ralston, Samuel 17, 24
Reardon Hotel (St. Paul) 203
Red Wing, MN 25, 27
Remington 6
Rice, Benjamin *116*
Rice County Journal (Northfield, MN) 27, 39–40
Rich Hill, MO 163–164
Richmond Democrat 178
Risty, A.G. 90
Ritter, Richard 180
"Roan Charger" 191
Robert, Richard 66
Robin Hood 155
Robinson, Charles 46
Rock River 74, 106
Rockwood, George "Elder" 68, 87, 111
Rogers, F.A. 79
Rogers, Will 61
Rolph, Charles B. 74–77, 94
Rolph, Sarah 74, 76
Rongstad, Ole 104–105
Rose, Arthur P. 74
Rossteuscher, Charles 103
Roundtree, R.H. 192
Rudolph, O.A. 106
Russellville, KY (bank robbery) 23, 67, 201
Rutledge, Thomas 131

Sager, Levi 52
St. James, MN 113
St. Joseph, MO 22, 145, 153, 161, 169–173, 197–198. 210
St. Louis, MO 25, 30, 120, 126, 143, 146–149, 152, 162, 185, 191, 201–202
The St. Louis Globe-Democrat 125, 149, 175
St. Olaf College (Northfield, MN) 20
St. Paul, MN 25, 26, 29–31, 49, 53, 76, 83, 111–113, 117–118, 120, 122–125, 128–130, 152, 203
St. Paul Pioneer 132
St. Paul Pioneer and Press 81, 133
St. Paul Weekly Dispatch 30, 71, 112, 120, 122, 129
St. Peter, MN 20, 57, 58, 71, 78, 79
St. Peter Tribune 128
Salzman, Henrietta 176–177
Samuel, Archie 26, 163
Samuel, Johnny 175
Samuel, Dr. Reuben 10, 12, 152, 175; death 210
Samuel, Zerelda 8, 9–10, *11*, 12, 26, 153–154, 163, 172–176, 179, 185, 192, 194; death 210, *211*
Samuelson, Anna 99
Samuelson, John 99
Sanders, W.W. 92–93
Schaffer, John 58–59
Sedalia, MO 180
The Sedalia Weekly Bazoo 79, 81, 149–150, 163–164, 172–173, 183
Severson, S.J. *116*

Sexton, George 51
Seymour farm 68
Shaubert, Henry 57
Shelby, Joe 154–155
Shepherd, George 157–159, 164
Shieldsville, MN 51–52
Shindlar, SD 103
Shulson, Andrew 104–107, 138
Siedenfaden, William 171
Sioux City, IA 27, 63, 79, 102–103, 107, 111, 118, 136–137, 139, 141–145, 147–149
Sioux City Democrat 144
Sioux Falls, SD 50, 75, 87, 92, 94, 137, 145, 206
Sioux Falls Daily Press 91
Sioux Falls, Dakota Territory 82, 84, 86, 88–89, 98–103, 105–106. 206
Sioux Falls Independent 88–89
slaves and slavery 9, 10, 23
Sleepy Eye, MN 70
Smith, R. 184
Sorbel, Axle Oscar 112–113, 117–118, 120, 121
Sorbel, Mary 113
Spink, Dakota Territory 145–146
Split Rock River 77–78, 84, 87, 89–91, 94, 105
Springfield, Dakota Territory 101, 145
Stacy, Elias 41
Stafford, Harvey 105
Stevens, Henry H. 169
Stevens, W.H. 30
Stiles, Bill 26, 42–44, 47–48, 51
Stiles, Elias 47
Stillwater prison 132–133, 154, 192, 202
Streeter, Col. 53
Sutley, Zack T. 108
Swain, Asa 53
Swain, W.I. 204–205
Swan Lake Era 108
Swan's homestead and ford 70–71, 73
Syverson, Amos 104

Talley, Dick 146
Taylor, Charles Fletcher *13*
"Texas Jack" 201–202
Thomas, Chauncey 75
Thompson, Horace 114–115, 122
Thompson, J.C. 142–143
Thompson, Thomas 70
Tilden, Samuel 37
Timberlake, James H. 167–168, 170, 175
Townshend, M.M. 202
Traverse, Kitty 30
Triplett, Frank 61–62, 185
Twain, Mark 159
Twyman, Fanny C. 97, 128, 131

"Uncle Dan's Ford" 77
Untome 89

Valley Springs, SD 75
Valley Springs, Dakota Territory 83–84, 88, 94, 99

Vermillion, Dakota Territory 101–103, 108–109
Vermillion River 103, 108–109
Vincent, John 66–67
Vought, T.L. *116*, 120, 131

Wahl, Peter 104–107, 138
Wallace, William H. 155–156, 174
Waseca, MN 55
Waterville, MN 52
Watonwan River 114–116
Webber, Martin 75–76
Webster, Madison 100
Webster, SD 112, 120
The Weekly Butler Times 189
Weekly Pioneer Press (St. Paul) 58
Wentworth News 92
Westfall, William 161, 174
Wheeler, Henry M. 41, 49, 50, 124
Wilcox, Frank J. 34–35, 37, 39, 124, 188
Wild West Shows 8
William Jewell College 9
Willoughby, Dick 90–91
Wilson's Creek, battle of 12, 13
Winchester 6
Winston, MO 161
Winston train robbery 161–163, 166–168, 174, 188

Wisty, Oke 120
Worthing, SD 75
Worthington, MN 70, 72, 77, 84, 90, 105
The Worthington Advance 71

Yankton, Dakota Territory 25, 78, 82, 98–103, 108, 138
Younger, Henrietta "Retta" 128, 131, *134*
Younger, Henry Washington 23, 128
Younger, James Hardin "Jim" 15, 22, 25, 28; as "Al or Cal Carter" 126–128; in court 131–132; death 203; Northfield bank robbery 34, 61, 64–65, 70, 112, 117–118, 120–121; paroled 202; Stillwater prison 133–*134*, 135, 154
Younger, "Judge" 27, 118,
Younger, Robert "Bob" 22, 26–27, 28; in court 131–132; death 202; Northfield bank robbery 33–34, 37, 39, 45, 50–52, 55, 57–58, 61, 64–66, 70, 117–122, 124–128; Stillwater prison 133–*134*, 135, 154, 193
Younger, Thomas Coleman "Cole" 8, 12, 14, 21, 22–25, 27, 28, 29, 31, 32; in court 131–132; death 212; Northfield bank robbery 33–35, 37, 40, 45, 48, 50, 52, 54, 61, 64–66, 70, 95, 97, 114, 117–118, 120–124, 126, 128–129; paroled 202–204, 211; in Stillwater prison 133–*134*, 135, 136, 154, 193
Younger brothers: capture 111–118, 139, 155

www.ingramcontent.com/pod-product-compliance
Ingram Content Group UK Ltd.
Pitfield, Milton Keynes, MK11 3LW, UK
UKHW041942140426
5217IPUK00014B/613